THE RESURRECTION OF GOD INCARNATE

The Resurrection of God Incarnate

RICHARD SWINBURNE

CLARENDON PRESS · OXFORD

*This book has been printed digitally and produced in a standard specification
in order to ensure its continuing availability*

OXFORD
UNIVERSITY PRESS

Great Clarendon Street, Oxford OX2 6DP
Oxford University Press is a department of the University of Oxford.
It furthers the University's objective of excellence in research, scholarship,
and education by publishing worldwide in
Oxford New York

Auckland   Cape Town   Dar es Salaam   Hong Kong   Karachi
Kuala Lumpur   Madrid   Melbourne   Mexico City   Nairobi
New Delhi   Shanghai   Taipei   Toronto
With offices in
Argentina   Austria   Brazil   Chile   Czech Republic   France   Greece
Guatemala   Hungary   Italy   Japan   South Korea   Poland   Portugal
Singapore   Switzerland   Thailand   Turkey   Ukraine   Vietnam

Oxford is a registered trade mark of Oxford University Press
in the UK and in certain other countries
Published in the United States
by Oxford University Press Inc., New York

ISBN 978-0-19-925746-1

Preface

IN THE COURSE of the past thirteen years I have written a tetralogy of books concerned largely with the philosophical issues involved in specifically Christian (as opposed to general theistic) doctrines.[1] I was concerned to spell out these doctrines (for example, the doctrine that Jesus was both divine and human) in a coherent way, and to provide some initial a priori probability for supposing them to be true. However, I always emphasized that to show these Christian doctrines to be more probable than not we require some evidence (though not an enormous amount of evidence) of a detailed historical kind to support the claim that Jesus of Nazareth led a certain sort of life, gave certain teaching, died on the Cross, and rose bodily from the dead on the first Easter Day. In this book I seek to provide that evidence, in particular evidence for the Resurrection which—if it occurred—would be the divine signature on the teaching of Jesus and the teaching of the Church which he founded.

I have used in this book material from two previous papers of mine: 'Evidence for the Resurrection', in S. T. Davies, D. Kendall, and G. O'Collins (eds.), *The Resurrection* (Oxford University Press, 1997), and 'Evidence for the Incarnation', in M. Meyer and C. Hughes (eds.), *Jesus Then and Now* (Trinity Press International, 2001). My thanks to the publishers concerned for permission to reuse this material.

Very many thanks to Mrs Chio Gladstone for her patient typing and retyping of versions of the book. I am most grateful to Professor Christopher Tuckett (and also to two anonymous referees for the Oxford University Press) for reading an earlier version of the book and producing most useful comments. My greatest gratitude is to Professor Chris Rowland, with whom I gave classes on the

---

[1] *Responsibility and Atonement* (Clarendon Press, 1989); *Revelation: From Metaphor to Analogy* (Clarendon Press, 1992); *The Christian God* (Clarendon Press, 1994); and *Providence and the Problem of Evil* (Clarendon Press, 1998).

Resurrection on two occasions, who guided me on what I should read on the detailed historical issues, and commented most valuably on an earlier draft of the whole book as well as on yet earlier drafts of parts of it.

Contents

Introduction

The initial topic of this book is the examination of the evidence for the core physical element of the Resurrection of Jesus understood in the traditional sense—of Jesus being dead for thirty-six hours and then coming to life again in his crucified body (in which he then had superhuman powers; e.g. he was able to appear and disappear). Of course, the Resurrection is traditionally supposed to have a cosmic significance which goes infinitely far beyond this core physical element. The Jesus who died and is risen is Jesus Christ, Messiah and the Word of the God, the second person of the Trinity. His Resurrection constitutes God the Father's acceptance of the sacrifice of Christ on the Cross for the sins of the world; and the initiation of a process of redeeming humanity and nature in respects both physical and spiritual.

But the Resurrection has—it is traditionally supposed—this cosmic significance only because of its physical core. The Word of God is risen from the dead only because the human Jesus is risen from the dead (only *qua* human can the Word rise); a human can be resurrected fully only if he is resurrected in an embodied state (for although, I believe, we can exist without bodies, bodies make for the fullness of human existence—such is the traditional Christian and Jewish view) and, although Jesus could have risen in an embodied state with a totally new body, resurrection of a changed old body would manifest 'resurrection' as opposed to mere coming-to-life again most eminently. The Father accepts the sacrifice of Christ by bringing to life what had been sacrificed; thereby he proclaims that suffering and death have been overcome. To initiate the redemption of humanity and of the natural order, he needs to bring to life a previously damaged body, not only a soul. And he gives his signature of approval to the teaching and sacrifice of Christ by doing an act which God alone can do—of interfering in the operation of the natural laws by which he controls the universe. For the coming-to-life again of a body dead for thirty-six hours is undoubtedly a violation of natural laws. The core physical element in the Resurrection of Jesus has for these reasons been supposed to be a very important element in the Christian creed. I shall in future understand by 'the Resurrection' simply the core physical element.

This present book is very different from the writing of a typical New Testament expert (whether radical or conservative) on this issue, because only the final third of the book deals with the kind of evidence normally thought by such an expert to be relevant to this issue: what the New Testament and other early documents had to say about what happened after the death of Christ. I argue that we need to take into account a far wider range of evidence than that. To start with, we need to take into account what I shall call the 'general background evidence', evidence (the data) about whether or not there is a God able and likely to intervene in human history in a certain kind of way. I shall not in this book consider whether or not generally available public evidence (not directly concerned with the Christian tradition) favours the claim that there is a God of the traditional kind—omnipotent, omniscient, perfectly free, and the perfectly good. This evidence is the evidence of natural theology: that there is a universe, that it conforms almost invariably to simple natural laws, that these laws and the initial state of the universe are such as to lead to the evolution of human bodies, that these are connected to souls, that humans have great opportunities for helping each other, and there there is widespread religious experience (all this to be balanced against the existence of much human and animal suffering). I have written a lot about the force of this evidence in other books.[1] Here I shall simply draw out the consequences of supposing that such evidence does or does not give a significant degree of probability to the claim that there is a God. Clearly, if there is an omnipotent God, there is a God able to bring about a miracle such as the Resurrection of Jesus. I shall argue that, in so far as the evidence is against the claim that there is such a God, then the occurrence of such an event as the Resurrection is improbable. If the evidence suggests that there is such a God, then it will give some probability to the occurrence of such a miracle in so far as God has reason to bring about such an event. I shall argue that he does have such reason.

---

[1] See esp. my *The Existence of God*, rev. edn. (Clarendon Press, 1991); and my short *Is There a God?* (Oxford University Press, 1996).

Then we need to consider whether, if there is a God with reason to bring about such a miracle, Jesus was the sort of person whom God would have reason to resurrect—and this is a matter of considering the sort of life he led and what he taught. Assessing this will be what I shall call assessing the prior historical evidence. This evidence of how Jesus lived and what he taught is, of course, investigated in great detail by New Testament scholars; but they do not normally consider it relevant to the issue of whether the Resurrection occurred. That is a serious mistake. For, I shall argue, the Resurrection only occurred if God brought it about, and so we need to consider whether the life of Jesus is the sort of life which God would resurrect. In so far as we have reason to suppose that it is, we will need less detailed evidence in the form of what documents have to say—what I shall call the posterior historical evidence—about what happened after the death of Jesus in order to support the claim that he rose from the dead, than we would need otherwise.

New Testament scholars sometimes boast that they inquire into their subject matter without introducing any theological claims. If they really do this, I can only regard this as a sign of deep irrationality on their part. It is highly irrational to reach some conclusion without taking into account 95 per cent of the relevant evidence (which includes the existence of a universe, its conformity to scientific laws, etc., and what this shows about whether or not there is a God). But of course they couldn't really do this if they are to reach conclusions about whether the Resurrection occurred (or whether the Virgin Birth, or some of the lesser miracles attributed to Jesus, occurred). For you couldn't decide whether the detailed historical evidence was strong enough to show that such an event as the Resurrection occurred without having a view about whether there was prior reason for supposing that such an event could or could not occur. What tends to happen is that background theological considerations—whether for or against the Resurrection—play an unacknowledged role in determining whether the evidence is strong enough. These considerations need to be put on the table if the evidence is to be weighed properly.

Chapter 1 assesses the kind of evidence we can have about historical events, and develops the point that, when we have an event of possible cosmic significance, we need to take into account general background evidence, as well as detailed historical evidence (prior as well as posterior). Since the Resurrection, if it occurred in the way traditionally believed, would be a violation of natural laws and so brought about by some supernatural agent such as God, and so a miracle in a traditional sense of that word which I shall follow, I consider briefly the arguments of Hume against the possibility of there being evidence in favour of such an event. I also emphasize, contrary to the procedures of the more radical New Testament scholars, that—in the absence of counter-evidence—we must assume that what looks like testimony to a historical event really is testimony to a historical event; it is the claim that some historical event occurred. And—in the absence of counter-evidence—testimony ought to be believed. If someone says, 'I saw so-and-so happen', we ought to believe that they saw so-and-so happen, unless we have positive reason to suppose that they didn't.

Chapter 2 considers reasons which God might have for becoming incarnate, that is, acquiring a human body and a human nature. The relevance of this is brought out in Chapter 3, where I argue that, if he did become incarnate, he would need to live a certain sort of earthly life and God would need to put his signature on that life by culminating it with an event which (if it occurred) would be evidently a miracle—what I shall call a super-miracle, such as the Resurrection. So God has a reason for bringing about the Resurrection if it is the Resurrection of God Incarnate, and—I claim—in so far as there is evidence that someone did live the requisite sort of life, it would be deceptive of God to raise that person from the dead unless he was God Incarnate. Chapter 3 goes on to argue that (if we leave aside the possible exception of Jesus) there is in all human history no known religious figure—I shall call such a figure a prophet—who is a serious candidate for having lived the requisite sort of life. Hence, if evidence supports the claim that Jesus did live that sort of life, it gives us reason to suppose that Jesus was God Incarnate, and so that God would sign this life with a super-miracle. I go on to claim that there is no known prophet in all human history apart from Jesus who had his or her life signed in this way by a super-miracle. A coincidence in one prophet of the only serious candidate for living the right sort of life being the only serious candidate for having a life thus authenticated would be very improbable indeed unless God brought about the coincidence. He would not have brought about such a coincidence unless that prophet was God Incarnate. Chapters 1–3 constitute Part I and thus provide a framework showing that, in so far as there is evidence of natural theology favouring the claim that there is a God, we don't need too much detailed historical evidence to show that the Resurrection occurred. We need only to show that Jesus is a serious candidate on normal historical grounds both for having lived the right kind of life and for being raised from the dead: that there is this unique coincidence of significant historical evidence in Jesus.

Part II (Chapters 4–8) then argues that the detailed historical evidence is such that it is not too improbable that you would find it if Jesus Christ did lead the relevant sort of life, and hence that there is a significant prior probability that God would raise this human being from the dead. Part III (Chapters 9–12) then finally considers the posterior historical evidence of what witnesses reported after the death of Christ. I argue that there is evidence which it is not too improbable to find if indeed Jesus rose from the dead. Because, for the reasons which I have outlined and shall be developing, the Resurrection of Jesus Christ is far more likely to have occurred if he was God Incarnate than if he was not, and he was far more likely to be God Incarnate if he was raised from the dead than if he was not, my discussion of the Resurrection of Jesus gets inseparably entangled with a discussion of whether Jesus was God Incarnate. The topic of this book unavoidably expands to include the Incarnation. A conclusion on one issue leads to a conclusion of the other. Hence the title of the book. My conclusion is that, given that general background evidence makes it at least as likely as not that there is a God, when we add the detailed historical evidence, the total evidence makes it probable that there is indeed a God who became incarnate in Jesus Christ and rose from the dead on the first Easter morning.

I have written above in a vague way of there being a 'significant probability' of this or that, or of evidence 'supporting' this or that. In order to provide more rigorous justification for a claim that it is or is not more probable than not that Jesus was God Incarnate who rose from the dead, we need to give rough values to the probabilities discussed, say that one is at least a quarter, or no higher than a tenth, or something like that. And to show how such probabilities add up, we need the probability calculus—the mathematical calculus of probability considered as a calculus for measuring evidential support. I therefore show in the Appendix at the end of this book how the calculus enables us to put the above probabilities together so as to yield a fairly precise result about how probable it is that Jesus was God Incarnate who rose from the dead. My reason for putting

this more formal demonstration into an appendix is that some readers may be intimidated by the introduction of mathematical probability into historical discussion. However, since the mathematics is
very simple, I hope that many readers will read that Appendix.
There is an enormous modern literature analysing the detailed
historical evidence about the life, death, and purported Resurrection
of Jesus. In order to make this book of readable length, where most
scholars agree on some relevant point which I am happy to endorse,
I have often simply stated the point; and, where the point is not very
generally known, I have referred to some textbook or commentary
where the evidence and arguments supporting the agreed view may
be found. Sometimes too, for amplification of a line of argument
which has been put forward by someone else and which I endorse, I
simply refer to a book where the author has developed that line of
argument. Although there are, I believe, a number of original
detailed historical arguments in this book, its main task is to put
arguments developed by others into a wider frame so as to form an
overall picture.

PART I

GENERAL BACKGROUND EVIDENCE

1

Principles for Weighing Evidence

Detailed Historical Evidence: Memory

IN ASSESSING what happened on some particular occasion in the past we have to take into account both detailed historical evidence and general background evidence. The detailed historical evidence may be of three kinds: our own personal (apparent) memories, the testimony of witnesses, and physical traces. The general background evidence will be evidence of the sort of thing that is likely to happen. This may be evidence of observations of what happened in cases similar to that under investigation, supporting a generalization about what normally happens; or evidence of observations over a wide range of cases, some of them rather unlike the case under investigation, supporting some deep theory which in turn has consequences for what might be expected to happen on the particular occasion.

Let me illustrate with a detective example. A detective investigating a safe robbery may have himself a relevant memory. By a 'memory' I mean what should be called, more strictly, an 'apparent personal memory', one which seems to the subject to be a genuine memory of having done something or having perceived something. The detective may have thought that he saw Jones robbing the safe. More likely, there may be the testimony of other witnesses who report that they saw Jones robbing the safe. And there will often be physical traces—fingerprints on the safe, or money stashed away in Jones's garage. The detective's own apparent memories or the testimony of witnesses may, more likely, be not of seeing the safe being robbed but of other events which in turn provide evidence of who robbed the safe.

That memories are to be trusted—i.e. that they make it probable that that which they report occurred—in the absence of counter-evidence is a fundamental a priori principle. You might think that memory is to be trusted only if independently confirmed. One thing that could confirm a memory would be some generalization about how the world works, together with present perceptual experience. My memory that I put the book on the table is confirmed by seeing it on the table now and the generalization that books usually stay where they are put. But why should I believe that books usually stay where they are put? Because I apparently remember that they do so in my experience, or that others have told me this. Those others must rely on their memories for the justification of what they tell me. And even if something is written in a book, I depend on my memory of what the words mean, and that most things in my experience written in books are true. There is no escaping the conclusion that if memory does not provide reliable evidence of what we did and experienced, we could have no knowledge of the world beyond what we immediately perceive, experience, and do. You might say that no one memory is to be trusted until confirmed by another. But think how little knowledge we would have if we really thought thus. We don't think that, and we must draw the consequences of our secular thinking: that memory as such, all memory, is to be trusted in the absence of positive counter-evidence that it is untrustworthy; e.g. that it concerns an occasion or matter on which that subject or all subjects tend to misobserve, or that there is strong independent evidence that what the subject apparently remembers did not happen. That positive counter-evidence will ultimately rely on other memories (or the testimony of others; see below) which clash with the given memory and are stronger or more numerous.

Detailed Historical Evidence: Testimony

When people tell us things, there is a normal meaning which their sentences have independently of the context in which they are uttered; and so a particular meaning which the words composing a sentence have independently of the context, which we may call their 'literal' meaning. Sometimes there may be more than one normal meaning of a sentence (and so more than one literal sense of the component words); but usually there is only one such meaning. A sentence must be assumed to have its normal meaning unless the context indicates that it does not have its normal meaning. Thus, 'this room is colder than usual' has as a normal meaning that the temperature of the room (of the kind measured in degrees centigrade) is lower than it normally is. If you do not know by whom the sentence was uttered, to whom, in what room, that is the meaning you must suppose the sentence to have. Context includes the literary context (the surrounding sentences), the social context (the authorship and intended audience), and the cultural context (the wider culture within which the sentence is uttered). However, any of these contexts may indicate that the sentence cannot be taken in its normal sense. It cannot be taken in its normal sense if literary and social contexts indicate that, so taken, it would be totally irrelevant to the conversation or implied something obviously false (obviously so to speaker and hearer alike). Thus, if, looking at my boss in the distance, I say in 2002 to my colleagues, 'There goes Stalin', this cannot be taken in its normal sense since it would be obvious to everyone that in that sense it is false. It cannot be taken in its normal sense also if the various contexts together show that it is part of a work of a style in which fictional works were written in that culture; or works of some other genre such as allegory, or apocalyptic or historical novel. When the context indicates that the sentence cannot be taken in its normal sense, there are then various rules determining just how it should be understood, into which we need to not go now.[1]

If you deny this role to normal meaning, and suppose that we cannot have any grounds for saying what a sentence means independently of knowing its context, you would never know what any sentence means. Providing more literary context would not help to discover what the sentence means. That could only help if you knew what the sentences forming the literary context meant. And if you do not know what the original sentence meant, how could you know what the additional sentences meant? Nor would it help if you knew by whom and to whom the sentence was uttered. It would only help if you knew that normally they uttered sentences with a certain kind of meaning, and then you could infer that the original sentence would be more likely to be uttered in this context if it had a certain

---

[1] For fuller discussion, see my *Revelation: From Metaphor to Analogy* (Clarendon Press, 1992), pt. I.

meaning than if it had a different meaning. If it occurred as part of a lengthy piece of writing by someone who usually wrote fiction, it was probably meant as fiction. But you could not know the genre of sentences normally written by a certain person unless you could determine that genre by a test other than the test of who wrote it. And so, generally, there has to be a presupposition, if you know nothing about its context, that the sentence means so-and-so if we are ever to understand language at all.

Sometimes, of course, a sentence may have two or even more normal meanings. This usually arises when a word (in the sense of a symbol pronounced and written in a certain way) has two quite different etymological origins: 'The bank is just round the corner', has two normal meanings, because 'bank' may mean river bank or the place where you deposit money. But the surrounding context can quickly disambiguate this if it contains sentences which themselves have only one, or perhaps two, normal meanings, such that the original sentence would only be a relevant thing to say in that context if it had a certain meaning and not a different meaning. But if any meaning were possible, context could never disambiguate.

The one and only normal meaning of a sentence which says that so-and-so 'saw' something or 'went' somewhere, or that there occurred a 'marriage' between some man and some woman on a certain day, or in other ways makes an apparently historical claim, is the historical meaning. The speaker or writer is saying that some person saw something or went somewhere or that a marriage took place. That such historical sense is the normal sense can be seen from the fact that in every culture people need to make such claims very frequently in the course of ordinary conversation, where there is very little evident surrounding context—when they do not, for example, form part of a lengthy conversation or a large literary work. 'Where were you yesterday?' and 'I went to Oxford yesterday' may be the only sentences uttered between two people on a certain occasion. If it were as likely that the sentences concerned someone's spiritual progress or someone's intellectual development at an immediately prior stage ('yesterday') as that they had their down-to-earth historical meaning, ordinary day-to-day business could not be transacted.

It is a further fundamental epistemological principle additional to the principle that other things being equal we should trust our memories, that we should believe what others tell us that they have done or perceived—in the absence of counter-evidence. I call this principle the principle of testimony. It must be extended so as to require us to believe that—in the absence of counter-evidence—when someone tell us that so-and-so is the case (e.g. that Washington is the capital of the United States), they have perceived or received testimony from others that it is the case. Without this principle we would have very little knowledge of the world. For, clearly, most of our beliefs about the world are based on what others claim explicitly to have perceived or tell us to be the case; beliefs about geography and history and science and everything else beyond our own experience are thus based. There is a philosophical dispute, into which there is no need to enter here,[2] as to whether—like the principle of the trustworthiness of memory—this principle is a priori, or whether it is a principle which is shown to be true by our general knowledge of the world available to us through memory. But the centrality of the principle of testimony for any knowledge of the world beyond our own present and past experience is evident. Again there can be positive evidence that certain witnesses, or witnesses positioned in certain circumstances, or a particular testimony by a particular witness, are unreliable. But the evidence will only have force on the assumption that most other witnesses are trustworthy. We can show that Smith is an utterly untrustworthy witness on certain matters only if we can trust the combined testimony of other witnesses about what happened. Conjoint testimony can defeat single testimony.

Just as positive evidence can on its own show a certain piece of testimony to be unreliable, there can also be additional positive evidence in favour of the truth of a particular piece of testimony (and evidence to counter-evidence against its reliability). Testimony by more than one witness to the occurrence of the same event makes it very probable indeed that that to which they testify is true—to the extent to which it is probable that they are independent witnesses (that is, that there is no cause of their saying the same thing other than they or their sources having witnessed what happened at the time and place in question). And solemn affirmation that the witness 'really' saw the event in question, 'himself' or 'herself', and promises or swears that his testimony is true is further reason for

---

[2] See my *Epistemic Justification* (Clarendon Press, 2001), 123–7, for discussion of this issue.

supposing that it is: it shows both that the apparent testimony was testimony and that it was not given casually. Conversely, testimony by one witness to the testimony of another witness (or testimony implying that the first witness is dependent on another witness for his information) that he observed something happening must be less strong evidence in favour of what is claimed to have happened than is the testimony of a witness who claims to have observed it himself.

Detailed Historical Evidence: Physical Traces

While there are or may be a priori reasons for trusting memory and testimony, that physical traces are evidence of this or that is, however, something to be established by empirical investigation. That fingerprints of the same pattern as those of Jones are (strong) evidence that Jones put his fingers where the prints are follows from the theory that fingers leave prints uniquely characteristic of their owner established in the nineteenth century on the basis of a very wide range of evidence. This evidence itself is available to us by the testimony (written or oral) of those who have studied it. That a particular piece of physical evidence *a* shows what it does, *b*, is something to be established inductively (i.e. as something entailed or rendered probable by a theory which is itself rendered probable by other pieces of evidence). We need to show that *a* would probably not have occurred unless *b* occurred; and that will be only if *a* would probably not have occurred unless *b*, or a cause of *b*, caused *a*. And to show that you need a theory of what causes what. An explanatory theory is rendered probable by observed data in so far as the theory is simple, and there are many data, all of which it leads us to expect (that is, whose occurrence is probable given the theory), and in so far as no other theory is simple and leads us to expect just those data (in the light of any 'background evidence', which I shall discuss shortly).[3] It must also be the case (barring a qualification to which I shall come in a moment) that there are no data whose non-occurrence it leads us to expect.

Apparent memories, testimony, and physical traces will often be evidence of certain other things which in turn are evidence of the

---

[3] For a full discussion of the criteria for determining when evidence renders some hypothesis probable, see ibid., ch. 4.

matter of interest to us—say, that Jones robbed the safe. Here the above pattern of inductive inference will again be evident. Two witnesses may report that Jones was in the neighbourhood of the robbery at the time it was committed, another one may report that a little later Jones boasted about having won the National Lottery and had a lot of money to spend, and lottery officials testify that he did not win the lottery. The traces may include Jones's fingerprints on the safe. So we infer that Jones was in the relevant neighbourhood, boasted later, and had handled the safe. These inferences must be accepted in the absence of counter-evidence that on this occasion the witnesses or fingerprints are untrustworthy. With the aid of other traces—say, the discovery of much of the stolen money in a garage, of which Jones possessed the key—we move to construct an explanatory theory. A theory immediately suggests itself which leads us to expect all these data, when the combination of all the data together would be otherwise unexpected; namely, the theory is a simple one—that one person caused all these effects. Another theory which would also lead us to expect the data with equal probability would be that the fingerprints were planted by Smith, the money stolen by Robinson who dropped it, Brown picked it up and hid it in the garage of which coincidentally Jones had the key; and so on, to deal with the other data. But the latter theory is not supported by the data, because it is complicated, and the former theory is simple.

Background Evidence

All the detailed 'historical' data considered so far are causal evidence in the sense that they are data caused by what happened at places and times relevant to our investigation; the data are effects from which we infer back to their causes (or to other effects of their causes). Thus, if Jones had robbed the safe, he would have caused the fingerprints to be on the safe. If someone had seen him rob the safe, that would (we suppose, by the principle of testimony) be part of the cause of their testifying that they saw him rob the safe. But now background evidence enters in. The background evidence is not, in the sense delineated, causal evidence relevant to a detailed historical hypothesis; but evidence from a wide area supporting (that is, making probable) a theory or theories which have consequences for how likely it is on other grounds that an event of the kind alleged would have occurred. In our example it will include evidence of Jones's behaviour on other occasions supporting a theory of his character from which it would follow that he is or is not the person who normally robs safes.

All these kinds of evidence are relevant to determining whether some historical event occurred and need to be weighed against each other; and the most interesting clashes of evidence, for our purposes, occur when detailed historical evidence points to something which background evidence suggests is most unlikely to have occurred. Your physical theory supported by background evidence from a wide field may suggest that stars cannot explode, but you see through your telescope a pattern of lights which could have been caused by the debris of an exploding star (a supernova), and for which there is no other simple explanation. Or, to take an older and more detailed example, consider the sixteenth-century Danish astronomer Tycho Brahe making observations of comets and measuring their angular distance from various stars at different hours of the nights and days of the year. The background evidence in the form of all that had ever been observed in the heavens, and especially the movements of sun and moon and planets relative to Earth and relative to the 'fixed stars', supported the Aristotelio-Ptolemaic astronomical theory, which held that the heavenly region beyond the moon was occupied by crystalline spheres in which there was no change, and which carried sun, moon, and planets round the Earth. It followed from Tycho's observations that comets change their apparent positions relative to the stars and planets during the year in such a way that if they were situated in a heavenly region beyond the moon, and the Aristotelio-Ptolemaic theory was true, they would be passing through the crystalline spheres—which would, of course, be impossible. But if, on the other hand, comets were situated in the region between the moon and the Earth, they should show a diurnal parallax, i.e. as the Earth rotates daily (or, alternatively, as all the crystalline spheres rotate daily around the Earth), comets should change their apparent positions during the course of the night relative to the background of the stars. Tycho Brahe had very accurate apparatus by which he could have detected any diurnal parallax. He observed the absence of such parallax. So the detailed historical evidence of the relative positions of comets during the year, together with the absence of diurnal parallax, were such as would be expected if comets move through the region beyond the moon but not otherwise.[4] In this situation of a clash between the historical evidence and the theory supported by background evidence, it must be the case either that the background theory is false, or, more limitedly, that there is an isolated exception to it, or that the historical evidence is misleading. In this example it was, of course, the background theory that was eventually found to be at fault (on the basis of a new theory supported by much new evidence added to the old evidence).

Miracles

But if the theory tells us, as scientific theories do, not just about what normally happens (most of the time, on the whole) but about what the laws of nature make inevitable or immensely probable, and if we accept that the historical evidence shows what happened, can we really say that there is an isolated exception to the theory? Must we not say straightforwardly that the theory is certainly or very probably not true, since an event has occurred that is incompatible with the theory or very improbable given the theory. In his discussion of miracles Hume was concerned with a clash of just this kind, for he understood by a miracle 'a transgression of a law of nature by a particular volition of the Deity, or by the interposition of some invisible agent'.[5] He assumed that there was no logical incompatibility here: a law could be a law even if there was an isolated exception caused by an agent from outside, although he had an argument to which we will come shortly to the effect that there could never be good evidence for such an occurrence. But is he right to assume that the notion of a miracle in this sense is even logically coherent? That depends on how one understands a 'law of nature'.

Laws of nature are principles embedded in nature determining what happens. They may be fundamental or derivative. Derivative laws (such as Kepler's laws of planetary motion) are consequences of fundamental laws, which determine what happens under limited conditions (e.g. in certain spatio-temporal regions) in the absence of

---

[4] For more details of Tycho's discovery and its significance, see e.g. S. Sambursky, *The Physical World of the Greeks* (Routledge & Kegan Paul, 1956), 218–20; and T. S. Kuhn, *The Copernican Revolution* (Random House, 1957), 206–9.

[5] D. Hume, *An Enquiry concerning Human Understanding* (1777 edn.), ed. L. A. Selby-Bigge, 2nd edn. (Clarendon Press, 1902), x. i. 90 n.

intervention. Exactly what the fundamental laws of nature are we do not yet know. In the eighteenth and nineteenth centuries people believed that Newton's laws of motion were the fundamental laws, but we now find that they too operate only under limited conditions, for bodies of medium mass which are not moving with high velocity. Newton's laws, we now know, follow—for these conditions—from Einstein's laws of relativity and the laws of quantum theory; these, we hope, will eventually be shown to be derivative from a much more general 'Theory of Everything' not yet formulated.

Laws may be deterministic or indeterministic (probabilistic). Let us consider first deterministic laws. They have the form 'As necessarily do X', e.g. 'photons necessarily travel at 300,000 km/sec.', and seem to be principles determining what happens inevitably; and if we construe this literally there can be no exception to their operation. And if we assume that laws of nature are the ultimate determinants of what happens, this seems a natural way to construe them. For nothing can be the ultimate determinant of what happens, if there is some event that happens not determined by it. But since it is at least logically possible that the way things behave depends on God (or some other supernatural agent) and he can alter this on an isolated occasion, while conserving the normal way things behave on other occasions, we need a looser conception of a law of nature so as not to rule out in advance that logical possibility. So I suggest that we understand by a deterministic law a principle which determines what happens inevitably unless God (or some other supernatural agent) intervenes to set the law aside temporarily. (I will not normally repeat but take for granted this clause 'or some other supernatural agent' for the next few pages, before returning to the issue of who, if miracles occur, is their agent.) That allows the logical possibility of a 'transgression', or, as I shall call it, a violation of a 'law of nature' which will inevitably be 'by a particular volition of the Deity, or by the interposition of some invisible agent'.[6]

---

[6] Note that this definition insists that any intervention from without that disturbs the operation of a fundamental law must be by an 'agent', and that means intentionally brought about by some personal being. If an impersonal force intervenes to prevent the operation of a law, either such an impersonal force operates in some lawlike way, in which case the 'fundamental law' is not really fundamental; or the operation of the force is a completely chancelike event—but if such an event can happen, the true fundamental law must be indeterministic or probabilistic (so as to allow for that possibility). For the sharp

The grounds for believing a purported law to be really a fundamental law is that it is part of a simple theory of a wide scope which is rendered probable in the way stated earlier: it leads us to expect all of many relevant data and no other simple theory of similar scope leads us to expect all of those data. It must also be the case, I suggested initially, that there are no data whose non-occurrence it leads us to expect. But this requires qualification if we adopt the above looser conception of a law of nature. There will now be two possible kinds of exceptions to purported laws: ones brought about by the operation of the true more fundamental law (itself conserved in operation by God, if there is a God), and ones brought about by a direct divine intervention, setting aside the operation of laws. To the extent to which an exception to a purported law (the occurrence of an event contrary to its predictions) is repeatable (that is, would sometimes regularly occur again under similar circumstances), that is evidence that the purported law is not a fundamental law; it is at best a law which holds only under limited circumstances. It is evidence that the purported law does not capture the regularities in nature. While the occurrence of any exception to a purported law caused by God is compatible with its still being a true fundamental law, only in so far as we have good reason to suppose the exception to be non-repeatable (and so not part of the natural order) could we still have reason to suppose the purported law to be a true fundamental law.

A stronger definition than mine of a fundamental law of nature would force us to say that any exception to the operation of a purported fundamental law would entail its not being a true law, even if the exception was brought about by God and would never be repeated. Yet if we said this of some otherwise enormously successful law, that would not seem to do justice to its vast predictive success. For if the exception is not repeatable, there will be no other candidate for being the fundamental law in the field (not even an indeterministic or probabilistic law allowing such events occasionally), and we would have to say that the field was not governed by law—which hardly seems to give a fair account of the situation. I suggest that my definition of a fundamental law of nature enables us to describe the

difference between the inanimate mode of causality, captured in laws of nature, and personal agency (the causing of an effect intentionally by an agent for a reason in the light of beliefs), see e.g. my *The Existence of God*, rev. edn. (Clarendon Press, 1991), ch. 2.

world more comprehensively, by allowing us to discriminate between two kinds of possible exceptions to a purported law: repeatable (because the result of processes inbuilt in nature, i.e. because of the operation of a more fundamental, possibly probabilistic, law) or non-repeatable (because the result of divine intervention from outside).

But what reason would we have to suppose that an exception to a purported law is to any extent repeatable? The evidence that the exception was repeatable would be either that we repeated it (found that we could sometimes, often, or always produce a similar event under similar circumstances), or that a new theory with a rival law could be constructed which was not too much less simple than the previous one but which predicted the aberrant event (which would give reason to suppose that a similar event would occur again under similar circumstances). But if the only way in which we could amend our theory so as to make it predict the aberrant event would be to make a far more complicated theory, that would be grounds for supposing such a theory not to be true and so the occurrence of the event not to be governed by law (in the absence, that is, of the amended theory making successful predictions not made by the old theory).

Here is an example. Suppose E to be the levitation (i.e. rising into the air and remaining floating on it, in circumstances where no forces of known kinds other than gravity (e.g. magnetism) are acting) of a certain holy person. E is thus a counter-instance to otherwise well-substantiated laws of nature L (namely, the laws of mechanics, electro-magnetism, etc.) which together purport to give an account of all the forces operating in nature. We could show E to be a repeatable counter-instance in so far as we could construct a formula L^1 which predicted E and also predicted some other divergencies from L, as well as all other tested predictions of L; and the new predictions were observed to occur, or L^1 was comparatively simple so that we had good reason to believe that they would occur. L^1 might differ from L in postulating the operation of an entirely new kind of force, e.g. that under certain circumstances bodies exercise a gravitational repulsion on each other, and those circumstances would include the circumstances in which E occurred. If L^1 satisfied either of the above two conditions to some reasonable extent (e.g. many of its new predictions were successful), we would adopt it, and we would then say that under certain circumstances people do levitate and so E was not a counter-instance to a law of nature. However, it might be that any modification which we made to the laws of nature to allow them to predict E might not yield any more successful predictions than L, and they might be so complicated that there was no reason to believe that their predictions not yet tested would be successful. For example, we could perhaps modify our theory, our system of laws, by postulating as a law of nature that L holds except when holy men utter certain words on a Tuesday. The last clause would be so different from the kind of interconnected mathematical scheme of the theory containing L as to make such a vastly ad hoc and thus complicated kind of theory that we would have no reason for believing it true. Under these circumstances we would have some reason to believe that the levitation of the holy person violated the laws of nature, and so was caused by an intervention from outside.

Laws of nature may be indeterministic as well as deterministic. Indeterministic (or statistical or probabilistic) laws have the form 'As have a probability p of doing x', e.g. 'atoms of C_{14} have a probability of ½ of decaying within 5,600 years', and they seem to be principles determining the physical probability of what happens. Most physicists believe that the statistical laws of quantum theory are fundamental laws of nature, and so that nature on the very small scale is indeterministic. Although such laws are formally compatible with the occurrence of any of many incompatible possible events, they make the occurrence of certain kinds of event very probable (relative to alternative events described equally specifically) and the occurrence of other kinds of event very improbable. Thus, if it was a purported fundamental law that a tossed coin has a probability of ¾ of landing heads, any result of a million tosses would be formally compatible with the purported law. But certain results would be a lot more probable than others; it would, for example, be much more probable that the result would be 750 heads and 250 tails than that it would be 250 heads and 750 tails.

If the laws of nature on the very small scale are indeterministic, it follows from them that certain macroscopic events (i.e. events observable by humans with the naked eye) are (relative to alternatives) very probable and others very improbable. When a kettle of water is put on a fire, the fire causes the water molecules to move around in various ways and is itself affected by the kettle. It follows from the laws of statistical mechanics that almost all of these exchanges of energy will lead to the water boiling and the fire getting

cooler. But a very few exchanges will lead to the water freezing and
the fire getting hotter. Yet so few are they that it is vastly improbable
(though compatible with statistical mechanics) that this will happen
even once in human history.

The occurrence of events that are very improbable (relative to
equally specific alternatives), given some purported indeterministic
law, is strong counter-evidence to that law. If we think of an indeterministic law as a principle determining the physical probability of
what happens, there are then just two possibilities: that the very
improbable has occurred, or that the purported law is not a true
fundamental law and so we must look for a better one. Either way,
the improbable event will be a repeatable exception to the purported
law, either in virtue of that law (despite the improbability) being the
true law or in virtue of its being produced by a different true law.
But if we wish to allow the possibility of God making an isolated
intervention to alter the way things happen, then we need to amend
our understanding of an indeterministic law in a way analogous to
that in which we amended our understanding of a deterministic law.
We should understand by our indeterministic law a principle which
determines the physical probability of what happens unless God
intervenes to set it temporarily aside. If God does so intervene, the
event he brings about will be a non-repeatable exception to the
purported law, which would indeed be the true law. We may call it a
quasi-violation of that law ('quasi' because formally compatible with
the law; 'violation' because the law was in fact set aside to bring it
about).

The evidence that an event was a quasi-violation of an (indeterministic) law would then be that it was vastly improbable (relative to
equally specific alternatives) given the purported law, and that any
attempt to replace the purported law by a better one ran into difficulties analogous to those described earlier with respect to deterministic laws—the only alternative 'laws' compatible with
observations made so far being highly complicated, and the ones
which are tested being no more successful in their predictions.
Under these circumstances we would have some reason for supposing that a quasi-violation had occurred; the laws had been temporarily set aside by the lawgiver.

So in a clash between historical evidence and background theory
where the theory consists of purported laws of nature, on a reasonable understanding of laws of nature, one can hold both that the

theory is true and that the historical evidence was correctly reported—either because the very improbable has for once occurred, or because a violation or quasi-violation has occurred. I have analysed the kind of detailed scientific evidence there could be for this in a particular case.

All claims about what are the laws of nature are corrigible. However much support any purported law has at the moment, one day it may prove to be no true law. Similarly, all claims about what does or does not violate the laws of nature are corrigible. When an event apparently violates such laws, the appearance may arise simply because no one has thought of the true law which could explain the event, or, while they have thought of it, it is so complex relative to the data as rightly to be regarded as too improbable to be worth testing. New scientific knowledge may, however, later turn up which forces us to revise any such claims about what violates laws of nature. But then all claims to knowledge about the physical world are corrigible, and we must reach provisional conclusions about them on the evidence available to us. We have to some extent good evidence about what are the laws of nature, and some of them are so well established and account for so many data that any modifications to them which we could suggest to account for the odd counter-instance would be so clumsy and ad hoc as to upset the whole structure of science. In such cases there is significant evidence that, if the purported counter-instance occurred, it was a violation (or quasi-violation) of a law of nature. It is enormously probable—so probable that I shall treat it as certain—that the following events if they occurred would be violations (or quasi-violations) of natural laws: a man whose optic nerve had wasted away suddenly becoming able to see; a man walking for a long time on water; a woman instantaneously growing a new limb; and a man dead for thirty-six hours as a result of crucifixion coming to life again and able to appear and disappear at will.

Hume would, I think, have been satisfied with my amended understanding of a law of nature—because he did not wish to rule out the notion of a miracle as logically impossible. What he did claim was in effect (to fill out his words a little) that, to be justified in claiming some generalization to be a fundamental law of nature, we need to show that it operates without exception in a wide range of cases. That evidence will be very strong evidence that it will hold in the case in question. If the historical evidence suggests that some event occurred contrary to a fundamental law, we have at best a standoff; we cannot say what happened, certainly not with enough certainty to provide 'a just foundation for any . . . system of religion'.[7] And the normal situation, Hume considers, is that the background evidence, in the form of evidence of the universal conformity to the purported law in many different areas investigated, will outweigh the historical evidence; and so show that what happened accorded with a law of nature and so was no miracle.

Hume's discussion suffers from one minor deficiency, one medium-sized deficiency, and one major one. The minor one is that the only kind of historical evidence of which he takes account is testimony. He doesn't consider what someone ought to believe who thinks that he himself has seen a miracle. Nor does he consider the possibility of physical traces, e.g. X-rays of the internal state of someone before and after a purported healing (whose status as X-rays taken at the time and of the patient in question is evidenced by many witnesses and much theory). But the addition of these important kinds of historical evidence would not affect the shape of Hume's argument. Far more important is the point that Hume seems to regard the situation as static. We have a certain number of witnesses, and their testimony has a certain limited force against the background evidence, and that's that. But that need not be the situation at all. Evidence can mount up both for the background theory and for the reliability of the detailed historical evidence. Evidence could mount up in favour of the biochemical theory that people cannot pass from the kind of state recorded by the earlier X-ray to the kind of state recorded by the later one. Evidence could also mount up in favour of a healing having occurred on the particular occasion. True, there could not be an indefinite increase in the number of physical traces and witnesses in favour of a healing; but what could mount up indefinitely is evidence in favour of the reliability of X-rays of the kind in question (and of the reliability of the witnesses who testified to their status). Evidence could mount up that X-ray pictures are, interpreted in a certain way, never misleading; and hence that the two pictures show how things were. And evidence could mount up that certain witnesses or certain kinds of witness (e.g. those testifying to events of great importance to them, where affirming the event

---

[7] *Enquiry*, x. ii. 98.

could lead to their death by execution) are reliable. And when the evidence on both sides does mount up, the situation—given the logical possibility of miracles—would not be a standoff, but evidence both that the purported law is a law and that there has been a unique exception to its operation, which, if brought about by God (or 'some other invisible agent'), would be a miracle in the Humean sense.

But Hume's worst mistake was to suppose that the only relevant background theory to be established from wider evidence was a scientific theory about what are the laws of nature. But any theory showing whether laws of nature are ultimate or whether they depend on something higher for their operation is crucially relevant. If there is no God, then the laws of nature are the ultimate determinants of what happens. But if there is a God, then whether and for how long and under what circumstances laws of nature operate depends on God. And evidence that there is a God, and in particular evidence that there is a God of a kind who might be expected to intervene occasionally in the natural order, will be evidence leading us to expect occasional violations of laws of nature. Any any evidence that God might be expected to intervene in a certain way will be evidence supporting historical evidence that he has done so. To take a human analogy: suppose we have background evidence supporting a theory about some person that he behaves normally in highly regular ways; Kant, say, going for a walk at totally predictable times through the streets of Königsberg (so that the citizens could set their watches by his walk). Then suppose there is historical evidence of many witnesses that on one day his walk was half an hour late, and other witnesses reported that he had been told just before beginning his walk that a friend of his was sick. We might at this point have a standoff. But suppose that we have other evidence strongly supporting a theory that Kant was normally always a compassionate friend; then we might expect him to change his otherwise inflexible habits to visit a sick friend. The total background evidence together with the historical evidence that Kant had been told that his friend was sick supports the historical evidence that, on the occasion in question, the regularity was broken.

The more evidence we have of some other kind for the existence of a God able to produce violations of natural laws, the stronger will be the case that one has occurred on a particular occasion. In so far as one has evidence not merely that there is a God, but that there is a God likely to intervene in nature, especially in this kind of way on this kind of occasion, the evidence will be even stronger that he has done so on the particular occasion. Why people believe that such events as I listed earlier (a man whose optic nerve has wasted away suddenly becoming able to see, etc.) would, if they occurred, be violations is not merely that (as I claimed) their occurrence does not fit into the scientific scheme of things, but that they are events which, they believe (rightly or wrongly), God (if he exists) might wish to bring about. Conversely, the more evidence one has that there is no God, or that, if there is, he is not likely to intervene in nature at all or in this kind of way on this kind of occasion, the weaker will be the case based only on detailed scientific evidence about the otherwise inexplicability of the particular event.

Background evidence supporting a theory that some event is or is not likely to happen can naturally be construed as evidence supporting a theory that a certain kind of event is or is not likely to happen under certain circumstances. The detailed historical evidence can then be subdivided into the prior historical evidence about whether the circumstances were appropriate, and the posterior historical evidence about whether that kind of event then happened. Both kinds of historical evidence are causal evidence of effects to be expected if certain things happened. The Aristotelio-Ptolemaic theory predicted that a certain comet which showed no diurnal parallax would not change its apparent position during the year. The prior historical evidence is the causal evidence about whether the comet showed diurnal parallax; the posterior historical evidence is the causal evidence about whether its apparent position changed during the year. The theory about Kant's character held that he is normally inflexible but also compassionate, and so has the consequence that there is quite a chance that he will change his otherwise inflexible habits when he believes that some friend needs him. So in order to have reason to expect an exception to his otherwise inflexible behaviour, we need prior historical evidence that he believed that some friend needed him. That is provided in my example by the testimony of witnesses that he had been told just before beginning his walk that a friend was sick. Both to predict regular behaviour and to predict exceptions to it, we need prior historical evidence as well as general background evidence.

The Structure of Resurrection Evidence

Evidence that the Resurrection in the traditional sense occurred—which, we have noted, would have been an evident violation of natural laws, a super-miracle—will consist in the first instance of apparent memories, testimony, and physical traces. No one alive today has any relevant apparent memories; and it does not look as if (given that we ignore the Turin shroud) there are any relevant physical traces, other than written testimony, though it is just possible that archeological work on the alleged tomb of Jesus in the Church of the Holy Sepulchre or on supposed remains of the 'true Cross' may one day yield something interesting. But there is the apparent testimony of witnesses—of an indirect character. There is the apparent testimony of witnesses (the writers of the various books of the New Testament) to the testimony of other witnesses. For the reasons I gave earlier, apparent testimony to historical events must be regarded as real testimony—in the absence of evidence to the contrary. There is evidence in the case of some apparent testimony in the New Testament that it should not be so interpreted. There are, for example, grounds, which I shall discuss in Chapter 4, for supposing that some of the apparent descriptions of the 'signs' in St John's Gospel (e.g. the healing of the paralytic at the pool of Bethesda) were not intended by the author to be understood as historical narratives. But there is not, I shall urge, general reason for supposing that much of the apparent testimony to historical events in the New Testament was not so intended; and in the absence of such reason we must interpret apparent testimony as testimony. It looks as though St Paul, St Luke, etc. purport to tell us what they have been told, both by witnesses who purported to see the tomb empty, and by witnesses who purported to have met the risen Jesus; and, in the absence of counter-evidence, we must suppose that these writers are telling us just that. Let us call the New Testament writers the indirect witnesses and their informants the direct witnesses. The principle of testimony requires us to believe the indirect witnesses, and so in turn the direct witnesses, in the absence of counter-evidence. As I wrote earlier, the testimony of one witness about what another witness claimed to have happened is not as strong evidence about what happened as is more direct testimony; but any diminution of trustworthiness by indirectness is compensated by quantity. In this case there are several indirect witnesses and two at least of them claim to have heard their news from more than one direct witness.[8] In such circumstances positive counter-evidence is needed for not believing the news. The most obvious kinds of counter-evidence of a historical kind in this case are, first, the existence of counter-testimony and, secondly, the existence of discrepancy in the positive testimony. St Matthew's Gospel records that the Jews claimed that the dead body of Jesus was stolen by his disciples.[9] Then there are discrepancies implied by the positive testimony, as to where the Resurrection appearances occurred, to whom, and over how long a period. I shall examine these in detail in due course. The existence of counter-evidence means that we need to construct a hypothesis to explain all the data—the main testimony, its discrepancies, and the counter-testimony—which is the most probable theory. A theory of given scope is probable in so far as (given background evidence) it is a simple theory and makes it probable that many observed data will occur (and does not make it improbable that any observed data will occur) when it is not otherwise probable that these data will occur (that is, it is not probable given any other simple theory of similar scope). Other things being equal, we must assume as much as possible of the testimony, especially the most direct testimony, to be true; otherwise we violate the principle of testimony described earlier.

Apparent discrepancies in the details require to be explained by the witnesses being deceitful, bad observers, careless reporters, or witnesses whose testimony is not intended to be taken in a fully literal sense; and any such explanation casts some measure of doubt on other details of their testimony and to some extent (dependent on the kind of explanation given) on their whole testimony. But evidence can only fail to render a hypothesis probable if it renders probable instead the disjunction of all alternative hypotheses (that is, renders it probable that one—we don't know which—such hypothesis is true). And if none of these has any great probability, the original hypothesis must retain its overall probability—which is a more careful and precise way of putting Sherlock Holmes's famous remark: 'When you have eliminated the impossible, whatever remains, *however improbable*, must be the truth.'[10]

---

[8] See Luke 1: 2; Gal. 1: 18–19.
[9] Matt. 28: 15.
[10] Arthur Conan Doyle, *The Sign of Four* (Spencer Blackett, 1890), ch. 6.

Alternative hypotheses will need to explain both why false testimony or inaccurate or misleading reporting was given, and also the absence of any positive testimony in their own favour, e.g. testimony to have seen the dead body of Jesus after the first Easter Day.[11] But it might be that some of the evidence is best explained by an alternative hypothesis, including perhaps the absence of certain evidence which one might expect if the traditional account is correct, for example St Paul's failure to mention the empty tomb when he cites, as evidence of the Resurrection, witnesses who saw the risen Christ. (I shall argue later that we do not need an alternative hypothesis to explain St Paul's failure to mention the empty tomb.) However, when all that is taken account of, I can only say that alternative hypotheses have always seemed to me, for reasons which I shall give in detail in due course, to give far less satisfactory accounts of the historical evidence than does the traditional account, in the sense of being much less simple hypotheses or ones that lead us to expect the evidence we find with much smaller probabilities. Most people who think that the total evidence is against the traditional account do so, I believe, because they think the background evidence makes a Resurrection very improbable. There is, in my view, so much testimony to the main outlines of the traditional account that if this event was of a kind which we might expect occasionally to happen, one licensed by our overall background theory, we would have no problem whatever in accepting the main point of that testimony. If the testimony to Jesus being crucified was only of similar amount and quality to that about Jesus having risen from the dead, there would be no problem (despite the discrepancies of detail) in accepting it.

The problem arises because the (physical core of the) Resurrection is supposed to be very improbable given the laws of nature—and, as I suggested earlier, rightly so. If the laws of nature are the ultimate determinants of what happens, there is at best a standoff. (That is, the counter-evidence from laws of nature that this sort of thing virtually never happens at best balances the detailed historical evidence that it has happened on this occasion, and maybe is considerably stronger than the latter.) True, we might be able in principle

[11] Arthur Conan Doyle, 'Silver Blaze', in *The Memoirs of Sherlock Holmes* (George Newnes, 1894), 24: ' "Is there any other point to which you would wish to draw my attention?" "To the curious incident of the dog in the night-time". "The dog did nothing in the night-time". "That was the curious incident", remarked Sherlock Holmes.'

to multiply evidence about the reliability of the witnesses or kinds of witness with whom we are concerned. The witnesses included some whose life was in danger if they testified to the Resurrection and (plausibly) some whose religious upbringing would have led them to expect that no crucified rabbi would rise again. And perhaps the evidence could become immensely strong that people of that kind could never have testified to the Resurrection unless they believed it to have occurred after having checked the matter our thoroughly by standards as good as those of the best modern historian or detective. Then maybe the detailed historical evidence would be so strong, despite the fact that such a Resurrection would have been a unique exception to natural laws, that Jesus had risen that the balance of probability would favour the latter.

But this simply is not going to happen. We simply do not know enough about the characters, let alone the investigative abilities, of the witnesses to the Resurrection. I shall suggest, when we come to the detailed historical evidence, that although there is quite good detailed historical evidence in favour of the Resurrection, it is not strong enough to equal the very strong force of the background evidence—if the latter is construed only as evidence of what are the laws of nature. But in my view that is not the right way to construe the background evidence. My belief is that there is a lot of evidence for the existence of God—a being essentially omnipotent, omni-scient, and perfectly free and perfectly good. This evidence, to repeat it, is the evidence of the existence of a complex physical universe, the (almost invariable) conformity of material bodies to natural laws; these laws, together with the initial state of the universe, being such as to lead to the evolution of human organisms; these humans having a mental life (and so souls), and having great opportunities for helping or hurting each other and having experiences in which it seems to them that they are aware of the presence of God. In my view these phenomena are best explained by the causal agency of a God (with the properties stated) and hence provide good inductive evidence for his existence. This general evidence, the evidence of natural theology, provides general background evidence crucially relevant to our topic. I have argued at length elsewhere the case for this evidence giving substantial probability to the existence of God.[12]

---

[12] See esp. my *The Existence of God* and the shorter *Is There a God?* (Oxford University Press, 1996). Evidence in favour of the existence of God has to be balanced against

I cannot, for reasons of space, argue that case again here. But to get my argument going here, I will make only the moderate assumption that the evidence of natural theology makes it as probable as not that there is a God (with the stated properties). I am also going to assume that, if there is no God, there are no other lesser deities with power to intervene in nature.[13] If there is a God with the stated properties, it will follow that the laws of nature depend for their operation from moment to moment on God, who, in virtue of his omnipotence, can suspend them as and when he chooses (and any violation of laws must then be caused by God, or by some lesser agent allowed by God to cause it). I will come in Chapters 2 and 3 to the question of whether and when he is likely to do this. But in so far as there is evidence that there is a God, there is evidence that a violation of natural laws is a serious possibility. In so far as there is evidence that there is no God or other supernatural agent, there is evidence that the laws of nature are the ultimate determinants of what happens, and so that there can be no exception to the operation of the fundamental laws. To the extent to which my background theory of the existence of God has a lower probability than the moderate value which I have ascribed to it, to that extent we would need much more detailed historical evidence in favour of the Resurrection to make its occurrence overall probable.

evidence against the existence of God, the most significant of which is the occurrence of suffering. I argued in *The Existence of God* that this in fact does not count against the existence of God, but feeling the need for a more thorough discussion of the 'problem of evil' I wrote subsequently *Providence and the Problem of Evil* (Clarendon Press, 1998), to substantiate that view. I argued in *The Existence of God* that it is 'more probable than not' that there is a God. However, my subsequent more satisfactory argument in *Providence and the Problem of Evil* to show that suffering does not count against the existence of God relied in part on the supposition that God would become incarnate to share our suffering and to make atonement for our sins. My argument for there actually being such an incarnation depends on an argument for the Resurrection. Although, in order to reach my conclusion in *The Existence of God*, I gave some very small weight to evidence connected with the Resurrection, that must be laid aside at this stage in this book, since this book is concerned with giving far fuller consideration to this evidence. For this reason, and because I do not wish the conclusion of this book to turn on giving a high value to the arguments of natural theology, I make only the more moderate initial assumption that the background evidence (now solely the evidence of natural theology including the evidence of suffering and the evidence of the widespread phenomenon of religious experience) makes the existence of God as probable as not. I do actually think that this is an underestimate, but for the purposes of the present argument, the more moderate supposition will suffice.

[13] A hypothesis that there are many lesser deities who keep the universe in being, but no God in the stated sense, is, I claim, much less simple than traditional theism and for that reason much less likely to be true. On this, see my *The Existence of God*.

2

God's Reasons for Incarnation

God's Perfect Goodness

SUPPOSE THAT I am right in claiming that the evidence of natural theology gives support to the claim that there is a God, that is, a personal being essentially omnipotent, omniscient, perfectly free, and perfectly good.[1] At the end of the last chapter I made the provisional assumption that this evidence makes it as probable as not that there is a God. A perfectly good being will in any situation do the best possible act, if there is such an act. But there may not be a unique best possible act (that is, an act better than any other act available to the agent). Often the choices before us ordinary humans are between incompatible equal best acts (that is, acts each as good as each other, where there is no better act available to the agent, and he or she cannot do both acts). We may be able to give money to pay for an operation to save the life of this poor African child or of that poor African child, but not have the money to provide for both. It may be an equal best act to provide money for this child as to provide money for that child. The choices before an omnipotent being (who can do anything logically possible) may also be sometimes of that kind: whether, for example, to provide all humans always with plenty of food, or sometimes to permit floods and famines in order that humans may have the opportunity to provide for their own future and to help each other in need. But the choices before an omnipotent being may also include a kind of choice which

---

[1] See my *The Coherence of Theism*, rev. edn. (Clarendon Press, 1993) and *The Christian God* (Clarendon Press, 1994) for different ways of understanding these properties and for my preferred account. Little in this book depends on exactly how we understand God's 'omnipotence', 'omniscience', or whatever.

(in virtue of our limited powers) we do not have, a choice between an infinite number of acts each less good than some other possible act (where the agent can only do one of the acts). God has a choice of how many humans to create. Given that human existence is a good thing, and that God can space out the humans throughout an infinite universe so that they do not crowd each other out, the more humans God creates the better. So, however many he creates (even if he creates an infinite number), he could do a better act by creating one more. For this reason alone there can be no best of all possible worlds.

While God cannot always do the best, what he can do is to fulfil all his obligations. There is a difference between an act which is obligatory to do, and one which is good but not obligatory to do. (The latter kind of act is supererogatory; doing it goes 'beyond obligation'.) That there is such a difference is recognized by most people, though there is great disagreement about exactly where the boundary lies between the obligatory and the supererogatory. Most people would accept that (subject to possible qualifications) I have an obligation to keep my promises, not tell lies, care for my aged parents, and feed and educate my children. I have an obligation too not to kill or hurt others. And most people would accept that I have no obligation to sacrifice my own life to save that of some stranger, supererogatorily good though it is that I should do so. Obligations are obligations to someone. Obligations of a positive kind typically arise from commitments we make (explicitly or implicitly) or benefits we receive. We must pay our debts because we have undertaken to do so, and care for our parents because they have cared for us. Obligations of a negative kind are typically obligations not to act so as to make someone who does not owe us anything worse off than they would otherwise be. Hence we must not kill or hurt. To do what you have an obligation not to do, or to fail to do what you have an obligation to do, is to do wrong.

What obligations does God have towards us? God had no obligation to create us, any more than we have any obligation to produce children. For he cannot owe it to anyone else to create us, and he cannot owe it to us while we do not even exist. He gives us a finite gift of life, and he has no obligation to make it a long one or a short one (I do not wrong you if I give you a gift smaller than the gift which I give to someone else). But plausibly he has obligations to us if he does create us—e.g. to ensure that on balance our life (which may or may not extend beyond life on this Earth) is a good one. A perfectly good being will surely, if he can, fulfil all his obligations. Since it is an obligation on everyone not to get oneself into a situation where one cannot fulfil all one's obligations, and since obligations typically arise from commitments undertaken or benefits received, and since whether God undertakes a commitment or receives a benefit depends on him, it is plausible to suppose that he can and so will fulfil all his obligations. So he would only create us if he could fulfil all his obligations towards us. For these various reasons the perfect goodness of some being can only be construed as his fulfilling all his obligations, doing no bad acts, doing the best or some one of incompatible equal best actions where there are such, and doing many good acts. One who does all that does the best that it is logically possible to do.

So an omnipotent and perfectly good God will inevitably do any act that is a unique best act, and that will include fulfilling all his obligations. He will do one of any incompatible equal best acts open to him; and, since all such acts are equally good, the probability if there are n such acts that he will do one particular one must be $1/n$. Where there are an infinite number of incompatible good acts, each less good than some other one, it will be equally probable that he will do any one such act, and so the probability that he will do a particular one will be infinitesimally small. But if there is a least good act and all the other incompatible acts can be ordered in a series each less good than the next, it will follow that there is a probability infinitesimally close to 1 that he will do an act better than any particular act you care to name. God will do an act in so far as he has reason to do so. He has a reason to do an act in so far as and only in so far as it is good, and overriding reason to do the unique best act or one of the equal best acts, if there is one.

God's Reasons for Becoming Incarnate

What reasons does God have for bringing about the Resurrection of Jesus Christ? There will need to be reasons why he should raise this particular person from the dead rather than any other one. I shall argue in Chapter 3 that there are good reasons for God to raise Jesus from the dead if Jesus was God Incarnate, God who had taken to himself a human nature and a human body, and lived a certain sort of human life. I shall also argue there that God has very good reason not to raise Jesus if Jesus was not God Incarnate. So in this chapter I shall give reasons why God should become incarnate, and incarnate in a certain sort of way leading a certain sort of life. When I give these reasons, the reader will be right to feel that I would not have given them if I had not derived them from the Christian tradition. Indeed, I shall be arguing later that neither Jews nor pagans of the first century AD expected an incarnation of the sort I shall describe. It needs the Christian tradition to make us aware of a theory—a particular theory of the divine nature and of what a being with that nature might be expected to do, to be found in the New Testament but articulated more fully by such writers as Athanasius, Augustine, Anselm, and Aquinas—before we can judge whether or not, by objective standards, the evidence supports that theory well. Most physicists could never have invented the general theory of relativity for themselves, but once it has been proposed for discussion, they can then assess whether in fact the evidence supports it. Or again, Inspector Lestrade and the bumbling police of Victorian Scotland Yard so often saw everything Sherlock Holmes saw. But they could not see its inductive implications, what it made probable. It needed Sherlock Holmes to suggest a theory to account for the data; and once they had heard his theory, then they came to see that the evidence supported that theory. But the evidential relations were there, whether or not they saw them. I shall be arguing that the Christian tradition of what God might be expected to do is correct.

So how should a God of perfect goodness and total power relate to the human race? What needs initially to be explained is not why God should occasionally intervene in human history, but why he is not in constant manifest loving interaction with all humans all the time; why he did not take all of us to Heaven straight away. And there can, I think, only be one answer to that: that he wanted us to choose over a significant period of time the kind of people we are to be (to form our own characters) and to choose how to influence the kind of other people there are to be (to help them to form their own characters) and the kind of world in which we are to live. Therefore, he gives to us free will and much responsibility (our free will makes big differences to others and the world). He gives us this responsibility by making a world governed (almost totally) by regular laws of nature, so that our actions have predictable effects.

But if we are to have a real choice between good and evil, God must withdraw; he must put a certain 'epistemic distance' between himself and human beings. For humans have two natural desires: to be thought well of by the good and the great; and to go on living good lives for ever. Without these elements of character, we would be subhuman. Those who really 'couldn't care less what other people think' of them do not want love. And those who want neither love nor life are tragic specimens indeed. But, given those desires, inevitably if the presence of God were known for certain, that would make choice between good and evil impossible. How could one choose deliberately over a period to make oneself evil if one wanted to be thought well of by the ever present good God? And since one might reasonably conclude that a good God might not think one was worth keeping alive with a life in any way good if one did choose to become evil, one has a further motive for choosing the good. But someone has a good character only if he is naturally inclined to do what is good for its own sake and not merely in order to secure a reward. So God must not deter us from forming such a character by making it too obvious that we will be rewarded for well-doing, for then there will be no opportunity to do acts solely because they are good and so form a character naturally inclined to do such acts. God must stand back if we are to choose; just as the parent must leave the children in the nursery for a short while on their own if they are to form their own characters. While God will want to provide for those who have formed a good character the enormous reward of his everlasting friendship, the only way in which he can do so is to make the reward uncertain. So he will put us in a world with death as its normal end, and not give us too much information about what happens afterwards.

But like a good parent, God will want to help us to make the right choices; and, if we make a mess of things, he will want to help us to sort out the consequences—if we choose to accept that help. And, like a good parent, he will want us, if not to know for certain all the time that he is there, at any rate to have a reasonable belief for some of the time that he is there, caring and ready to help. And he may encourage us with some less than certain information about the reward of Heaven for the good. And all that is reason why he should interfere in our individual lives to help, teach, and encourage from time to time. But too frequent interference would produce that 'culture of dependence' which we all now so rightly abhor.

One of the greatest gifts that any parent can give to their children is responsibility for others—the elder child responsibility for the younger child, for example. The whole way the world is organized indicates that, if God made it, he made it the sort of world in which how people flourish depends in considerable measure on other people. For our sake (to allow us to help each other) he deals with us corporately as well as individually. And so, when help, teaching, and encouragement are required, one might expect a public act or acts which are given for whole cultures or for the whole human race, and about which some can tell others.

So, more precisely, how will a particular form of divine intervention—God becoming incarnate—assist him in forwarding his purposes for the human race? In three basic ways: to provide a measure of reconciliation with God for a broken relationship, to identify with our suffering, and to show and teach us how to live and encourage us to do so.

To Provide Atonement

Let us begin with our need for reconciliation with God, which, I shall be arguing, could be effected by God Incarnate making atonement (or rather, I shall want to say more carefully, making available to us the means for us to make atonement) for our sins. The primary reason which Christians have almost always given for God becoming incarnate in Jesus Christ, and all that flowed from it, was in some sense to reconcile us to God by making atonement for our sins. There are, of course, in the Christian tradition many different theories of what precisely is wrong with the human race and how the life and death of God Incarnate dealt with it.[2] In making a claim about how God did deal with the bad state of humans, each of these theories suggests a different reason God would have for becoming incarnate and the kind of life or death he would in consequence have to live or undergo; and then goes on to claim that in Jesus he did become incarnate and live the required life or undergo the required death, and thus dealt with the bad state. My concern in this chapter is only with these suggested reasons which God might have for

---

[2] See e.g. L. W. Grensted, *A Short History of the Doctrine of the Atonement* (Longmans, 1920).

becoming incarnate and living or undergoing a certain kind of life or death. I come later to the claim that he did become incarnate in Jesus and made atonement in a certain way.

There is first the view that the death of God Incarnate would be a victory over the Devil or perhaps over impersonal evil. But that does not explain why the victory had to be so costly. Why could not God just annihilate evil or the Devil? Then there is the view that the death of God Incarnate would be a ransom paid to the Devil to release God from his promise to the Devil that he would allow the Devil to control the fate of those who rebelled against God. But then why would God have made such a foolish promise? Then there is the view that the life of suffering and death of God Incarnate would be a punishment for sin which humans should have undergone, but which God Incarnate would bear instead of us. While this theory is closer than the others to the theory which I wish to support, it does not make clear what good would be served by God imposing such a punishment even if it was deserved; or if God does provide atonement in this way, why we need have any involvement in this process at all. God could punish God Incarnate instead of us and then let us off our punishment without our being involved at all. Most of these and other accounts of how God Incarnate could make atonement are mutually compatible. You can believe *both* that the death of Jesus was a victory over evil, *and* that thereby God paid a ransom to the Devil. So, in order to justify my own account, I do not need in general to exclude other accounts. But I am going argue that something is wrong with the human race, namely, sin, which needs God Incarnate to live a perfect life which we can offer to God as a sacrifice for that sin. My theory of God's reasons for becoming incarnate to make atonement is, I believe, that of Aquinas and substantially (under the name of 'satisfaction' theory) that of Anselm.[3]

All ordinary humans (that is, all humans other than God Incarnate) suffer from sin, actual and original. Actual sin is simply wronging God. To wrong someone is to do something which you have an obligation to them not to do; or to fail to do something which you have an obligation to them to do. Objective wrongdoing is doing such an act (or omission), whether or not you realize you are doing this or realize that in doing it you are wronging anyone. When we

---

[3] For a full account of this theory, see my *Responsibility and Atonement* (Clarendon Press, 1989), esp. ch. 10.

fail in our obligations, we have done wrong, whether or not we realize that we were doing wrong. If I seek to repay my debts but the cheque miscarries, I have still wronged my creditor, even if I do not realize this. But if we have done our best to fulfil our obligations as we saw them, we are not culpable or blameworthy. Yet when we do what we believe to be wrong we are indeed culpable, and such wrongdoing I will call subjective wrongdoing. Objective wrongdoing puts one in a state of objective guilt; subjective wrongdoing puts one in a state of subjective guilt. Guilt which is both subjective and objective is the worst; after that comes guilt which is merely subjective, and then, the least bad, guilt which is merely objective.

Guilt has to be dealt with. I shall call what needs to be done making atonement. Atonement has four parts: repentance, apology, reparation, and penance—though not all are needed in all cases. If I wrong you, I must make reparation for the effects of my wrongdoing. If I have stolen your watch, I must return it and compensate you for the inconvenience and trauma resulting from my thieving. If the watch has been destroyed, I must give you something of equivalent value. When I have deprived you of a service I owe you, I must perform the service and compensate you for the delay. But what needs to be dealt with is not merely the effects of wrongdoing; there is also the fact of wrongdoing—that I have sought to hurt you. I must distance myself from that as far as can be done. I do this by sincere apology, and that, where the wrongdoing is subjective, involves repentance as well as public apology. But for serious wrongdoing, mere words may sound empty. I can make the apology sincere by doing something extra for you—doing for you more than is needed to compensate for the effects of my wrongdoing; a small gift, an extra service as a token of my sorrow—which I shall call penance. Where the guilt is only objective, repentance is not required (I cannot repent of something for which I am not to blame); and where the wrongdoing is not serious, penance is less needed. The process is completed when the wronged person agrees to treat the wrongdoer, in so far as he can, as one who has not wronged him; and to do that is to forgive.

It is not necessary, in order for the wronged person to forgive the wrongdoer, that the latter should make a full atonement. In my view some apology and (if the wrong is subjective) repentance is always required, but the wronged one can determine how much and can waive the need for reparation. To treat someone who has wronged you seriously and makes no serious apology as one who has not wronged you is in my view wrong. It is not to take his hostile stance towards you seriously; it is to treat him as a child not responsible for his actions. It is condoning, when condoning is wrong. We could call it forgiving, but I suggest that we confine 'forgiving' to those cases where treating the wrongdoer as one who has not wronged you is right, i.e. to cases when it is in response to some repentance and apology.

Now it does look as if almost all humans have wronged God, directly and indirectly. We wrong him directly when we fail to pay him proper worship. Deep reverence and gratitude is owed to the holy source of our existence. We wrong him indirectly when we wrong any of his creatures. For thereby we abuse the free will and responsibility we have been given by God—and to misuse a gift is to wrong the giver. And in wronging God's creatures, we wrong God also in virtue of the fact that he created these creatures. If I hit your child, I wrong you, for I damage what you have exercised your loving care upon. Such wronging is actual sin—sometimes only objective but often subjective. It is subjective sin if the wrongdoer believes that he is doing wrong to someone, even if he does not realize that he is doing wrong to God. But it is, of course, far worse if he realizes that he is wronging the good God who created him and keeps him in being from moment to moment.

But there is more to our bad condition than mere actual sin. There is an element inherited from our ancestors and ultimately from our first human ancestor, whom—defined as the first of our ancestors who had free will and moral concepts—we may call Adam. There is first a proneness to wrongdoing which I shall call original sinfulness; and I will come to that in due course. But there is also something analogous to the guilt of our actual sin. All our ancestors have done wrong, and in consequence owe God atonement; but they have not (at any rate in general) made that atonement: it still needs to be made. We owe our ancestors our life and so much of what we are. For God in creating us has acted through them who have (in general) not merely brought us into the world by accident, but lavished much care on our nurture. Those who have received great benefit from others owe them, where it is possible, a smaller benefit in return. What we could do for our ancestors is to help with their atonement. We who have inherited from them so much positive have inherited a debt also. Even the English law requires that before you can claim your inheritance you must pay the debts of the estate. To inherit a debt is not to inherit guilt. For we were not the agents of our ancestors' wrongdoing, but we have inherited a responsibility to make atonement for this debt of 'original sin', as far as we can.

It is beginning to look as it we humans are in no very good position to make proper atonement for sins, good though it would be that we should make our atonement. We owe much by way of service to God our creator, who has given us so much. We owe a lot more in virtue of our own actual sins; and yet more in virtue of the sins of our ancestors. And we suffer from original sinfulness, a proneness to do wrong against which we have to fight, a proneness to seek our immediate well-being in lesser respects, at the expense of others and at the expense of our ultimate well-being. We are hardly in a position to make atonement for ourselves. We need help.

How can someone else help us to make atonement? Aquinas, as so often, sees the answer. He writes that although confession has to be made and contrition shown by the sinner himself, 'satisfaction has to do with the exterior act and here one can make use of instruments'[4]—i.e. one can make use of reparation provided by others.

'No one can atone for the sins of another.' Taken literally, that remains profoundly true. You cannot make my apologies, or even pay my debts. If I steal £10 from Jones and you give him an equivalent sum, he has not lost money; but it remains the case that I still owe £10 to Jones. You have not changed that. But one human can help another to make the necessary atonement—can persuade him to repent, help him to formulate the words of an apology, and give him the means by which to make reparation and penance. Individual humans can be helped to make their atonement and so also to fulfil their obligations to help others make their atonement.

So what would be a proper reparation (and penance) for us to offer to God, if someone else provided the means of reparation? What has gone wrong is that we humans have lived bad human lives. A proper offering would be a perfect human life, one that was not owed to God anyway, which we can offer to God as our reparation. The only human life not owed to God would be a human life led by God himself, God Incarnate that is; for God can owe nothing to God. But how can we offer God's own life to God? It is possible for *A*

---

[4] *Summa Theologiae* 3.48.2 ad 1.

to give something to *B* which, if he chooses, he can give back to *A*. I can give you a banker's cheque payable to myself; you can choose whether or not to return it to me. But the model becomes more obviously comprehensible if we take the separateness of the persons of the Trinity a bit more seriously. The Christian doctrine of God is that the one God consists in some sense of three persons, Father, Son, and Holy Spirit, of which the second person, the Son, voluntarily became incarnate.[5] Using that doctrine, we can then say that we can offer to God the Father the incarnate life of God the Son, who, because necessarily—i.e. not voluntarily—begotten by the Father, does not owe him that life. Maybe one human life, however perfect, would not equate in quantity of goodness the badness of so many human lives. But it is up to the wronged person to deem when a sufficient reparation has been made;[6] and one truly perfect life would surely be a proper amount of reparation for God to deem that reparation (and penance) enough had been made.

But why would God go to all this trouble, when he could simply forgive us in response to some minimum amount of repentance and apology? Well, he could have done so—almost all theologians agree on that. But they also say that there is much good in him taking our wrongdoing so seriously as to insist on some reparation. When serious wrong has been done, parents and courts rightly insist on some minimum amount of reparation by the wrongdoer. It involves him taking what he has done seriously. And if the wrongdoer has no means to make reparation, a well-wisher may often provide him with the means; the wrongdoer can then choose whether or not to use that means for that purpose. Could God not have sent some angel, or created some human in an adult state free from responsibility for the sins of ancestors, to make this atonement? No. That would have been

---

[5] I do not, however, wish to assume the doctrine of the Trinity at this stage, as I believe that the doctrine of the Incarnation can be spelled out without making the assumption that God consists of more than one person. However, it seems to me that taking seriously the sort of thing written in the Gospels and other New Testament books by those writers who affirmed most clearly the divinity of Jesus leads us to think of him as in some way a separate person from the Father. (See, further, Chapter 8.) I have argued on quite independent a priori grounds that God consists of three persons in *The Christian God*, ch. 8.

[6] Duns Scotus saw this clearly as regards God; that what counts as a sufficient reparation to God depends on what God deems sufficient. See the quotations and discussion in Grensted, *A Short History of the Doctrine of the Atonement*, 158–60. In this way Scotus took the discussion away from talk of the need for a sacrifice of infinite goodness to make reparation for our sins of infinite badness.

wrong. The officer has no right to command (or even permit) a private to fall on a grenade to save other soldiers if he could fall on it himself. God cannot command or even permit some volunteer to undertake so serious an act. If it is to be done, he must do it himself.

A perfect life need not end in a death by execution, but in so many human societies that might well happen; those who protest too strongly against injustice get executed. If God is to live a perfect life among us, just once for the sins of the world, it is plausible to suppose that he might choose to live in a society where it is highly probable that living a perfect life would involve bearing serious suffering, and where protest pays the highest price. 'No one has greater love than this, to lay down one's life for one's friends.'[7]

If the life of God Incarnate is to be available for us to offer back to God as our atonement, God Incarnate must intend that life to be used by us and so must show us how to join our repentance and apology to it; and God must tell us or show us that it is a pure offering acceptable to him as adequate reparation. From that, and from the fact that God would not allow anyone else to do such a serious act, and from the fact that the only human life not already owed to God would be God's own life, and so it would be very difficult for anyone else to live the requisite perfect life, we can conclude that the life which God intends us to offer is his own life. Providing atonement cannot be a totally incognito affair.

Is this first reason why God should intervene in human history in a public way—to make available to us, by becoming incarnate, a means of reconciliation to God by atonement for our sins—an overriding reason? Given that God creates us and that we sin, will he necessarily provide a means of atonement? Clearly he has no obligation to do so. No wronged person has any obligation to help the wrongdoer atone for their wrongdoing. If you steal my money, I have no obligation to you to help you cope with the consequences. But it might be generous of me to do so. So would it be the unique best action for God to do, to become incarnate and live a perfect human life? One alternative would be for God to insist on our making considerable atonement ourselves, and then forgiving us in the light of that. That insistence would make the obtaining of divine forgiveness very difficult indeed for most of us, although it would make us take our sins even more seriously. The other alternative

[7] John 15: 13.

would be to forgive us without requiring any reparation, but that has the disadvantage which I have stated, that our sins are not taken seriously enough. But perhaps a reasonable conclusion would be that it would be at least one of a few equal best acts for God to become incarnate in a perfect human life very probably ending in a death by execution; and maybe this would be a unique best act.

To Identify with our Suffering

A second reason why God might become incarnate in a human life very probably ending in a death by execution is this. God made humans subject to pain and suffering of various kinds caused both by other humans and by natural processes. God, being perfectly good, would only have permitted this subjection if it served some greater goods. Theodicy seeks to explain what are the relevant greater goods[8]—for example, the great good of humans having significant free choice that involves the possibility of their doing considerable harm to each other. We ordinary humans sometimes rightly subject our own children to suffering for the sake of some greater good (to themselves or others); for instance, make them eat a plain diet or take some special exercise for the sake of their health, or make them attend a 'difficult' neighbourhood school for the sake of good community relations. Under these circumstances we judge it a good thing to manifest solidarity with our children by putting ourselves in somewhat the same situation: share their diet or their exercise, or become involved in the parent–teacher organization of the neighbourhood school. A perfectly good God would judge it a good thing to share the pain the suffering to which he subjects us for the sake of greater goods, by becoming incarnate in a life that ends paradigmatically badly. If we ordinary humans subject our children to serious suffering for the sake of a greater good to others, there comes a point at which it is not merely good but obligatory to identify with the sufferer. Given the amount of pain and suffering which humans endure involuntarily, it seems to me highly plausible to suppose that, even if not obligatory, it would be a unique best act for God to share that sort of life, including the paradigm crisis which humans have to face: the crisis

---

[8] For my theodicy, see my *Providence and the Problem of Evil* (Clarendon Press, 1998).

of death. And the sharing needs to be not entirely incognito. The parent needs not merely to share the child's suffering, but to show him that he is doing so.

This reason is connected with a number of reasons which Christian theologians have given as to why, even if there was no need for atonement, God might well have become incarnate; but it is not quite the same as them. Aquinas lists ten such reasons, giving for each a supporting quotation from Augustine.[9] The nearest of these to the reason which I have just given is that, by becoming incarnate, God shows us how much he loves us.[10] He manifests his love by getting as close to us in our condition as possible. Under this heading it is appropriate to mention Kierkegaard's parable of the king and the maiden. The king seeks to win the love of the humble maiden, but if he appeared to her as a king he might elicit her love for the wrong reason. So he comes as a servant—not in disguise, for that would be deception, but really becomes a servant.[11] This reason is a reason for incarnation, quite independently of whether our condition involves suffering to which God has subjected us. Like the former reason, however, by acting on it God does not merely show us some truth which holds independently of being shown, but performs an act manifesting love. It has been the very widespread Christian experience that a God manifested only through the orderly behaviour of the natural world is a God 'afar off'. Few Christians have rich enough ever-present religious experiences which might seem to bring them into constant contact with God. The Jesus of the Gospel stories, believed to be in essence historical and believed to be about a Jesus who was God as well as human (as Christians have almost always believed), has, rightly or wrongly seemed to so many Christians to provide solid, reliable, public access to a God who was close enough to them to be their friend, and the comfort of knowing that God too suffered the human lot.

[9] *Summa Theologiae* 3.1.2.

[10] Aquinas cites Augustine, *De Trinitate* 13.10: 'nothing is so needful for us to build up our hope than for us to be shown how much God loves us'.

[11] S. Kierkegaard, *Philosophical Fragments*, trans. D. F. Swanson (Princeton University Press, 1962), ch. 2.

To Provide Information and Encouragement

The other reasons which Aquinas gives are ones in virtue of which a God Incarnate could show us things more fully than words could; for example, to show us how great is the dignity of human nature (because God took it on), and show us by example what a perfect human life amounts to.[12] To some extent humans can find out for themselves the most general moral truths: that we ought to keep our promises and pay our debts, care for our children and parents, and not kill or hurt others; and that beyond that it is supererogatorily good to care for others in innumerable ways. But we have a natural bias towards concealing these things from ourselves; and the teaching and example which we have provided for others have often been such as to prevent them from finding these things out. Original sinfulness has played its role. We need to be reminded of the moral truths which we can find out in theory for ourselves; and there are other moral truths which we cannot find out for ourselves, and we need to be told them by some authority. And in virtue of being our creator who keeps us in being from moment to moment and gives us so many good things, God has the right to impose further obligations on us—as do lesser benefactors such as parents or the State; to make, that is, acts which otherwise would be merely supererogatorily good or even morally indifferent into obligations. And God has good reason to do this; for example, to get us into the habit of doing the supererogatorily good, or for purposes of coordination (that is, for ensuring that someone does each job which needs doing). Even if it is not otherwise a duty to care for the poor in distant lands, God could make it our duty and thus oblige us to live better lives than we would live otherwise, and so become better people—something which is ultimately a good for us. If there is a job which needs doing by one person, and there is no evident way of determining who should do it, it will probably not get done. In such a case God has good reason to decree who should do the job. Nineveh needs to be preached to, but unless God tells Jonah to preach to Nineveh, either no one or too many people who could be better employed elsewhere will preach to Nineveh. So it is good for God sometimes to impose

---

[12] Aquinas quotes a sermon of Augustine (Sermon no. 371.2 (PL 39: 1660), *De Nativitate Dei*): 'It was in order that God might be shown to man and seen by man, and that there might be someone for man to follow, that God became man.'

duties, and we need to know what they are. While duties which concern only particular individuals do not need a general revelation, there may be reasons of coordination why particular classes of people should have particular duties. (For example, if families are to be a stable unit, they may need a head; and then God could lay down that wives ought to be the heads of family, or alternatively that husbands ought to be the heads of family.)[13]

For all of these reasons we need propositional revelation to tell us how to live. While nothing turns on whether the true answers to the moral problems which I am about to list are truths which we can but don't discover for ourselves, or are ones about which we need revelation or divine decree, there is so much about morals that we need to know. We need to know how to worship (and that, if God has made available a perfect life for us to offer in atonement for our sins, includes how to join our repentance and apology to that offering). We need to know whether abortion is always or only sometimes wrong; whether euthanasia or lying is always or only sometimes wrong; and whether there is a best form of government (e.g. democracy). We need to know whether the State has a duty to educate children if parents do not do so; and at what stage it has the right to intervene when parents abuse their children. And we need to know when countries have the right to interfere in the internal affairs of other countries.

Yet while we need all this moral information and we clearly need help in getting it and so a propositional revelation, there is no reason to expect that God would provide for us a total moral code. He needs to provide a lot of information, a lot more than we would have without a propositional revelation, but perhaps leaving some scope for ourselves to work out the detailed consequences of what he tells us. The purpose which we must attribute to God of giving us choice is compatible with him helping us to form right choices when we prove unable to do so, but not with him taking away totally our freedom to refuse to do so. We might therefore expect him to give us a lot more moral information than we would have on the basis of natural reason alone, but not perhaps so much as to deprive us of the possibility of choosing whether or not to work out the more detailed consequences for our lives of what he has told us.

---

[13] For my more detailed account of how God can impose obligations, see my *Responsibility and Atonement*, esp. ch. 8. For the importance of coordination as a reason for God to impose obligations on particular individuals, I am indebted to my former doctoral student Joseph Shaw.

And we need not merely revelation but encouragement. It is good that we should aim at long-term goals for the human (and animal) races. Not merely is it good that we should help this poor man and that poor woman, but it is good that we should work towards the alleviation of world poverty in decades to come. And for this purpose we need reason to believe that our efforts will have some success, that human suffering is a temporary and removable phenomenon. God needs to tell us or show us that that is the case. And it is also clearly good that, through doing good acts often, we should make ourselves naturally good people. In that moral struggle we need encouragement; and a major way of providing encouragement is to provide incentive. It will help us in our struggle if we believe that our efforts to be good people, good for their own sake, will be good for other reasons also which have a more natural appeal to us; e.g. that they will lead to us living for ever in the presence of God. Parents rightly encourage the faint desires of children to do what is right by tying their doing what is right to other goods which the children more readily desire. We can only know that God offers us the prospect of Heaven (and perhaps the risk of Hell) if he tells us or shows us this. But, for reasons given earlier, he cannot make this prospect too obvious.

God could certainly provide propositional revelation in words without himself becoming incarnate, and other religions (e.g. Islam) claim that this has happened. But words have to be understood, and definitions in terms of other words have to end somewhere (you could not understand any talk of colour, smell, or taste unless you were presented with examples of various colours, smells, etc. in terms of which other colours, smells, etc. could be defined). And I see every reason to believe that fundamental moral notions such as 'good', 'right', etc. can only be grasped if we can be shown examples of what goodness, oughtness-to-be-done, etc. amount to, by means of which we can recognize other examples of goodness etc. If these paradigm examples are not themselves examples of perfect worth, we would need to be told how a perfect life would differ from these less than perfect ones. And the words in which this difference was stated would themselves need to be understood. It is, I hope becoming clear that the least ambiguous grasp of what the goodness of human nature and the perfection of a human life amounts to would be provided by showing us an example of a perfect life, rather than describing it by words ultimately cashed out by inferior examples of good living. The example will be most relevant to our condition if it is an example of living perfectly in circumstances similar to the most difficult circumstances in which we have to live; and such a life must end in a death, plausibly the hard death of execution, involving rejection by one's fellows. And again, as with providing atonement, God has no right to send (or permit) someone else to do this job for him, although if some other human had lived a perfect life not being sent by God for the purpose of being our example, God could certainly tell us to copy him. However, for reasons considered earlier, there is not likely to be such a human. God has good reason to become incarnate in order to show us how to live, and we have good (though not conclusive) reason to suppose that any life which he commands to us as a perfect life is his life. In becoming incarnate, he could also provide encouragement to us in our long-term work of curing the world's ills by making his own efforts as a human at removing human ills to have considerable success; and he could show that death was not the necessary end of our lives by showing us that death was not the end of his human life. However, this latter encouragement could also be provided by a mere propositional revelation.

I should add that there are one or two respects in which it would be wrong for God Incarnate to live in the way that it would be good for us to live, and so respects in which, being perfectly good, God Incarnate would not live as it would be good for us to live. For example, I shall be arguing below that it would be wrong of God to become incarnate in such a way as to be capable of doing wrong. Hence, being unable to do wrong, he would not do wrong—to humans or to God. We humans, having done much wrong to God, have a duty to repent and apologize to God. But if God Incarnate were to confess having done wrong, he would be uttering a falsehood. Knowingly to utter a falsehood is to do wrong. So it would be wrong of God Incarnate to repent and apologize during any period of his life in which he showed awareness of being God Incarnate; that is, any period in which he sought to show us this (and I have argued that we have reason to expect that God Incarnate will seek to show us who he is).

Even if God Incarnate did live a perfect life (as near as possible to the kind of perfect life it would be good for us to live), humans do nevertheless need a lot more information of how to live than mere observation of one perfect life could provide. For that life would be the life of one human—of one sex, one age range, one race, in some very special circumstances, and with a very special job to do. We need guidance as to what a good life would be for us who are inevitably different from him in so many varied ways. So should not God become incarnate innumerable times in different kinds of human lives? Even if he did, they would still be the lives of God Incarnate, for whom, in virtue of his being God, slightly different acts would be good from those which would be good for ordinary humans. And too many examples of how to live would reduce the 'epistemic distance' from God which we need for free will and responsibility; and would deprive us of much responsibility for telling others about what God Incarnate had done. The more appearances God makes, the less need there is to tell others about it. Help enough to apply the perfection of the exemplary incarnate life would be provided by God-authenticated sentences describing what the perfection of a human life amounts to when it is the life of one of another sex, age, culture, and race to the exemplary life. I suggest that for God to become incarnate once in order to show us how to live and encourage us to do so would be at least an equal best act— as good that God should do it as that he should not. So long as there was only one incarnation and not too obvious a one, quite enough epistemic distance would remain.

I have given three groups of reasons why it would be a good thing for God to live an incarnate life among us. Taking the reasons of each group together as one reason: they are to provide a means of atonement; to identify with our suffering; and to show us how to live and encourage us to do so. I have suggested that each separate reason makes it at least an equal best act for God to become incarnate, and the second reason plausibly makes it a unique best act. Human judgements about such big moral issues as what would be the best act for God to do are inevitably going to be somewhat tentative. But obviously we do know something about the difference between good and bad, and more particularly about what makes for a good parent, when the parent–child relation is similar to the relation of God to humans. So, taking my three kinds of reasons together, it would seem fairly plausible to suppose that together they do provide strong reason for God to become incarnate. Again, so as not to exaggerate my case, let me suggest that these reasons make it as probable as not that, if there is a God, he will become incarnate (in order to identify with our suffering and for at least one of the other two reasons).

None of the reasons why God should become incarnate provides much by way of grounds for expecting more than one incarnation. It trivializes the notion of a perfect human life to suggest that three lives, say, might be a suitable reparation for God to accept, whereas one would not. We live but one human life; he shows his love and identifies with our suffering fully by living one human life. And, as I wrote above, too many examples of a perfect life believed to be that of God, given in order to show us how to live, would reduce too much God's 'epistemic distance' from us. But there is no need for me to prejudge the issue of whether there has been more than one incarnation by claiming that God would have no reason to become incarnate more than once, for, as we shall see in due course, there is no significant historical evidence that he has done so more than once.

The Kinds of Incarnation Required

What would incarnation involve? God being essentially omnipotent, omniscient, perfectly free, perfectly good, etc.—which I summarize as being essentially divine—his incarnation could not involve his ceasing to be divine. It must, rather, involve God taking on additionally a human body and a human nature understood as a human way of thinking and acting.[14] This is what the Council of Chalcedon, as I read it, affirmed in AD 451 had actually happened when God did become incarnate in Jesus Christ; and the Chalcedonian definition has become the hallmark of orthodoxy for mainstream Christianity (Catholic, Orthodox, and Protestant). But it can be understood in different ways. You can think of God having a human nature as him acting and thinking in a human way, and while doing so being fully aware of his divine nature, acts, and thoughts, and this is the understanding of Chalcedon of those who added to the Chalcedonian definition St John Damascene's doctrine of the περιχώρησις φυσέων, the interpenetration of the two natures of Christ. Such an incarnation we may call a unified incarnation. Alternatively, while remaining one subject of thought and action, he could act and react

---

[14] It needs to be argued that the concept of an incarnation, God essentially divine taking on a human nature and body, is a coherent one. I have argued that it is in *The Christian God*, esp. ch. 9.

in his human life in partial ignorance of, and so with only partial access to, his divine powers. As Freud taught us, we often put ourselves into a situation of partial ignorance of our desires and beliefs voluntarily, for bad reasons. But God could put himself in such a situation for good reasons, if there were good reasons for that. And just as we, or at any rate some of us, can carry on a telephone conversation while writing a letter at the same time, and in each action act and react with quite distinct beliefs and desires, so God could act simultaneously with a divine nature doing divine things and with a human nature doing human things (not acting with awareness of his divine nature). Such an incarnation we may call a divided incarnation. One who claims that Christ's incarnation was divided stresses Chalcedon's affirmation that the union of natures was ἀσυγχύτως ('without confusion'); one who claims that Christ's incarnation was unified stresses Chalcedon's affirmation that the union was ἀδιαιρέτως ἀχωρίστως ('without division, without separation').[15]

Now what sort of incarnation do these various reasons for incarnation suggest that God would adopt? They all, except the reason of giving propositional revelation, suggest that God should live a life as close as possible to our human life, and live that life—not a superior human life—to perfection. That requires living under our conditions of ignorance (of things other than those which he needs to reveal) and unawareness of powers beyond ordinary human powers (except when these are required to fulfil the reasons for incarnation). There are certain human limitations which, being God, he cannot take on. He cannot take on a proneness to sin (because sinning is wronging God and no one can wrong himself), nor, more substantially, can he take on a proneness to wrongdoing. For to put yourself in a position where you are liable to wrong others (when you would not otherwise be liable) is itself wrong. (That is why it is wrong to drink alcohol before driving a car.) And so, in virtue of his essential perfect goodness, God could not become incarnate with such a proneness. But it is not wrong, and it may sometimes be very good, to put yourself in a position where (with the foreseen consequence though not the intention that) you have a proneness to do less than the best, e.g. to give away so much money that you are prone to

---

[15] I summarize here two different possible ways in which Chalcedon could be satisfied, spelled out more fully in my *The Christian God*, ch. 9.

become stingy. And it would not have been wrong, and in fact for the reasons I have set out it would have been very good, for God to become incarnate, sharing our lot so much that he became liable not to act for the best. In that respect, and that respect alone, he would suffer from original sinfulness. So prone, his overcoming that proneness and forcing himself to act heroically would have enabled him to live a perfect life of the kind that we humans live imperfectly; and hence a life suitable for out atonement and example.[16] I conclude that the reasons which I have addressed as to why God should become incarnate lead us to expect a divided incarnation.

If God is to become incarnate for all these reasons, he will have to do so when at least some part of the human race is intellectually and spiritually fairly well developed. It needs a clear concept of morality, that is, not concerned merely with ritual or family issues, but with justice and the needs of the poor; and a sharp awareness of the difference between knowing wrongdoing and inadvertent wrongdoing, and the sense that the really bad form of guilt requiring considerable atonement is that resulting from wrongdoing knowingly. And humans need the concept of God, our omnipotent, omniscient, perfectly good creator if we are to realize that we have a duty to God to worship him and a duty to care for our fellow humans; not just a duty to those humans, but a duty to God to care for our fellow humans. Many humans need to have knowingly done much wrong over a considerable period and have failed to make proper atonement to God for their wrongdoing (and for that of their ancestors). For God would surely prefer us to take our own wrongdoing seriously by ourselves making atonement—for that is our duty, and the paradigmatic way of taking our wrongdoing seriously. Plausibly, only if most humans over a considerable period of knowing wrongdoing failed to make proper atonement would God see fit to intervene. And if God is to identify with our sufferings and show us how to live, for this reason, too, humans need to have the concept of God, our omnipotent, omniscient, perfectly good, etc. creator, and not just the concept of a god, a powerful supernatural being. For only if we understood *who* has become incarnate would we know the kind of identification involved (that it was he who allowed us to suffer for

---

[16] If he had yielded to the proneness and so not have lived heroically, no wrong would have been done, but a new incarnation would have been required to produce a perfect life suitable for atonement and example.

the sake of greater good who suffered with us), or have great reason to follow his teaching and example. Now for this purpose (though not for the purpose of making atonement, where we need to have had the concept much earlier) an incarnate God could teach us about who God is, at the same time as teaching us other things. But clearly there is good in humans finding this out for themselves if they are capable of doing so; and clearly many individual thinkers and at least one individual culture (the Jewish people in the half-millennium before Christ) were monotheistic, without deriving their views from the teaching of an incarnate God.

3

The Marks of an Incarnate God

SUPPOSE THAT for all of the reasons set out in the last chapter God did choose to become incarnate and lead a human life. What would be the marks of that life by which we could recognize it if it was to succeed in providing atonement, identifying with our suffering, and providing information and encouragement? Let us call a candidate for being God Incarnate a prophet.[1] What observable features would we expect a prophet's life to have if it was to be the life of God Incarnate?

The Prior Requirements for being God Incarnate

In order to provide atonement and to provide information by showing us how to live, God Incarnate would have to live a perfect human life; and so the first requirement is that a prophet's public behaviour would be (in so far as we have knowledge of it) characteristic of a perfect human life. I argued earlier that God would not become incarnate in a way which made him liable to do wrong. But acts which are wrong for ordinary humans to do are not always wrong for God to do. God, for example, has the right to terminate an ordinary human life—for such a life is God's gift, and so he can limit the length of the gift as he chooses. So God Incarnate could kill. But if he did, while incarnate, acts which though permissible for him are not permissible for us, he would not be living the sort of life we have failed to live, nor would he have identified with us in our difficult

---

[1] I shall use the personal pronoun 'he' to refer to such a prophet, in view of the clumsiness of the more precise 'he or she', but I am not assuming that any prophet will be male.

human situation (where so many actions are not permissible) as fully as possible, nor would his life be an example to us—and so none of the three main purposes of an incarnation would have been fulfilled. Likewise, even if he fulfilled all the obligations we would have in his situation (apart from any that involve actions which he would have an obligation not to do; see p. 49), his life would still not serve two of those three purposes unless it manifested supererogatory goodness. It is a perfect life which would make a proper atonement; and since God seeks the best for us, he will want us to live lives of supererogatory goodness and so he needs to show such a life to us.

Perfection involves helping others, and encouraging some to help others improve the human condition massively damaged by disease, death, and sin. So the prophet must provide us with encouragement in our efforts to improve the human condition, showing us that God supports and will forward these efforts. He can do this most obviously by actually improving the human condition in ways that are beyond the capacity of ordinary humans to do. Let us call this requirement the healing requirement, without assuming that it will necessarily include healing physical disease. It may involve psychological healing or healing some of the evils of society. Such healing might or might not involve violation of natural laws. If it did, it would constitute more evidence that God was at work here, but unless God was going to violate natural laws often in future when humans asked his help,[2] this healing would not in this respect provide a recipe for ordinary humans to follow. Perhaps some miraculous and many non-miraculous healings would be the best combination.

As I noted in the last chapter, a perfect life led for the purposes of exemplifying and showing us how to exemplify coping with the worst that life throws at people might well be expected to end in a death by execution. This symbolizes the final rejection of the prophet by other humans, something so many humans experience to a lesser degree when rejected by their family or community, belonging to a family or community being so central to a full human existence.

Secondly, if God Incarnate is to provide moral guidance, the prophet needs to teach us by word how to live in order that we may

---

[2] And to do so would be to deprive humans of many opportunities to sort out their own problems.

see how to apply his pattern of life to the circumstances of our lives, when we will be for the most part humans of different age, sex, class, or culture from him. This teaching would include teaching about how we are to worship and otherwise interact with God; and teaching about the afterlife, that there is Heaven for the good and (if that is how it is) the possibility of Hell for the bad; for, as noted in the last chapter, we need encouragement to do good and deterrence from doing bad. It will thus include teaching (e.g. about Heaven) whose truth we could not discover for ourselves, but it must be such as—in so far as we can judge for ourselves—is plausibly true and deep. A prophet who taught that rape and murder were good would disqualify himself from being a serious candidate for being God Incarnate. In respect of things that humans cannot discover for themselves, the prophet must claim God's authority for his teaching; he will claim our assent to it as something 'revealed'.

Thirdly, the prophet must show us that he believed himself to be God Incarnate. I do not wish, however, to claim that the prophet must say, at any rate at the beginning of his ministry, 'I am God'. For the natural way to understand God becoming incarnate is to suppose simply that he operates temporarily through a human body, without his whole way of thinking and his susceptibility to feeling being affected. Allegedly, the Greek gods often took on human bodies and lived among humans in disguise. Unless people had the concept of a divided incarnation of the kind described in the last chapter, the statement by the prophet 'I am God', if believed, would be so badly misunderstood as to defeat some of the purposes of an incarnation. For people would suppose that when nails were hammered into his body he did not suffer, or when he uttered sentences like 'My God, my God, why have you forsaken me',[3] he did not really feel that he was deserted by God (that is, they would not believe that he was unaware, in his human way of thinking, of the fact that he was God). They would suppose that, knowing his nature and the outcome of his life, he would see with total clarity that all would be well in the end. But someone who lived a human life of this kind would not suffer the pain and uncertainty which we suffer, and so people would not believe that his kind of life was a life which manifested his identification with their suffering or which they could imitate under the circumstances of their life.

[3] Mark 15: 34.

One way out of this would be for God to ensure that the doctrine of the possibility of the divided kind of incarnation was available for ready application to a prophet who claimed to be God, thus preventing misunderstanding of the kind of incarnation he was affirming. The alternative way out of this would be for people first to realize that many of the purposes which would be served by an incarnation had been fulfilled, and then to conclude from less evident parts of the prophet's teaching and actions that it was indeed God who had fulfilled them. The prophet could be shown evidently to suffer, and then the less evident part of his teaching could be shown to entail his divinity, and so show that he was God Incarnate in the divided way. To a society initially ignorant of the possibility of a divided incarnation, this second way would seem the only one possible. This, perhaps, in any case is the only way in which God can get close to us in the kind of way in which Kierkegaard's parable of the king and the maiden suggests: he cannot initially reveal his identity.

Nevertheless, God Incarnate must reveal his identity in the end. For we will reflect (if my reasoning in Chapter 2 is correct) that God had no right to send someone else to lead an atoning life on his behalf, and so if there really was an atonement, it must have been God himself who made it. And although God could share the suffering to which he subjects us for the sake of a greater good without showing that he was doing so, we should still doubt whether those evils had been brought about by God for the sake of a greater good unless we have reason to believe that he had shared that suffering. And we would have little ground for believing either of these things unless the prophet eventually made it clear that he was God himself.

However, fourthly, what the prophet can teach without initial misunderstanding and so (if he is God Incarnate seeking to provide atonement) must teach is that his life (and death) do provide a means of atonement making God's forgiveness available for those who repent of their sins. For an atoning life of which we are ignorant is not one to which we can join our repentance and apology. And finally there is no point in God teaching or showing all the things which I have set out to a small community unless (barring innumerable incarnations) he makes provision for his teaching (including his teaching about his incarnation and atoning life) to be handed on to new generations and cultures. So the prophet must found a church in which these things are to be handed on, and he must teach that what it teaches and provides is what he teaches and provides. And it would have to be the case that the church did continue to teach what he taught (including the doctrines of his incarnation and atonement) and provide what he claimed to provide (forgiveness of sins for penitent sinners), and did spread and make it available to new generations and cultures. For otherwise the incarnation would only have been of use to one generation and culture; and God would have achieved very little of his purposes by the incarnation. The alternative of a separate incarnation to each culture and generation seems, as I claimed in the previous chapter, to trivialize the notion of the perfection achieved for atonement and identification by one perfect life, and to deprive other human beings of the enormous responsibility of spreading the divine message widely or failing to do so.

No Other Prophet Satisfies these Prior Requirements

If God is to become incarnate in order to fulfil all the purposes for becoming incarnate listed in Chapter 2, we would expect his life to show these five marks. His life must be, as far as we can judge, a perfect human life in which he provides healing; he must teach deep moral and theological truths (ones, in so far as we can judge, plausibly true); he must show himself to believe that he is God Incarnate; he must teach that his life provides an atonement for our sins; and he must found a church which continues his teaching and work. Let us call a prophet who does all this one who satisfies the prior requirements for being God Incarnate. If God became incarnate only to fulfil some of the purposes described in Chapter 2, then we might not expect quite all of these requirements to be fulfilled. But I urged that identifying with our suffering was plausibly a unique best act and so one which God would have to do; and many of these requirements are to be expected for that reason alone. And even if, for each of the other two purposes, it was as good to fulfil them as not to fulfil them, then, I claim, it would be as probable as not that God would fulfil at least one of them, in addition to the purpose of identifying with our suffering. So God's nature is such that we can expect him to fulfil most of the purposes through some prophet.

Despite this, I do not know of any prophet in human history about whom we have significant positive evidence that he is a serious candidate for fulfilling even most of these requirements, if we leave aside for the moment Jesus of Nazareth. Many prophets have led good lives—the Buddha, for example—though for none of the founders of major religions (major in terms of number of present-day adherents) other than Christianity did their life end in an execution. Among medium-sized religions the Bab, the founder of Baha'ism, was executed by Shi'ite Islam (and possibly Zoroaster was executed). Many prophets have taught important moral and theological truths; though Muhammad and (if we count him as the historical founder of Judaism) Moses and some founders of smaller religions taught that their teachings were revealed by God, the Buddha did not. Large-scale bodily healings were not characteristic of the foundation of any other major or smaller religion. But one could regard the liberation of the Jews from Egypt (as a result of the plagues prophesied by Moses), or the conquests resulting from the work and teaching of Muhammad, as initiating new eras of divinely governed society. Yet force of war is dominant in both these events, and even if the end product is good, the means are not obviously ones by which human society is healed.

None of the major religions, apart from Hinduism (and Christianity), have claimed for their founders or any prophet that he was God Incarnate. Hinduism has claimed that God became incarnate in many prophets in human history. However, the knowledge of the lives of these prophets comes from writings far more remote from the events with which they are concerned than are the books of the New Testament. There is no serious historical evidence of the details of the lives of any of these purported Indian prophets whose lives are recorded in the Hindu Scriptures, nor evidence that they claimed, or led their contemporaries to believe, that they believed themselves to be God Incarnate. So if there was any claim by any significant religious figure of the past (apart from Jesus) that he was God Incarnate, we have no serious evidence of it, and the major benefits of such an incarnation are not available to subsequent generations. Certainly, very many people other than founders of major religions have claimed to be God Incarnate (there were plenty of them in the twentieth century). But when we learn the details of their lives, they have been found to have serious blemishes (often in the form of many mistresses and expensive motor cars).

No founder of a major religion (or established medium-sized religion) other than Christianity has claimed to provide an atonement for human wrongdoing. Neither Moses nor Muhammad nor the Buddha made such a claim. Certainly all the founders of major religions founded institutions to carry out their work. But neither Judaism nor Hinduism provide obvious signs of having a church founded to proclaim their teaching (including teaching of an atonement and incarnation) to others beyond their own culture. Jews have usually seemed to regard proselytizing as a somewhat peripheral activity, and many Hindus hold that you cannot become a Hindu—you have to be born as one.

I conclude that, if we leave aside for the moment the case of Jesus of Nazareth, there is no known serious candidate in all human history for satisfying even most of the prior requirements for being God Incarnate. In so far as this claim concerns significant known historical figures, I am not making a recondite historical claim. It would in general be agreed by defenders of non-Christian religions: they do not commend their religion, for example, on the basis that God became incarnate and made atonement for the sins of the world. That is not their grounds for claiming human allegiance. The major religions (and medium-sized established religions) other than Christianity claim either that there is no God or that he is not able or has no need to become incarnate in such a way as to satisfy these prior requirements or that he has not done so yet.

No Other Candidate Satisfies the Posterior Requirement

But even if the prior requirements were known without any possible doubt to have been satisfied by some prophet, that perhaps would not be overwhelming evidence for his divinity. He could live a perfect life (unlikely though that is), teach great truths, perform works of healing, teach that his life was an atonement, and found a church (which taught his incarnation and atoning work) without being God. He could even, perhaps, make it evident that he believed himself to be God; this belief could have been the result of a misunderstanding of his inner experience which was not his fault. However that may be, it is surely not enormously unlikely that, in the course of the three or so millennia about which we have reasonably good detailed historical knowledge of human events, there should be a prophet about whom there was quite good but not incorrigible evidence that these requirements were satisfied, even though he was not God Incarnate. It could certainly happen if there was no God that such a prophet appeared through natural processes—though the fact that (with our one possible exception of Jesus) there is no such prophet suggests that natural processes do not readily throw up such a prophet. However, it is possible (though not, of course, in my view, probable) that there is no God. So we must take seriously the possibility that there could be a candidate who satisfied the prior requirements moderately well and yet was not God Incarnate.

If God is to give us good grounds for believing that some prophet is God Incarnate, he must provide some further evidence, evidence of some kind of divine signature on that life which could not be produced by normal processes but only by God himself (or by some agent permitted to do so by God). That involves the success of the life being made possible only by an evident violation (or quasi-violation) of natural laws—for God, who keeps the laws of nature operative, alone can permit them to be set aside—and the contemporaries of this event having the concepts to recognize this intervention as God's authenticating approval of the life. (I write 'the contemporaries', for it is they who in a church would have the responsibility of handing on the good news to later generations.) A violation brought about by God which is large in the sense of one which if it was known to occur would be manifestly a violation I call a super-miracle. The prophet's life needs to be signed by a super-miracle. There are different ways in which this could be done, but, I shall be arguing, one very obvious way would be by God bringing to life again him who was killed for leading a perfect life.

Let us call a prophet with whose life such a super-miracle is connected in this way one who satisfies the posterior requirement for being God Incarnate. There is again (with the same one possible exception, Jesus Christ) no prophet for whom there is serious evidence that this posterior demand is satisfied. No other of the major (or medium-sized) religions is founded on a purported miracle for which there is even a moderate amount of historical evidence. Muhammad claimed to perform no miracles except the writing of the Koran—and however great a work that is, there is little reason to suppose that for an uneducated prophet to write it constitutes violating a law of nature. And although the Israelite religion may have been founded on a miracle (such as the crossing of the Red Sea), the detailed historical evidence for it is simply not in the same league as the evidence of the Resurrection—whatever particular value one gives to the strength of the latter evidence.

Jesus as a Candidate for Satisfying both Requirements

Now of course it may be that there is some small religion making claims about its prophet, for which there is significant historical evidence which it can produce that both the prior and posterior requirements for being God Incarnate are met. But, if so, it is somewhat surprising that this religion has remained so inconspicuous; and clearly it has not so far even begun to fulfil the major purpose of an incarnation, to make various good things, including atonement, accessible to all humanity. So, in the absence of such evidence being produced, I shall assume that there is no such religion. Christianity, however, is different; in the case of Jesus, unlike other prophets, I shall be arguing, there is significant historical evidence that both the prior and posterior requirements for being God Incarnate are met. That the one and only one prophet in the history of the world who satisfied the prior requirements for being God Incarnate should also satisfy the posterior requirement would be impossible unless God brought about the latter for the purpose of making it clear that that prophet was God Incarnate. For violations (or quasi-violations) of laws of nature cannot (given my assumption of the non-existence of lesser deities) occur unless there is a God who controls the laws of nature. Otherwise laws of nature provide the ultimate explanation of what happens and no one can set them aside; but if there is a God, he (or someone else permitted by God to do so) can set them aside. It would be a massive deception on his part to set them aside by putting a divine signature on the life of a prophet who was not God Incarnate, for whom all the prior requirements for being God Incarnate were satisfied; for that would amount to his saying falsely that that prophet was God Incarnate. A perfectly good God would not bring about a massive deception,.

It is not merely impossible that the prior and posterior requirements should both be satisfied in the same prophet unless God brought it about, but it is very unlikely that there would be the amount of evidence there is (to be spelled out in later chapters) that both requirements had been satisfied in connection with the same prophet unless God brought it about. For, as we have seen, there is significant evidence that the prior requirements have been satisfied by at most one prophet. We have also seen that there is significant evidence that the posterior requirements have been satisfied in connection with at most one prophet. And, I now add, there is no significant evidence of a super-miracle culminating the life of any major figure in world history, with again one possible exception. It is, therefore, very unlikely indeed that there would be evidence that both requirements have been satisfied in connection with the same prophet, by chance in a God-less universe. It would be very unlikely to happen unless God (or some lesser agent permitted to do so by God) had brought it about, given that there is a reasonable probability that there is a God, and that there is some good purpose for which he might choose to bring it about. Clearly, the obvious good purpose to bring about evidence that the posterior requirement had been satisfied in connection with a prophet for whom the prior requirements had been satisfied would be to show that he had put his signature on the life of that prophet and so declared him to be God Incarnate. If he brings this about when the prophet is not God Incarnate, God would be deceiving us (or agreeing to a deception by some devil on a matter of vast importance for the human race). It would be like leaving someone's fingerprints at the murder scene when they had not committed the murder, or spreading a rumour that someone had won a presidential election and therefore had the right to give orders to soldiers to kill, when that person had not won the election. God would not thus deceive (or permit such a massive deception) and so we can reasonably conclude that, if there is a God, this evidence is not misleading.

It should now be clear that everything turns on relative probability: how much more likely it is that you would get the kind of evidence we have that the prior and posterior requirements are jointly fulfilled, if God brought about their joint fulfilment as a result of becoming incarnate, than if the occurrence of the two sets of evidence occurred by mere chance in a God-less world. If the former is a lot more probable than the latter, you don't require the theory that there is a God who becomes incarnate to be already very probable simply on the evidence of natural theology (in more technical terms, to have high prior probability). So what needs to be shown now is just how strong is the detailed historical evidence that the prior and posterior requirements for being God Incarnate were satisfied in Jesus, in the sense of just how probable it is that there would be the sort of historical evidence there is if Jesus was God Incarnate who rose from the dead. Even if it is only moderately probable that there would in this case be that sort of evidence (even if it was more probable than not that the evidence would not be of this kind) it may still exceed by a long way the great improbability of the coincidence of evidence in connection with a prophet who was not God Incarnate.

Before I turn to the detailed historical evidence about Jesus, it is worth noting that it would be very difficult for God to fulfil all the purposes of an incarnation by becoming incarnate long before the time of Jesus or among most peoples other than the Jews. I argued in Chapter 2 that an incarnation for the purpose of making atonement required that the human race should be at a stage where they had sinned knowingly and badly for a considerable period of time against a deep understanding of the moral law and proved unable to make adequate atonement themselves; and that an incarnation to identify with our sufferings and to teach us how to live required a community capable of understanding that it was God (omnipotent, omniscient, etc.) who was doing these things, and not just a powerful supernatural being. No whole community (as opposed perhaps to isolated thinkers) understood both the bindingness of morality and the nature of God (as I am assuming him in this book to be) better than the Jewish people of the later part of the first millennium BC. That the moral law was concerned not merely with ritual purity but above all with justice (to be practised by kings as well as subjects) and caring for the poor was a central message of the Jewish prophets of the middle of that millennium (Isaiah, Jeremiah, Ezekiel, Amos, Hosea, Micah, etc.). If that message was not always very central in subsequent Jewish thinking, it was there as part of the Jewish Scriptures to be heard regularly by all the people. Jesus may have extended the normal understanding of who is the 'neighbour' whom we ought to help[4] and the goodness of helping him, far more than obligation requires,[5] but he was building on a tradition. Morality mattered, and to break the moral law was to wrong the one God all-powerful and all-good who created us from nothing. But inadvertently breaking the moral law was not nearly as important a sin as breaking it knowingly.[6]

---

[4] See the parable of the good Samaritan; Luke 10: 29–37.

[5] See Matt. 5: 38–42.

[6] See the distinction, made in Num. 15: 22–31, between the kind of response appropriate to unintentional sin (an animal sacrifice to God to make atonement) and the kind of response appropriate to sin 'with a high hand' (the sinner to be 'cut off from among the people').

I now add that if God Incarnate is to found a church which will continue his teaching and give to people of new generations and cultures reason to hold beliefs about him and his teaching, there are similar constraints on when he can become incarnate. He needs to live on Earth when there is travel and writing (without which messages are bound to get distorted), a sharp awareness of the difference between myth and ancient history and of ways of testing historical claims (e.g. that you can trust a witness of this sort and not of that sort). Only so will he provide those new generations and cultures with good reason for belief. This sharp awareness of the difference between myth and ancient history and how to test for it was evident, as far as the cultures of the Mediterranean and Middle East are concerned, as far as we can judge for the first time among the Greeks of the later half of the first millennium BC, peoples among whom travel and writing were widespread. This culture came to permeate the whole Mediterranean area, including Palestine, in the two centuries before Christ.

It would need a long historical discussion to substantiate the claim that it was in Palestine in the last two centuries BC for the first time in human history that both of these sets of conditions for the suitability of an incarnation were well satisfied. I have not made the comparison with China or India. But it is commonplace to observe that these conditions were not well satisfied among so many earlier and distant peoples. Palestine in the two centuries BC was among the earliest if not the earliest place in the world well suited for an incarnation for the purposes discussed in Chapter 2. And in fact many Jews of the first century AD expected God to intervene in human history through some agent: the human race (or at any rate the Jewish people) were in such a bad way that they needed help. But, as we shall see, despite the variety of expectations about the kind of human who might be God's agent, they did not expect God himself to become incarnate; nor, as we shall see, did they expect that his agent would behave much like Jesus.

So I turn now to consider the evidence that the prior historical requirements for being God were satisfied in the life of Jesus of Nazareth.

PART II

PRIOR HISTORICAL EVIDENCE

4

The Historical Sources

Their Genre

ALMOST ALL the evidence about the life and teaching of Jesus of Nazareth is in the form of written testimony; and by far the most important evidence is that contained in the books of the New Testament. The vast majority of scholars agree that almost all the books of the New Testament were written within the first 110 years of the Christian era, that is, within eight-five years of the events which are their primary focus, the last three years of the life of Jesus and what happened immediately after that; and that most of the books were written much earlier than that. There are a few other extant Christian writings probably written at the end of this period. Of these the First Epistle of Clement is generally dated at about AD 96 and the Epistles of Ignatius of Antioch about AD 106. The 'Gospel of Thomas' is a collection of parables and short sayings of Jesus (and so somewhat misleadingly entitled a 'Gospel') to be dated somewhere between AD 60 and 140. There are also a few brief references to Christianity in Jewish and pagan writings of this period,[1] though some of them may be quite significant. But the fact remains that by far the most important evidence is contained in the books of the New Testament. So much is going to depend on what we judge the conventions of genre, the trustworthiness of the authors, and sources of those books to be.

By the 'conventions of genre' I mean how far the authors of those books intend their sections, which seem to narrate some event, to be taken as an accurate, detailed report of a historical event. To illustrate what I have in mind, note that there are books of the Old Testament

---

[1] For descriptions of these, see G. Thiessen and A. Merz, *The Historical Jesus: A Comprehensive Guide* (SCM Press, 1998), ch. 3.

which, many scholars agree, are not so intended. The books of Jonah and Daniel are not, for example, in the view of many, intended to give accurate historical reports. They are works of fiction intended to encourage. The book of Daniel contains stories of the heroism of Jews taken captive to Babylon in maintaining their religious practices in the face of attempts by King Nebuchadnezzar to force them to sacrifice to his gods. These stories were written 300 years after the captivity in Babylon in order to encourage Jews in Palestine facing a similar persecution from the Syrian King Antiochus Epiphanes. The book of Jonah is a story of a prophet who tried to escape his vocation from God to preach to the Gentiles but finally did preach, designed to encourage Jews to proselytize. New Testament scholars raise the issue of how much of the apparently narrative parts of the New Testament was written in a similar vein.

I argued earlier that, in the absence of counter-evidence, apparent testimony should be taken as real testimony and so apparent historical claims as real historical claims. Given that, and the fact that they are in many respects in a style similar to many other letters of the ancient Graeco-Roman world, the genre of many of the 'epistles' of St Paul as letters is unquestionable; they are paradigm examples of letters where any brief narrative contained within them is intended to be taken as history. Scholars are virtually unanimous both in attributing many of the epistles of St Paul (1 Thessalonians, Galatians, Philippians, Romans, 1 and 2 Corinthians, and Philemon) to Paul of Tarsus and in dating them between AD 49 and 58. And not merely is the genre, author, and date of these documents clear, but the character of the author jumps out of the pages. No one can read the more personal letters—Galatians, 2 Corinthians, and Philemon—without getting a very strong impression that Paul is a totally honest and generally very compassionate man (willing to rebuke those who he thinks have been deceitful or otherwise immoral, but keen for reconciliation with them; and keen not to get involved in matters which he thought relatively unimportant). What he says in his letters, above all what he gives his solemn word about, he means. He may or may not have been deceived by others or misled by appearances, but he is certainly not attempting to deceive us. He is telling us what he believes. And on the few occasions when he gives us narrative, he means it to be taken as a literal historical truth. If we question the genre of those letters, we would have to question the genre of every historical document ever written.

The genre of the other 'epistles' as (purported) letters is also reasonably clear (though they may include elements of liturgy). What is less clear is who wrote them and when. The last book of the Bible, the book of Revelation, purports to be a vision. The elements of the vision (horses, colours, Babylon, etc.) clearly have great symbolic significance, not all of which is clear to modern readers. It is similar in genre to one or two books of the Old Testament (especially books of the Apocrypha), and close to many other Jewish books in circulation at the time. And that leaves us with the four Gospels and the Acts of the Apostles, on which we are so largely dependent for our knowledge of Jesus. How far were they intended to be taken as literal history?

It seems fairly clear that the main body of the Acts of the Apostles is intended to be taken as literal history. It reads like any other contemporary work of history, and the later parts (which contain no reports of anything miraculous) are so detailed and matter-of-fact as to have a diary-like quality to them. In a number of passages when describing the travels of St Paul, the author speaks of 'we'.[2] Paul's letters describe events also described in Acts.[3] Further, it seems evident that Acts is the second part of a two-volume work, of which the first volume is St Luke's Gospel. There is a unity of style and thought between the two works, and the explicit affirmation of its second-volume status at the beginning of Acts.[4] That opening sentence of Acts describing the 'first book' as being concerned with 'all that Jesus did and taught from the beginning' indicates that the author thought of his earlier work as also basically historical, differing from the later work only in the period of history described by it. The opening sentences of St Luke's Gospel confirm that the author thought of his work as basically a work of history (though, of course, history of cosmic significance). He writes there that he sought to do the same as the many others who 'have undertaken to set down an orderly account of the events which have been fulfilled among us, just as they were handed on to us by those who from the beginning were eyewitnesses and servants of the word'.[5] The most

---

[2] Acts 16: 10–17; 20: 5–15; 21: 1–18; 27: 1–28: 16.

[3] See the Council of Jerusalem, described rather impersonally in Acts 15: 1–29 and from a very personal perspective in Gal. 2: 1–10; and the incident of Paul's escape from Damascus (Acts 9: 23–5 and 2 Cor. 11: 32–3).

[4] Acts 1: 1. Translations of biblical passages are all taken from the New Revised Standard Version of the Bible. [5] Luke 1: 1–2.

fundamental principles for interpreting sentences discussed in Chapter 1 force us to suppose that Luke is seeking to record contemporary history, in the absence of strong positive evidence to the contrary. He might have been misled, and he might even be seeking to mislead us (though I shall argue against that shortly), but what he is trying to do is get his reader to believe that what he records really happened in recent history.

Are there exceptions—passages in Luke or Acts not intended to be taken as literal history? The reports of long speeches (in Acts), though they purport to be verbatim accounts, are no doubt intended only as accounts giving the essence of what was said. Ancient writers do not distinguish sharply between the two kinds of account. And if the infancy narrative (Luke 1: 5–2: 52) is in general to be taken as purported history, the reports of the hymns sung are no doubt for similar reasons to be understood as giving the essence of someone's response to a situation rather than as verbatim. Is the infancy narrative in general intended as literal history, or perhaps as a myth conveying (via the story of the Virgin Birth) a deep truth about Jesus' nature—that his origin was from above? It does have a certain fairy story-like quality to it, suggesting that it may not have been intended to be taken as literal history. But the occurrence of this narrative immediately after the opening verses of the Gospel, on which I have just commented, forces us to suppose that St Luke intended us to think that the infancy narrative (at any rate in its essentials) was literal history; but, of course, he may have obtained his material from a source which did not think of the narrative in this way. As well as recording events, Luke's Gospel, like the others, contains much purported teaching of Jesus: explicit teaching about which actions and attitudes are right or wrong, pithy sayings, and parables. What Luke is claiming is again clear: that Jesus taught these things. However, the possibility remains that there are individual verses in Luke or Acts in which the author 'theologizes', that is, purports to record a deed or remark of Jesus which he does not believe that Jesus did or said in the literal sense, but which, in his view, expresses the essence of what Jesus was doing or teaching. But for all the reasons given previously we should only suppose that if we have positive evidence that that is what is happening.

Luke obtained much of his material (especially the purported history) from Mark's Gospel, and probably quite a lot of the rest (sayings and parables) from a source which Matthew also used and is traditionally called 'Q'. For his account of events in the life of Jesus, Luke to a considerable extent uses Mark's Gospel. This is sometimes misstated as Luke being dependent on Mark for his knowledge of these events; that, however, does not follow. Luke belonged to a local church, and clearly knows quite a lot about many cities, and so he would have been acquainted with other local churches. Churches were founded by evangelists who came preaching an oral message. That message must have contained some information about Jesus, for otherwise the evangelists would have given their hearers no reason to join a religion to which the person of Jesus (Christ) was so central. So Luke must have had other oral sources, but he may not have had any other written sources for the events whose description he takes from Mark; and so, naturally enough, having only one written source for certain events, he copied from it.

How did Mark intend his Gospel to be understood? It certainly purports to tell us about a large number of historical events and, by my argument of Chapter 1, purported testimony should be regarded as testimony in the absence of reason to the contrary. Luke understood Mark as telling us about historical events. Matthew's Gospel also purports to tell us about historical events; and since Mark is his primary source for these events, Matthew must have understood him in the same way. It would be very odd indeed if Mark, seeking to tell his readers something, and phrasing his Gospel as a historical narrative and so understood by two near-contemporaries (themselves familiar with other churches, some of whom must have read Mark and could have corrected any obvious misunderstanding of it by Matthew and Luke), was really doing something quite other than trying to record history.

There are a few events in the 'synoptic' Gospels (Matthew, Mark and Luke) to which Paul, or the author of the Epistle to the Hebrews, or the author of I Peter, or some non-Christian sources also refer—in particular, of course, the life, preaching, and death of John the Baptist, the Last Supper, the Crucifixion, and (in the Christian sources) the Resurrection. There is no reason to deny that, as appears, these other writers thought of those events as historical. So belief in their historical character was widespread. Hence there is no justification for thinking that Mark is trying to do anything else than record history when he writes about these events; and so, since he relates other events in the same style, about the other events which he records. Similarly, the Gospel of Thomas, for whose independence from the synoptic tradition (the sources which gave rise to the Gospels of Matthew, Mark, and Luke) there are strong arguments,[6] contains 114 sayings, some half of which have parallels in the synoptic Gospels including Mark. Thomas claims that Jesus said these things; and so they are the sort of things that people believed that Jesus said, for reasons other than that Mark said so. So when Mark said that Jesus said these things, there is no reason to suppose that he was doing anything else except claiming that (literally) Jesus said these things. I conclude that the three synoptic Gospels purport to be history (history of cosmic significance, but I repeat, history all the same). That is their genre. There remains the possibility of occasional 'theologizing', but we should not postulate it without positive evidence, given the overall genre of these works.

What about John's Gospel? There are, I think, some stories in this Gospel which the author does not intend to be read as history. It does rather look as if sometimes, at least, St John tells a story simply as a way of setting forward some deep theological truth. One obvious example is the story of Jesus' miracle at the pool of Bethesda.[7] The implication of the story is that the first invalid to get into the water when it is disturbed is cured. This is supposed to be a regular, predictable event (and so not a miracle, on my definition in Chapter 1) of a most extraordinary kind of which we know absolutely nothing from any other source. The evidence is therefore massively against it having happened. Perhaps John was deceived or is deceiving us. But then we learn that the sick man had been sick for thirty-eight years. The people of Israel wandered in the wilderness for thirty-eight years until Joshua (the Hebrew word for Jesus) led them through the River Jordan to the promised land.[8] No one can read St John's Gospel without realizing that symbolism is of immense importance to the author. So plausibly this story is just John's way of telling us that Jesus helps the sick in soul through the water of baptism of the kingdom of Heaven.

Another possible example of a story told by St John simply to make a theological point, and not as history, is the story of the raising of Lazarus.[9] Lazarus has been dead and buried four days, but the stone sealing the tomb is removed, Jesus calls Lazarus, and Lazarus

---

[6] For these arguments, see Thiessen and Merz, *The Historical Jesus*, 38–40.
[7] John 5: 2–18.   [8] Deut. 2: 14.
[9] John 11: 1–46.

walks out of the tomb bound in his grave clothes. John claims that this was a widely reported miracle, the influence of which the chief priests were anxious to counteract.[10] The problem is that the synoptics show no knowledge of this story, and yet (because Lazarus has been dead for four days) it is a greater miracle than the one or two raisings from the dead by Jesus which they record. If it really happened as John said, they would surely have wanted to record it.[11] Yet John may, as it were, be summarizing in one miracle story the general effect of the miracle-working of Jesus, and his assessment of its theological significance. It may also be the Johannine equivalent of the predictions by Jesus recorded in the other Gospels of his own death and Resurrection: it showed that God could and would do even that. There must be a reasonable suspicion that in these and some other places in John's Gospel, when John tells a long story about a miracle (in my sense) or (not always the same) about a 'sign' in John's sense, that he is recounting a story apparently as a historical incident only in order to illustrate a theological truth believed by the author.

On the other hand, John records or shows knowledge of the same main incidents as the other Gospels. He records the calling of the first disciples, the feeding of the 5,000, the ride into Jerusalem on a colt or donkey with the crowds waving branches, the overthrowing of the tables in the Temple, the Passion (with many details the same as in the other Gospels), and the Resurrection (with, as we shall see, many similarities to the other Gospels). He shows knowledge of the baptism of Jesus; for while not recording an actual baptism of Jesus by John the Baptist, he records the same surrounding events as the other Gospels: Jesus at the beginning of his ministry coming to John the Baptist when John was baptizing, and the descent onto Jesus of the Holy Spirit in the form of a dove. John's Gospel also, I shall argue in a later chapter, shows knowledge of the Last Supper. John is the latest of the Gospels, written for Christians who had by then clearly accepted from the other Gospels that such events formed the historical framework of Jesus' life. In recording them, and not disavowing the obvious interpretations, he cannot be represented as other than affirming that interpretation. Of course, he is also trying

---

[10] John 12: 9–11.
[11] For a defence of the story having a historical meaning, see J. A. T. Robinson, *The Priority of John* (SCM Press, 1985), 220–2.

to tell us a lot about the deep meaning of such events other than is obvious from the other Gospels. Further, John does tell us explicitly and solemnly that he has an eyewitness source for one event—that when one of the soldiers pierced the side of the dead Jesus, 'blood and water came out. He who saw this has testified so that you also may believe. His testimony is true and he knows that he tells the truth.'[12] That cannot be read except as a claim to have an eyewitness source who saw a historical event, and so provides reason for reading much else (but not everything) in John's Gospel as purported history. In the same spirit is John 21: 24 (John 21 is a chapter generally agreed to have been added to the main body of the text by the same writer or school of writers as was responsible for the latter). This penultimate verse of the Gospel, referring to 'the disciple whom Jesus loved', claims, 'this is the disciple who is testifying to these things and has written them, and we know that his testimony is true'. 'Testifying' to things is (as with the blood and water) to be read in this context (far more naturally than in any other way) as claiming to have seen historical events. John's Gospel purports to contain much history, but it is not always clear with respect to all the stories which it contains whether they are intended as history or not.

So much for the sources, and their character (in general) in purporting to tell us history. How reliable are they?

Their Reliability

Just as apparent testimony must be read as real testimony, so real testimony must be believed, in the absence of counter-evidence. I shall discuss whether there is any such counter-evidence in respect of particular important claims about Jesus when I come to discuss these claims. But is there any general reason for suspecting the reliability of the New Testament writers on historical matters? Sometimes they do give conflicting accounts of particular matters, but the discrepancies are not great, and what is more impressive is their agreement in respect of the framework of Jesus' life. Just as this agreement (on which I commented earlier) is further reason for taking their purported testimony as real testimony, so it is further reason for believing that testimony, to the extent that the testimonies

---

[12] John 19: 34–5.

are independent, that is to the extent that one account is not derived solely from another account. While the large dependence of Matthew and Luke on Mark for the written account of many events in the life of Jesus diminishes their status as independent witnesses, we need to bear in mind, as I wrote earlier, that they would have been Christianized through oral traditions, which might have been scant, but which would nevertheless have constituted an independent source. And clearly, too, they had a common independent written source for the sayings of Jesus ('Q') and further independent sources for passages dependent on neither Mark nor Q.

The agreement of the Gospels about the main incidents of the life of Jesus remains even when, as with the baptism of Jesus by John the Baptist, a main incident causes theological problems. The very high view of the status of Jesus as sinless, developing in the early Church, implied that he needed no baptism. And yet the writers learned of the baptism and recorded it, though Matthew's account showed his theological disquiet about it. And, as I commented earlier, occasional details mentioned in the Epistles coincide with ones in the Gospels, the preaching and Crucifixion of Jesus are mentioned in pagan sources, and there is considerable overlap of the purported teaching of Jesus between the synoptic Gospels and the Gospel of Thomas. This amount of agreement suggests the reliability of the synoptic Gospels in the very broadest outline, and so that they are reliable in other respects where some incident is recorded only in one Gospel. There are, of course, disagreements between them, and reasons for not believing them on particular matters, to which I will come in due course. But it is important to bear in mind, with respect to disagreements, that historical incidents inevitably get remembered better than the details of teaching, and the parables which are so frequent in the Gospels would have been remembered better than would have been their context in Jesus' teaching or any prosaic statements which he might have made about their application. And writers will be more free in the way they express what they see as the essence of Jesus' teaching than in the recording of historical incidents.

Whatever were their sources, Mark, Matthew, Luke, Paul, and the authors of the other relatively earlier New Testament works (Hebrews and 1 Peter)—or most of them—must, given their dates of writing (between twenty and seventy years after the crucial events), have known people who knew eyewitnesses of some of those events. For they were members of local churches, and knew about other churches and received written documents; and the churches were founded and documents brought to them, and for other reasons were visited by official and unofficial representatives of more central churches, themselves founded by or indirectly authorized by the apostles. Paul, of course, explicitly claims to have met Peter (whom he calls Cephas) over significant periods, and also James 'the Lord's brother' and other apostles; and Acts confirms such meetings.[13] Luke too claimed to have derived his information from eyewitnesses.[14] And so does the author of the Epistle to the Hebrews, who speaks of the message of salvation, 'which was declared at first through the Lord, and it was attested to us by those who heard him'.[15] All of this must lead to an assumption of general reliability, especially with respect to the matters to be investigated in Part II, where (with the possible exception of Jesus' 'healings') there is no issue of violation of laws of nature.

I have not so far discussed the reliability of John's Gospel as a historical source.[16] Most of the more liberal twentieth-century scholars have regarded it as in general a very unreliable source. Before we could settle finally just how reliable a source it is, we would need to be certain about which passages therein were intended as history, and that, I have claimed, is not always clear. John 21: 24, cited earlier, suggests that a witness ('the disciple whom Jesus loved') told what he saw and also wrote it down, but that a group ('we') edited what was written. And the other 'testimony' verse cited above (John 19: 35) is consonant with this account. The latter very solemn attestation concerns an event in the Passion, and 'the disciple whom Jesus loved' is referred to as prominent in the events of the Passion a number of times. An anonymous disciple is also responsible for securing entry for himself and Peter into the high priest's courtyard.[17] If the solemn witness affirmation of John 19: 35 and 21: 26 are to be taken seriously, clearly it is 'the disciple whom Jesus loved' who is the eyewitness source of a lot of information. If that is so, there seems no reason to deny the unanimous early Church

---

[13] e.g. Gal. 1: 18–20; 2: 1–14; Acts 9: 26–7; 15: 4–29.　　　　　　　[14] Luke 1: 2.

[15] Heb. 2: 3.

[16] My discussion in the next pages of the historicity of John's Gospel depends on points made in Robinson *The Priority of John*, where he develops the case made by C. H. Dodd in *Historical Tradition in the Fourth Gospel* (Cambridge University Press, 1963).

[17] John 18: 15–17.

tradition that the author, or at any rate the historical source of the Gospel's information, was the apostle John, the son of Zebedee. And there is a clue in the Gospel that that is what it is claiming. The two disciples never mentioned by name in the Gospel (and only as 'the sons of Zebedee' in its additional chapter[18]) are John and his brother James, although they clearly had a prominent place in the earthly ministry of Jesus. Only if John was the author would he hesitate to refer to himself as John. And he refers to himself as 'the disciple whom Jesus loved' only as a witness to the central events of the Passion and Resurrection—as the witness of Jesus' foreknowledge of his betrayal, as witness to the Passion (where he is entrusted with the care of Jesus' mother), and as a witness to the empty tomb. The final reference to 'the disciple whom Jesus loved' is by others (John 21: 24; see 21: 20) to his authorship of the Gospel.

Now all of this talk of 'testimony' and 'the disciple whom Jesus loved' might be no more than an artificial device used in a historical novel. But it should not be so regarded in the absence of positive evidence against taking the affirmations at their face value. The literal sense has priority, especially when expressed with the solemnity of John 19: 35. And there is more detailed evidence in the Gospel, both of its historicity and of its having a historical source independent of the synoptics. There are, to start with, indications that the author was familiar with the topography of which he wrote. There is a wealth of names of places in Galilee and Jerusalem, and details about them.[19] And on one crucial incident connected with the Passion—the date of the Last Supper—John's account is generally regarded as somewhat more plausible than that of the synoptics. The synoptics represent the Last Supper as a Passover meal, and so the trial of Jesus and his execution as also taking place on the Passover Day. (Jewish days began at sunset.) John dates it as taking place on the day before the Passover. Among the many arguments

---

[18] John 21: 2.

[19] See Robinson, *The Priority of John*, 52–9. Similar points are made by Robin Lane Fox in his *The Unauthorized Version* (Penguin Books, 1992), 204–9. He comments on the style of the author of John's Gospel as 'steeped in Jewish texts and piety' while never drawing on Greek thought or literary style. He writes that the author's understanding of Jewish practices also suggests an informed Jewish milieu, presupposing nothing which occurred after AD 70. Lane Fox concludes that he believes that John's Gospel 'is historically the most valuable', accepting that its immediate source was a disciple who witnessed the events of the Passion and 'saw into the empty tomb', while remaining agnostic about whether that disciple was John, the son of Zebedee.

against the synoptic dating are that it involves the trial taking place
on Passover Day, contrary to the law (as codified in the second-
century AD Mishnah); and that a Passover amnesty (which was given
in the end to Barabbas rather than Jesus) would make more sense if
the festival to be celebrated was yet to come (to be enjoyed by the
one amnestied).[20]

Then there is substantial evidence that if John's view of the
history involved in the life of Jesus was formed solely by reading the
synoptists, he read them a long time before he wrote his Gospel.
Their details had sunk into his consciousness—he was in no sense
copying their words. For example, all the isolated sayings which John
cites and which have parallels in the synoptists are given by John in a
different context from that in which they appear in the synoptists.[21]
One point which makes this very clear is that, at places where a text
of Mark or Luke would fit his theology very well, he does not use it.
After his long silence before the high priest's interrogation, in answer
to a final crucial question, 'Art thou the Christ, the Son of the
Blessed?', Jesus answers according to Mark:[22] ἐγώ εἰμι. Literally
translated, this means 'I am'. But it is also the name of God as
revealed to God in Exodus—and it is John's view that Jesus is God.
John reports Jesus as saying ἐγώ εἰμι in reply to the soldiers who say
that they have come to arrest Jesus of Nazareth;[23] but not at this all-
important point when he acknowledges his messianic identity to the
high priest. If John were copying the synoptics, he would have had
every reason to follow them verbatim at this point.

Still, maybe he had absorbed them years previously, and then
when he came to write the Gospel he depended only on his memory
of an overall pattern and individual phrases. Against that, however,
there remain the arguments of previous paragraphs in favour of
John having, and indeed being, an independent historical source.
More generally, it seems massively implausible on more a priori
grounds to suppose that John (even if he was not an eyewitness) had
no source on the life of Jesus additional to the synoptics. For, all
agree, John was the last Gospel to be written. I made the point
earlier that the other Gospel writers belonged to churches founded

---

[20] For a fuller account of these and other such arguments, see Thiessen and Merz, *The
Historical Jesus*, 426–7.

[21] Robinson, *The Priority of John*, 12 n. 32, citing and amending H. E. Edwards, *The
Disciple who Wrote these Things* (J. Clarke, 1953), 96–7.

[22] Mark 14: 62.   [23] John 18: 5.

and visited by representatives of more central churches, themselves founded or authorized indirectly by the apostles. They were founded and reinvigorated by a stream of oral tradition. Gospels were written to flesh out the tradition, and to ensure that, with the course of time, it did not get misreported. But they were not the primary vehicles of its transmission in the first fifty years. No one founded a church as a result of having bought a copy of St Mark's Gospel from the local bookstore and being impressed by its message! Early tradition is unanimous in claiming that John's Gospel originated from Ephesus, a thriving Christian Church in the mid-50s, much cultivated by Paul and visited by Apollos, who originally had a somewhat different message from Paul.[24] Is it really plausible to suppose that John (even if he was not an eyewitness) could have written his Gospel, having no historical sources other than the synoptics?

I have argued, however, that he was an eyewitness, indeed the apostle John. But I have also argued that it is not always clear when he is seeking to recount history and when he is telling a story with no historical basis solely to make a theological point. The arguments which I have given for suspecting the literal historicity of parts of this Gospel concern long stories for which there are no parallels in the other Gospels nor any evidence elsewhere of what they purport to record, and which might be susceptible of interpretation as parables designed to make a theological point. However, even if we treat such stories as fictions making theological points, they are valuable in showing the way that John, who had been the disciple of Jesus, came to understand the life of Jesus and who he was. The arguments which I have given for John's historical intentions and historical reliability concern incidents in which he represents 'the disciple whom Jesus loved' as present, or which largely coincide with incidents recorded by the other Gospels (where the additional testimony is thus confirming testimony), including, on the whole, respects in which he corrects the other Gospels on detail. His trustworthiness on detail is evidenced by his familiarity with Jewish places and customs and the greater plausibility of his dating of the Last Supper. John's Gospel must be used with care, but it is a historical source.

The other Gospels and Acts, however, and (in so far as they report or allude to historical matters) those Epistles of Paul which are clearly authentic, are, I have argued, far less open to the charge of

---

[24] Acts 18: 24–6.

making a theological point by telling a story which they represent as history, and must be taken as generally reliable sources for the life, death, and purported Resurrection of Jesus of Nazareth. There may indeed be particular reasons for doubting what particular sources appear to say, if understood in a literal sense, about particular matters. They may occasionally 'theologize'; and either they or their own sources may be unreliable (through misobserving, misremembering, or even deliberate deceit). But in the absence of such reasons, the rational assumption is that the sources are reliable.

Note that when Gospels (or other New Testament books) record an important incident for which they have independent sources (have not, for example, all copied their account from Mark), discrepancies of detail are to be expected for reasons which do not apply in the modern world. The Christian message was transmitted largely orally in the first decades of Christianity. It could take many weeks if not months to get from one Christian centre to another; and so many weeks to convey any Christian message from one centre to another. In these circumstances what would have been remembered most clearly and passed on would be a very short statement of central belief and of its grounds. The details of grounds for that short statement, although no doubt also passed on, would be remembered less clearly (because there were more of these grounds and their details were less important). The Gospels were written down in different places, and so it was almost inevitable that there would be a few minor differences in their detailed accounts. In the modern world, when modern historical works are published in different places containing different accounts of some incident, emails, television interviews, and newspapers are at hand to try and sort out which was the correct account—and, of course, even then disagreement often remains. The ancient world had no such resources. It would have taken a long time for two distant authors to sort out whose detailed account of some incident was correct—even if they had thought it worth while to attempt to do so. And by then their Gospels would be in circulation in forms almost impossible to correct. Add to the errors arising from the inaccurate memories about what they had been told by the indirect witnesses carrying the message from one church to another errors arising from the fading memories of the direct witnesses of those incidents, and it is almost inevitable that there will be more than a few discrepancies in the Gospel accounts.

5

The Life and Moral Teaching of Jesus

A Perfect Life

THE FIRST requirement for Jesus to be God Incarnate is that the life of Jesus should have been a perfect human life—a life which we can offer instead of our own life as our reparation for sin and a life which showed us how to live—and that he should have provided deep moral teaching. The evidence for the holiness of another person's life can, of course, come only from their public behaviour. But I suggest that such evidence as there is of Jesus' public behaviour is such as one would expect if he led a perfect human life. That Jesus had table fellowship with 'tax collectors and sinners', as well as with the Pharisees, seems virtually undisputed. On this it is appropriate to quote Geza Vermes:

In one respect more than any other [Jesus] differed from both his contemporaries and even his prophetic predecessors. The prophets spoke on behalf of the honest poor, and defended the widows and the fatherless, those oppressed and exploited by the wicked, rich and powerful. Jesus went further. In addition to proclaiming these blessed, he actually took his stand among the pariahs of his world, those despised by the respectable. Sinners were his table-companions and the ostracized tax-collectors and prostitutes his friends.[1]

The offence which Jesus caused by these actions to the more pious Jews was not, as E. P. Sanders emphasizes, that he sought to get the

[1] Geza Vermes, *Jesus the Jew* (SCM Press, 1994), 196.

'tax collectors and sinners' to repent and to repay those whom they had defrauded.[2] Rather it was in part (for the other part, see later) that he ate with them before they changed their lifestyle. The complaint is made that Jesus 'is gone to be the guest of one who is a sinner' before the sinner, Zacchaeus, publicly resolves to change his lifestyle.[3] And Jesus was prepared to touch lepers, whose disease was regarded both as contagious and as ritually unclean.[4] Jesus showed love towards the outcasts.

The life of Jesus was the life of a wandering teacher, and there seems no reason to doubt the genuineness of his saying about himself that 'the Son of Man has nowhere to lay his head'.[5] Like John the Baptist, but unlike the Essenes, he did not reserve his instruction to initiates, but taught publicly to anyone willing to listen. To teach people about God, his love towards them, and how they should live is obviously a good thing if what is taught is true, and I will come to that below. Obviously, prayer and religious experience played an important part in the life of Jesus.[6] He taught his disciples how to pray.[7] Clearly, too, he saw himself as having a calling from God, and that dictated the kind of perfect life he should live. See, to start with, his moment of commissioning. The synoptics report the descent of the Holy Spirit in the form of a dove onto Jesus as something which he saw, not as a public event. So their report could only have come from Jesus himself. Then there are the many sayings attributed to Jesus of the form 'I have come' to do so-and-so. This phrase 'I have come to . . .' (ἦλθον) is a formula, with which a messenger announces the message he has been told to bring or the task he has been told to perform, used by, among others, John the Baptist. In the context of Jesus' utterances, the implication is that he has been sent

---

[2] E. P. Sanders, *Jesus and Judaism* (SCM Press, 1985), 200–4.

[3] Luke 19: 7–8.

[4] Mark 1: 40–5; see too Mark 2: 15 and Luke 7: 37–9 on eating with and bodily contact with 'tax-collectors and sinners'.

[5] Luke 9: 58 (Matt. 8: 20).

[6] See the reports of their place in the life of Jesus at the crucial moments of the post-baptismal temptations in the Wilderness, the Transfiguration, and the Agony in the Garden of Gethsemane, reported (in most cases at some length) in all synoptic Gospels. And if he took his own reported teaching that his followers should pray in secret (Matt. 6: 5–6) at all seriously, prayer would have played a much greater role in his life than the Gospels would have been able to tell us.

[7] Matt. 6: 9–15; Luke 11: 2–4.

[8] See G. Thiessen and A. Merz, *The Historical Jesus: A Comprehensive Guide* (SCM Press, 1998), 525–6 for these sayings and the parallels to them in other writings.

by God the Father to do a certain task.[8] That Jesus should think of himself as having a divine mission is not something improbable on background evidence, and so the strong evidence of that provided by the account of his vision (the way it seemed to him) at his commissioning, and by the many 'I have come' sayings are to be taken at face value. All of this is indeed the sort of good life we should expect a prophet to live.

The Gospels abound with stories of miracles (in some sense)—so many that it would be totally implausible to suppose that they have no historical basis. Josephus refers to Jesus as a 'doer of startling deeds',[9] and the Gospels contain accounts of those who, while acknowledging Jesus' miracle-working powers, sought to attribute them to diabolic rather than divinely originating power.[10] The most commonly reported miracles were miracles of healing, either exorcisms or cures which did not involve exorcism which we may call 'therapies'.[11] In healing, Jesus was paradigmatically showing love. Were these healings miracles in my sense of violations of natural laws? In most cases it is almost impossible to say, because we know so little about the exact condition of the person being healed before Jesus acted, or indeed six months later. (The situation in this respect is, I shall be arguing, rather different in the case of the Resurrection of Jesus.) No doubt some of the cures of psychological or even neurological illness were caused by the sick person feeling that Jesus had given him the strength to live without his 'demons' and to live like other people. Some of those ill of fevers might have recovered spontaneously, and some of those whose fits ceased might have had other fits later. But there are stories of healings which are most naturally interpreted (if we take the Gospel record as accurate) as miraculous: the immediate healings of blind and deaf people, of the man with the withered hand, of lepers, and of the dead raised to life.[12]

Jesus was not the only person in ancient (or indeed modern) history to whom miracles have been attributed.[13] But there are two important features of his miracle-working. The first is the very large

---

[9] In a version of 'Testimonium Flavianum' (*Antiquities* 18: 63–4) which removes any possible Christian insertions.

[10] Luke 11: 15.

[11] See the classification of miracle stories by Thiessen, summarized in Thiessen and Merz, *The Historical Jesus*.

[12] Jairus' daughter (Mark 5: 35–43) and the widow of Nain's son (Luke 7: 11–17).

[13] Including some other Jewish miracle-workers later in the first century AD. See Vermes, *Jesus the Jew*, 50–63.

number of miracles attributed to him and their centrality in his activity. Thiessen and Merz comment that 'Nowhere else are so many miracles reported of a single person as they are in the Gospels of Jesus.'[14] Given that the 'nowhere else' concerns serious historical reports, this is surely no exaggeration. The other crucial feature of Jesus' miracles is that, as various Gospel sayings make clear, they are represented by Jesus as the breaking in of the Kingdom of God into a world which needed help. His response to those who accused him of casting out demons by 'Beelzebul, the ruler of the demons' was that this was implausible, since Beelzebul did not want the power of demons diminished; 'but if it is by the Spirit of God that I cast out demons, then the Kingdom of God has come to you.'[15]

Maybe none of the historical elements in any of these events involve violations of natural laws; but that does not seem to me very probable, unless we assume that such violations have enormous prior improbability. But if we have some evidence to suppose that there is a God with reason occasionally to intervene in the world through miracles, then we have some evidence that he has done so through Jesus. (Those who are rightly suspicious of the assumption that there exist demons to be exorcised can regard Jesus' exorcisms as ways of healing some psychological and other diseases described in that culture in terms of demon possession, and by us differently.)

As I wrote earlier, while God has reason to become incarnate and heal, he has some reason to do so via (in my sense) miracles and some reason to do so in a non-miraculous way. So my case does not depend on the healings of Jesus being in my sense miracles. But it is clear that, whether or not miraculously, Jesus healed many, was widely reported to do so, and saw his healing as God breaking into a world which needed help.

Jesus' life ended with his Crucifixion. A prophet who led a perfect life could not have been condemned to death justly. We need to show that either he did not do or say the things of which he was accused, or that doing or saying those things was not morally wrong (even if forbidden by law). It is a matter of considerable controversy why Jesus was crucified, and here the Gospel writers are open to the

---

[14] Thiessen and Merz, *The Historical Jesus*, 290.

[15] Matt. 12: 28. See too the charge to the Twelve sent out on a mission, which connects the proximity of the kingdom with healings: 'As you go, proclaim the good news "the kingdom of heaven has come near". Cure the sick, raise the dead, cleanse the lepers, cast out demons' (Matt. 10: 7–8).

accusation of reading back their own theology into the history. It seems fairly certain that Jewish authorities sought to have Jesus executed by the Romans, and that the Roman governor, Pontius Pilate, condemned him to death and executed him. Raymond Brown concludes that (despite the efforts of some scholars to show that the Jews were not involved), 'when the Jewish, Christian, and pagan evidence is assembled, the involvement of Jews in the death of Jesus approaches certainty'.[16] Perhaps the strongest evidence is St Paul's writing (*c.*AD 50) in 1 Thessalonians 2: 14–15 of the 'Jews' who 'killed ... the Lord Jesus'. Paul was in Jerusalem and hostile to Christians shortly after Jesus' death. This, together with the full unanimous testimony of the Gospels, Peter's sermons in Acts,[17] and a few pagan references, seems to provide overwhelming evidence of Jewish involvement in the death of Jesus. The Jewish proceedings, however, may or may not have been a formal trial before the Sanhedrin. The Jewish authorities condemned him on a charge; if they had not given out some public accusation justifying what they did (if their action had been a mere kidnapping), the Gospel writers would certainly have said so.

So on what charge did the Jews find Jesus worthy of death? Mark and Matthew are explicit that the charge was 'blasphemy' (insulting God)—not presumably that he cursed God directly, but in some way derogated him by claiming divine prerogatives. Mark and Matthew state that the 'false testimony' which led to the condemnation included the claim that Jesus would (Mark) or was able to (Matthew) destroy the Temple and build it again (or build another one not made with hands). I shall discuss both the authenticity and the significance of this accusation in more detail in the next chapter. I shall point out that the testimony may well be 'false' in that what happened is that Jesus predicted that others (not he himself) would destroy the Temple, but shall allow here the possibility that the accusation may be true, for the sole purpose of its relevance to our present topic—whether Jesus was condemned to death justly or not.

The charge at the Roman trial before Pilate on which Jesus was found guilty was presumably the accusation inscribed on the Cross—that he made himself 'the King of the Jews'—reasonably

[16] Raymond E. Brown, *The Death of the Messiah* (Doubleday, 1994), 382.

[17] In Peter's sermons in Acts 2 and Acts 3, addressing Jewish crowds, he says, 'you crucified' and 'you killed' Jesus (Acts 2: 23, 3: 15).

judged genuine since that particular phrase was never used of Jesus or by Jews in the Gospel accounts of his life before that time. It does, however, correspond to the 'anointed one', the Christ, the Messiah.

So Jesus was condemned for predicting or threatening or claiming the power to destroy the Temple; and claiming Messiahship or kingship, and divine prerogatives (by means of acts which I will consider in more detail in the next chapter). That he was silent or at any rate did not deny the charges is also common to the Gospels. Now either Jesus did not do and say the things of which he was accused, in which case he suffered judicial execution for crimes he did not commit (and so indeed his life was a suitable reparation— an innocent life taken away unjustly), or he did these things. As I remarked in the last chapter, if the perfect life was to be of use as an example and atonement, it must in general be the kind of perfect life we ordinary humans should have lived; and so he must not normally go about boasting of his status or threatening to destroy buildings. But, on the hypothesis we are considering, Jesus needed to claim divine authority for his teaching and to give some indication of his divine status. A claim to Messiahship will involve a divine authority for his teaching, and (as I shall be arguing in Chapter 6) the charge of blasphemy indicates that he made a rather higher claim than Messiahship for his status. On this hypothesis, he needed to make such claims in order to fulfil the purpose of his incarnation, and the claims were true. God Incarnate did no wrong in saying what was true of himself. My hypothesis is also that he was providing an atonement for sin. Hence he must make clear that older ways of attempting to make atonement are of no use; he must make clear that he replaces the Temple and its system of sacrifice. As God Incarnate he certainly has the right to allow others, or even himself, to destroy buildings—for he made the Earth and we live on it only by his permission. In threatening the destruction of the Temple, Jesus needs to do things which, as an ordinary human being living a perfect life, he would not have the right to do. His divine status gives him the right to do certain things to fulfil the purpose of his incarnation, which do not in consequence detract from the perfection of his life. Hence the Crucifixion was the Crucifixion of an innocent person, and so a proper culmination of an atoning life.

He bore it, as far as our evidence goes, bravely and without complaint. St Luke quotes Jesus as praying from the Cross, 'Father, forgive them for they do not know what they are doing.'[18] If he said these words, they were a supreme act of supererogation: no one has an obligation to forgive, good though it is that they should do so;[19] and no one has an obligation to ask God to forgive someone, good though it is that they should. Such a phrase is unlikely to have been quoted without historical basis;[20] for Christians had every ordinary unreformed human reason to hope that God would deal with the Jews in justice rather than mercy. So it looks as if 'the first word from the Cross' was indeed Jesus' supererogatory signature on his life.

I conclude from the very general aspects of the life of Jesus (agreed by almost all scholars) that he lived a good and holy life (by correct standards of human goodness) and was executed on a charge which could only be a just one if he was not God Incarnate, which is the very hypothesis which we are considering.

Almost inevitably, however, there are a few isolated incidents in the life of Jesus (different ones for each of us) where we wonder whether his action was a good one. I write 'almost inevitably' because with all the different views which there are among humans on moral matters, we are almost all likely to have some false views about what moral goodness amounts to in some particular cases and so are likely to judge some actions of Jesus to be bad, even if in fact they are good. That is not to say that we should not examine the particular incidents in detail, and if we have strong reasons to believe both that they are correctly reported in the Gospels and that our moral views on this particular issue are correct, then we have strong reason to believe that the life of Jesus was not in this respect a perfect one. The incidents reported in the Gospels about which people worry do, however, tend to be very untypical ones, such that there is doubt about the correctness of the reports or there is a certain ambiguity about their moral character.

I illustrate how we should react to such isolated incidents with

---

[18] Luke 23: 34.

[19] See my *Responsibility and Atonement* (Clarendon Press, 1989), 84–9, for amplification and qualification. I argue there that it is impossible (or at any rate bad) for anyone to forgive a serious offence without some apology from the wrongdoer. If that is right, either 'they do not know what they are doing' mitigates the offence sufficiently to make this possible; or the prayer is to be regarded as a request to God the Father to forgive as far as is conceivably possible.

[20] It is not found in some important manuscripts, but, for the reason given, it is more likely to have been omitted from these, although genuine, than added to other manuscripts. See Brown, *The Death of the Messiah*, 975–81.

perhaps the most striking example. There is no evidence that Jesus killed or injured any human being, but there is one incident where he appears to have agreed to a large slaughter of animals which impoverished their owners. He seems to have agreed to the demons which he cast out of the Gerasene demoniac entering a large herd of swine, which then rushed down a hill into the sea and were drowned.[21] The first thing to be emphasized about this reported incident is that it is not of a pattern with any other reported incident, and we have for it only one source, Mark's Gospel, on which Matthew is dependent at this point. Also, of course, the modern world is rightly suspicious of the existence of demons, and this story depends on that for its whole point. So the incident may well not have happened in quite that form or, indeed, may have been originally a parable of some kind which Mark has represented as history. But if it did happen in the way described, then we must take the whole story seriously, including the demons. The next thing to be said is that, if Jesus was God Incarnate, he certainly had the right to terminate the life of animals when he chose, and to reduce owners of such animals to a lower level of wealth than would otherwise be theirs. But what good would be served by his exercising these rights? If we take the story seriously, Jesus has powers over demons (and it would then be possible that some other humans also have such powers); and he is represented as having a choice between healing a madman and even showing some sort of compassion to demons (by finding a local home for them in the swine) on the one hand, and saving animal life and human wealth on the other hand. For a human who had the right to do so, his choice of the former act would plausibly be a good one; and plausibly Jesus himself would also think so since he seems to have taught that human life and health were very important, far more important than wealth and than animal life (valuable though that also was).[22] The act would then be not merely not wrong for God Incarnate to do, but would be good in showing people true values; but in doing it, Jesus was again claiming a more than ordinary human authority (something he would sometimes, though not too often, need to do).

---

[21] Mark 5: 1–20.

[22] For the value of animal life, and the value of human life being much greater, see Luke 12: 6–7 and 24 (parallels in Matt. 10: 29–30 and 6: 26). For the goodness of healing humans, even on the sabbath, see Mark 3: 4 (Luke 6: 9); and for the spiritual dangers of being rich, see Mark 10: 24–5 (and parallels).

There is no space here to discuss the morality of any other isolated puzzling acts in the life of Jesus. I emphasize their, in general, possible non-historicity, and suggest also that on reflection it may prove far from evident that they are not the acts of a perfectly good being. The evidence which we have about the general pattern of the life of Jesus, about which almost all scholars are in agreement, is, I suggest, in the respects in which we can judge it, the sort of evidence we would expect if that life was a perfect one.

The General Moral Teaching of Jesus

Much of the life of Jesus was devoted to teaching people about how to live and teaching them about God, his attitude to us, and his intentions for us. While the details of exactly what he meant may sometimes be unclear (especially because it is often difficult to know how to interpret the parables), there are, as with the life of Jesus, certain very general features apparent to anyone who reads the Gospels.

Jesus taught people that God loves them, that they should forgive each other and show supererogatory love to each other, should worship God, and ask him for good things. He taught that, for each of us, there would be a life after death where God would judge us and award a wonderful life to the good and a bad life to the bad.

It is difficult to interpret the parables of the prodigal son, the lost sheep, and the lost coin,[23] except as showing (among other things) the love of God for humans; as does the teaching of how much God loves us more than the ravens and the lilies, on whom he bestows much love,[24] That we should forgive each other 'not seven times, but, I tell you, seventy-seven times' is the way Matthew reports Jesus' teaching on forgiveness. That God is the master who forgives us much and expects us to forgive the lesser debts which we are owed by others is the obvious application, and drawn explicitly in Matthew's concluding verses.[25] This is borne out by the obviously remembered Lord's prayer, where the disciples were told to pray, 'Forgive us our debts, as we have also forgiven our debtors'[26]—we must forgive others before we can ask God's forgiveness for

---

[23] Luke 15: 3–32 (see also Matt. 18: 12–14).   [24] Luke 12: 22–34.
[25] Matt. 18: 21–35.   [26] Matt. 6: 12 (Luke 11: 4).

ourselves. That we should forgive is central to the teaching of Jesus; it was manifested by Jesus on the Cross, and seen by Luke as inspiring Stephen when he was stoned.[27]

Supererogatory love is, more than anything else, the theme of the Sermon on the Mount and the parable of the sheep and the goats:[28] loving one's enemies, going the extra mile, lending without expecting a return, feeding the hungry, clothing the naked, visiting the sick and imprisoned, etc. The observance of prayer, fasting, and almsgiving, with a proper attitude of humility before God[29] and avoiding using these as a means of acquiring a good reputation on Earth,[30] are also obvious Gospel themes. Jesus commended our relying on God and asking him for good things, mundane and spiritual.[31] It is, he taught, more important to show love to those in need than to conform to exact details of ritual. Jesus also is reported as having said a lot about the urgency of spiritual reform for each of us, and a coming judgement on all of us which would separate the good from the bad. This is a very frequent theme, but it suffices to cite the parables of the talents, the ten virgins, and the sheep and the goats, which together form Matthew 25.

That Jesus taught the things which I have mentioned is largely uncontroversial. There is dispute about how far he expected everyone to keep his most demanding requirements (e.g. by way of giving all one's wealth to the poor), or whether these were 'counsels of perfection';[32] and about whether this teaching was intended to be kept only for a supposedly short period before the Last Judgement. There is dispute, too, about when Jesus expected the Last Judgement to occur (an issue which I shall need to discuss in Chapter 8), and about whether he taught that there would be a series of intermediate crises and judgements before the Last Judgement. There is dispute also about the authenticity and meaning of innumerable other passages where particular theological or moral doctrines appear to be being taught. All I am claiming is that Jesus taught that a certain way of life described very broadly is good and also that God loves us and will judge us. To deny the authenticity of this teaching would be to deny any historical basis for themes constantly repeated in different books

---

[27] Acts 7: 60.   [28] Matt. 25: 31–46.

[29] See the parable of the publican and the Pharisee (Luke 18: 9–14).

[30] Matt. 6: 2–6.   [31] Matt. 6: 31–4; Luke 6: 38.

[32] Matt. 19: 16–22 might seem to suggest a two-level ethic: one set of requirements for everyone, a more demanding set for those who would be perfect.

which were at least trying to convey the historical core of Jesus' teaching and where we find similar teaching in St Paul's letters—all of which latter is most naturally explained by its common origin in the teaching of Jesus himself.

Given that there is a God who is perfectly good, he will love us; and given that, almost everyone would agree that the way of living towards God and our fellows which Jesus commended is a good way to live. So all this is the sort of teaching one would expect God Incarnate to give. But many modern people will not think it a good act for God permanently to separate the good and the bad (at the Last Judgement), and so they will find it strong evidence against Jesus being God Incarnate that he did teach this separation. For, they will say, a good God will not punish the bad but will reform them. So I had better say a little about this issue. The Gospels unanimously affirm that the bad will be punished and the good rewarded. For the bad there will be 'weeping and gnashing of teeth'.[33] With one or two possible exceptions[34] the Gospels certainly seem to teach that the separation will be permanent. But the fate of the wicked is normally described as destruction,[35] or as loss of the bridegroom[36] or of goods.[37] The metaphor of casting the bad into a fire is often used, but just how literally an element of sensory suffering is intended is unclear; the fire is sometimes described as αἰώνιός, 'eternal',[38] but sometimes rather as ἀσβεστός, 'unquenchable'.[39] But all that the latter implies is that the fire will leave nothing of the wicked unburned; and indeed, if we take such talk literally, and suppose the wicked to be ordinary embodied men, the consequence of putting them in such a fire will be their elimination. Only in one place in the Gospels is the punishment itself declared to be eternal.[40] I conclude that Jesus certainly taught that the bad would suffer in the afterlife, and the good rewarded; and it would be hard to deny that he taught that the separation would be permanent. Of course, the point of his preaching all this was to move all people to repentance, so that there would be no bad left to be punished.

---

[33] Matt. 24: 51.

[34] For example, there is the warning to men to be reconciled quickly with their adversaries lest they be thrown into prison: 'You will never get out until you have paid the last penny' (Matt. 5: 26). As John Hick comments, 'since only a finite number of pennies can have a last one, we seem to be in the realm of graded debts and payments, rather than of absolute guilt and infinite penalty' (J. Hick, *Death and Eternal Life* (Collins, 1976), 244.

[35] Mark 12: 9.   [36] Matt. 25: 12.   [37] Matt. 25: 28.

[38] Matt. 18: 8; 25: 41.   [39] Mark 9: 43, 48.   [40] Matt. 25: 46.

Why should a good God permanently separate the bad from the good, and give the bad a bad life? My answer to this in this context[41] must inevitably be only a brief beginning of an answer, but here it is. God gives humans a free will to choose between good and bad; but a good choice one time makes a good choice come more easily the next time, and a bad choice one time makes a bad choice come more easily the next time. By our choices we shift the range of possible choices, and the range within which choices are easy and the range within which they are difficult. People only ever have a temptation to choose the bad, because they desire it; though, while the good is still open to them, they can resist that desire. They only ever choose the good, because they see it as worth while and important; though while the bad is still open to them, they can yield to contrary temptation. It is a great good for us to be able to determine, through a succession of free choices during the course of our lives, the kind of person we are to be. In the course of their life someone may make so many bad choices that they form a character with not the slightest belief that the good is worth having remaining and no desire for it. People like that would not be happy in the Heaven of the Blessed— they have neither the desire for God nor the belief that to enjoy him is a good thing.

God could, it may be said, give these people new good desires. But that would be imposing on them a character which they have chosen freely over their whole life not to have; and plausibly, therefore, the imposition of such a character on them would be wrong—God respects a determined and persistent rejection of himself. The life such people will have will inevitably not be a good one, for it will involve the frustrations of their desires. On Earth people have not merely a choice between good and bad, but their bad choices as well as their good choices are allowed to have their effect. There is a point in giving people responsibility for things when there exists the possibility that they may make good choices. But when that possibility no longer remains, it would not be good to allow their bad choices to have bad effects. So the bad person may long to hurt others, but being unable to do so will inevitably be unhappy. Maybe God will indeed 'destroy' such people, in the sense of annihilate them, if that is what they want; or keep them alive unhappy, if that is what they prefer.

[41] For full discussion, see my *Faith and Reason* (Clarendon Press, 1981), esp. 167–72; and my *Responsibility and Atonement*, esp. ch. 12.

Anyone sympathetic to the kind of argument deployed in the last two paragraphs will see the teaching of Jesus on judgement as good, and the kind of teaching to be expected of an incarnate God. Anyone not sympathetic will have reason to believe that Jesus was not God Incarnate.

I have claimed that the life of Jesus and the teaching of Jesus were (in so far as we have clear knowledge of what these were) the sort of life and teaching to be expected of God Incarnate. I emphasize that I and my readers are in a position to make the moral judgement about the quality of this life and teaching and also the judgement that living a life of that kind and giving teaching of that kind was to be expected of God Incarnate, in virtue of a moral climate inspired in part by Christian tradition having opened our eyes to certain moral truths. That does not, however, in any way mean that the judgement that Jesus exemplified these standards which we have come to see as good is in any way a subjective or circular one. That 'moral climate' has caused us to recognize moral truths which we would not otherwise be able to recognize, but that does derogate from their status as truths. More precisely, some of the teaching of Jesus concerned moral truths which, I have claimed, hold independently of whether or not Jesus had taught them. He merely helped us to see them. Other of Jesus' teaching concerned actions which he claimed that God would do, although not ones which his perfect goodness required him to do; for example, allow the wicked to live after a Last Judgement. I have urged that moral reflection will lead us to see the goodness of actions of the latter kind; and so to see that they are actions which God would quite probably, though not certainly, do. So overall the teaching of Jesus was, I have claimed, of a kind to be expected if he was God Incarnate. Similarly, while not all the actions which Jesus did were ones which God Incarnate would have to do in virtue of his perfect goodness, my claim is that they are good ones and so ones which an Incarnate God would quite probably do.

What is, however, interesting is that while we now may expect that if God intervened in history he would do it by living this sort of a life and giving this sort of teaching, his Jewish contemporaries and his contemporaries of other cultures did not in general expect this at all. Many Jews of Jesus' time certainly expected God to intervene in history; and many of them held that God would intervene by means of an earthly agent. Sometimes this earthly agent whom they expected was called by them the Messiah (the anointed one, the

Christ), but sometimes he was given other names or descriptions: Son of Man, Son of God, etc. This figure was seen to have the role of establishing God's rule, but there were different views of how this was to be achieved and of what it would consist. 'God's rule' might be seen as either political independence for Israel, or as cultic purity, or as the establishment of justice, or as God's reign throughout the world (including sometimes the animal and plant kingdoms). The method of achieving God's rule might be force of earthly arms, or a completely supernatural intervention, or even perhaps the preaching of a prophet.[42] But while it was of course expected that God's agent would lead a good life, it was not expected that its goodness would consist in his healing, showing love to outcasts, and a life of hardship culminating in his execution. Just to take an extreme example to make this point; there is only one passage in the whole literature of early Judaism (Old Testament Apocrypha, Old Testament Pseudepigrapha, Dead Sea Scrolls) in which it is stated that the Messiah (called by that name) will die: 2 Esdras 7: 29. And this is just a matter-of-fact statement that this will happen; there is no suggestion that the death had any exemplary or atoning significance.[43]

And although there was some expectation that the divine agent would teach, this was expected to take the form of his teaching God's hidden purposes for the future, and also sometimes of a call to repentance. There was not the expectation that the preaching would consist of teaching or emphasizing a far higher moral code than was currently practised by the best citizens.

The fact that the life and teaching of Jesus as recorded in the Gospels is not what was generally expected of the divine agent is reason to believe that Christians gave this account of it only because they believed that it happened. They were not reading back into history some (in a wide sense) 'messianic' expectations current in their culture. Once Jesus had taught and lived and died as he had, and they had come to believe for other reasons that he was God's special agent, they then 'searched the scriptures' to find passages suggesting that the 'Messiah' would teach, live, and die in this way. But they were often not passages interpreted as 'messianic' prophe-

---

[42] For these points, see the articles in J. Neusner, W. S. Green, and E. S. Frerichs (eds.), *Judaisms and their Messiahs at the Turn of the Christian Era* (Cambridge University Press, 1987), esp. those by Green, MacRae, Kee, and Charlesworth.

[43] See the discussion of this passage in J. H. Charlesworth, 'From Messianology to Christology', ibid. 242–4.

cies in their culture, nor often naturally interpretable in this way. To take but one example: the 'Suffering Servant' passages in Isaiah[44] were not seen as prophetic of the Messiah by his Jewish contemporaries; but after Jesus had lived and taught, the New Testament writers saw them as foretelling him in a very large number of places.[45] Even so, according to St Luke, it needed Jesus himself after his Resurrection to explain to them that the Old Testament taught that Christ had to suffer.[46] We shall find this phenomenon when we come in the other chapters of Part II to the other aspects of Jesus' teaching and life, that the New Testament writers dug up Old Testament passages and represented them as predictive of Jesus, when contemporary writers did not find any 'messianic' (in a wide sense) significance in them.

[44] Isa. 42: 1–4; 49: 1–6; 50: 4–10; 52: 13–53: 12.

[45] See all the marginal references from these passages of Isaiah to New Testament passages in annotated Bibles.

[46] See Jesus' words to the two disciples on the road to Emmaus: 'O how foolish you are, and how slow of heart to believe all that the prophets have declared. Was it not necessary that the Messiah should suffer these things and then enter into his glory?' (Luke 24: 25–6).

6

Jesus Implied his Divinity

I ARGUED earlier that a God Incarnate, in order to fulfil the purposes which I described, could not, at any rate in a society which lacked the concept of a divided Chalcedonian incarnation, publicly and explicitly say that he was God before he had lived a perfect life to the full. Saying this would almost inevitably be misunderstood and defeat the purposes of the Incarnation. That could well happen even if the society did have the concept of a divided incarnation. But clearly first-century Palestine did not have that concept. Jesus even needed to downplay the expectations of a Messiah, not because he denied the title but because it immediately suggested the exercise of physical power. Peter's confession of Jesus as Messiah is followed immediately by Jesus' rebuke to Peter, 'Get thee behind me, Satan,'[1] when Peter objects to Jesus' predictions of his suffering. The claim of Messiahship needed to be heavily nuanced. But an explicit claim to divinity would be almost impossible to nuance: how could people understand that God had chosen to suffer and die as a human? Or how could people take seriously a claim which combined in one breath, 'I am God, therefore imitate me: be humble'? Vermes writes that 'it is no exaggeration to contend that the identification of a contemporary historical figure with God would have been inconceivable to a first-century AD Palestinian Jew'.[2] A claim to divinity would immediately be understood as the claim to be a pagan God, and not the God of Israel, without a full-scale Christian theology of two natures (divine and human) in one individual to explain it. Even today, most highly sophisticated people see a contradiction in God becoming incarnate as a human being.

[1] Mark 8: 3.
[2] Geza Vermes, *Jesus the Jew* (SCM Press, 1994), 186.

Jesus' technique with respect to many matters, including especially who he was, seems to have been to get the audience to think it out for themselves; see, for example, Jesus' refusal to answer the question about his own authority before his audience faced up to the need to have a view about John the Baptist's authority.[3] And even if we suppose that Mark has imposed on his history of Jesus his own theological view that there was a 'messianic secret' (Jesus keeping his identity as Messiah secret from the public until he revealed it at his trial), there are other passages (non-Marcan passages, and passages concerned with matters other than his identity) in which he seeks to make his audience reach their own conclusion. There is, for example, the question of the disciples of John the Baptist to Jesus asking whether he was the 'one who is to come' or whether they should expect someone else (a question recorded only in Matthew and Luke).[4] The answer given was 'Go and tell John what you hear and see.' And there is Jesus' action of riding into Jerusalem on the first Palm Sunday and cleansing the Temple, allowing the crowds to shout 'Hosanna', an event central to the tradition for which Matthew and Luke would probably have had other sources, when none of the synoptists records Jesus giving any explanation of his authority for such an act. This method of challenge was very much in line with Jesus' method of teaching by parables. Yet in the end, if Jesus was God Incarnate, he would need to ensure that his central claims were well understood.

So an incarnate God must leave plenty of clues in his life, reflection on which could give his followers after his life was finished the understanding of who he was—as well, perhaps, as explicit teaching after his life was finished. The arguments which I gave in Chapter 2 for expecting God to become incarnate were arguments for expecting a divided incarnation. We might expect him to live under conditions of ignorance except of those things he needs to reveal; of unawareness of his extra-human powers except when these are required to fulfil the reasons for his Incarnation; and of the possibility of his yielding to a temptation to do other than the best (though not to do wrong). In that case, we might expect not merely positive evidence of his divinity, but also some evidence of lack of access to knowledge which was God's, including knowledge of his powers

---

[3] Mark 11: 27–33 (Matt. 21: 23–7; Luke 20: 1–8).
[4] Matt. 11: 2–6; Luke 7: 18–23.

which were God's, and consciousness of a temptation to which he
might yield to do less than the best. Bearing in mind that we would
expect the positive evidence to be occasionally balanced by evidence
of this latter sort, let us consider what indication Jesus gave of his
divine status. I consider first what he explicitly said or allowed others
to express to him; secondly, the actions he did which might be
reasonably interpreted as making a claim to special intimacy with
God and having God's own authority; and thirdly, the explicit views
of the New Testament writers about his status.

Explicit Acknowledgements before Jesus of his Divinity

Fairly clearly, Jesus did not say 'I am God' before his (believed)
Resurrection;[5] none of the Gospels records such a saying. There are,
however, indications in two (and perhaps three) Gospels of Jesus'
acknowledgement of his divine status and its recognition by others,
after his Resurrection when the purposes of his Incarnation would
have been fulfilled and so when there was no need for the two
natures (divine and human) to be kept so far apart. Then he could
be fully aware of his divinity while doing human actions; and when
his followers had seen in his Crucifixion his manifest humanity, then
perhaps they could be introduced to a notion of divinity compatible
with that. If Jesus was to proclaim explicitly to the apostles his divine
nature, the time when they would be most receptive to that claim
would have been after his Resurrection. St Matthew's Gospel ends
with Jesus commanding the Eleven to baptize 'in the name of the
Father, and of the Son, and of the Holy Spirit'.[6] This saying puts 'the
Son' (Jesus) on a level with God the Father. Critics, rightly ever on
the watch for later interpolations, have, of course, cast grave doubt
on the authenticity of this verse; but the manuscript tradition is
unanimous and thus early. Then St John records the explicit confession by the formerly doubting, now convinced, Thomas, of Jesus as
'My Lord and my God'.[7] On two post-Resurrection occasions St

---

[5] My writing in this chapter and subsequent chapters of Part II of events having
happened 'before' or 'after' 'the Resurrection' is to be regarded as shorthand for the
events having happened before or after the time at which disciples later believed that Jesus
rose. I am not at this stage making any assumption about whether the Resurrection really
happened.

[6] Matt. 28: 19.   [7] John 20: 28.

Matthew's Gospel records that disciples 'worshipped (προσεκύνησαν) Jesus; and many ancient manuscripts record a similar 'worship' by the Eleven at the end of St Luke's Gospel.[8]

Is 'worship' (προσκύνησις) thought to be appropriate only to divinity? It certainly is so thought in several distinct New Testament passages. In Matthew 4: 10 (paralleled in Luke 4: 8) Jesus quotes Deuteronomy 6: 13, 'Worship the Lord your God and serve only him', in response to the Devil's invitation to worship him (the Devil). In Acts 10: 26 Peter stops Cornelius worshipping him with the words 'Stand up: I am only a mortal.'[9] And twice in Revelation the angel commands 'John' not to worship him with the words 'You must not do that! I am a fellow-servant with you ... Worship God.'[10] There are, however, two New Testament passages in which worship is used of a gesture to someone other than God or Jesus: Matthew 18: 26 and Revelation 3: 9. 'Matthew 18: 26 describes an abject gesture towards the creditor who has a debtor at his mercy (and "through" whom God himself is perhaps intended to be seen),'[11] though the parable expresses no approval of the 'worship'. Revelation 3: 9 is a quotation from Isaiah, used to describe an abject submission which opponents will have to make to the *Church* of Philadelphia; the context and use of this quotation need not, I am inclined to suggest, imply a literal act of worship. In neither of these cases is there any suggestion that literal worship is a *proper* attitude towards a good or powerful *individual* who is less than God. So there is no doubt that in general New Testament writers disapproved of worship of other than God. But it is not merely in post-Resurrection stories that worship is described as being offered to Jesus. There are quite a number of such occasions in Matthew and to a lesser extent in Mark; on one occasion the worship is by the disciples,[12] but it is offered mainly by those who had been healed or sought a favour of Jesus. Only some of these can be regarded as approved by the author

---

[8] Luke 24: 52.

[9] Analogously, when the people of Lystra concluded that Paul and Barnabas were 'gods ... come down to us in human form', Paul and Barnabas stopped them vigorously with the words 'We are mortals just like you' (Acts 14: 8–18).

[10] Rev. 19: 10, 22: 9.

[11] C. F. D. Moule, *The Origin of Christology* (Cambridge University Press, 1977), 176. For the point made in the parenthetical clause, Moule refers to an entry by E. Greeven in G. W. Bromiley (ed.), *Theological Dictionary of the New Testament* (Eerdmans, 1965–74), vi. 763. My discussion of προσκύνησις is very largely a paraphrase of pp. 175–6 of Moule.

[12] Matt. 14: 33.

of the Gospel as proper responses to Jesus. There is, however, a clear flavour of worship as an attitude appropriate to God being also appropriate to Jesus. And in no case, pre- or post-Resurrection, is Jesus (unlike Peter or the angel of Revelation) recorded as rejecting worship. Now, of course, both John and Matthew may be putting their own view into the mouths of Jesus and of Thomas, and Matthew (and Mark) may be expressing their own view of the response which the disciples ought to have had to Jesus. Still, there are clearly at least three independent sources here, that Jesus was worshipped and did not reject worship.

There are, however, two utterances of Jesus before his Resurrection which might be taken to imply that he believed himself less than divine. There is Jesus' claim in Mark (copied in Matthew) that he, 'the Son', does not know something which the Father knows: 'the day or hour' at which 'Heaven and Earth will pass away'.[13] However, in a divided incarnation an incarnate God acts and speaks only in the light of those beliefs which are his as a human and of those beliefs which he needs to know for the purposes of his Incarnation. 'The day or hour' seems to me not to be in that category.

The other utterance which might be taken to imply that Jesus believed himself less than divine is his 'cry of dereliction' from the Cross, as reported by St Mark, 'My God, my God, why have you forsaken me?'[14] which might suggest that Jesus at that moment ceased to believe that God was sustaining him and so did not then believe that he was divine. It seems to me doubtful whether the cry is to be read in this sense. It is, after all, the opening verse of Psalm 22, a psalm which describes what is happening to a victim whose fate is uncannily like what is happening to Jesus. ('All who see me mock me; they make mouths at me . . . My hands and feet have shrivelled,' and so on). What Jesus may be saying by quoting the opening verse of the Psalm is 'Can't you see Psalm 22 being fulfilled?' Nevertheless, if we do read the 'cry' as implying that Jesus did not at that moment believe that he was divine, that seems perfectly compatible with the fulfilment of the purposes of a divided incarnation. In order to share our suffering fully, he must experience the feeling of isolation from God which so many humans suffer; above all, he must suffer it at his supreme moment of crisis. But in order to tell and show us who he was, he must, of course, not experience it too much of the time. The

---

[13] Mark 13: 31–2.   [14] Mark 15: 34.

cry, like the claim of his ignorance about 'the day or hour', are what we might expect if the Incarnation was of the divided type, but they need to be combined with much positive evidence for his Incarnation if they are not simply to count against Jesus believing at all that he was God.

There are also two recorded questions by which Jesus challenged others, relevant to his status but which seem to me to show nothing either way about what he believed. There is the question to the rich young man who addressed him as 'Good Teacher'; 'Why do you call me good? No one is good, but God alone.'[15] And the question about why David (thought of as the author of the Psalms) addressed the future Messiah, believed to be the son of David, as 'Lord': 'David himself calls him Lord; so how can he be his son?'[16] You might suppose Jesus in the first quotation to be denying his divinity, and in the second to be affirming that the Messiah had a higher origin than from David alone, but in view of Jesus' method of challenging others to think things through by questioning them, these suppositions seem inadequately warranted. He might in the first case, for example, have been seeking the answer, 'but since you are good, you must be God'.

Actions of Jesus Implying Divine Authority

Although Jesus made no explicit pre-Resurrection claims to divinity in words, he claimed an intimacy with God and a great authority which he never explained in terms which would make it comprehensible against an Old Testament background (e.g. in terms of a prophetic call). By his 'Amen' he emphasized that authority. That is, many of his solemn sayings begin 'Amen. I say to you . . .'. (The 'Amen' is often translated in English 'verily' or 'truly'). 'Amen' is a response of assent to someone else's statement, and is never found except in the Gospels (in Mark and Q, and also in independent passages in Matthew and Luke) at the beginning of a statement where no other human has said anything. So perhaps Jesus is responding to what he takes God to be saying. In that case he is merely endorsing God's voice, as we do when we say 'Amen' at the end of a prayer uttered by someone else: we are not recognizing their

---

[15] Mark 10: 18.   [16] Mark 12: 37.

authority but merely endorsing their attitude (for example, their penitence or petition to God). If, instead of 'Amen', Jesus had said, following the prophets, 'Thus says the Lord', he would he handing on the command of a superior. He spoke of himself in relation to God as his son, in ways that contrast his sonship with that of others; for example, 'All things have been handed over to me by my Father; and no one knows the Son except the Father, and no one knows the Father except the Son and anyone to whom the Son chooses to reveal him.'[17] The unique relation is brought out by Jesus addressing his Father as 'Abba'.

On two occasions Jesus is recorded as forgiving sins;[18] though he used the passive 'Your sins are forgiven' to the person concerned, the bystanders are recorded as understanding this as his forgiving the sins himself, expressing wonder at his ability to do this. On the occasion when he was dealing with the paralytic, Jesus, recognizing the silent thoughts of the scribes who heard his words, goes on to heal the paralytic in order, he says, that 'you may know that the Son of Man has authority on Earth to forgive sins'. In John, Jesus hands on the power to forgive to his disciples.[19] Jesus claimed the power to interpret and even amend Mosaic law; for example, in respect of sabbath observance[20] and dispensation from the obligation to bury the dead.[21] Some have claimed that the stories of controversy with Pharisees over legalistic matters involve reading back later disputes between Jews and Christians into Jesus' time, but there is widespread agreement on the genuineness of the burial saying. And on the whole E. P. Sanders concludes, 'there is clear evidence that [Jesus] did not consider the Mosaic dispensation to be final or absolutely binding'.[22] Despite being a layman, Jesus cleansed the Temple (whether or not that was intended as a prophecy of doom). Jesus cast out many demons, but never invoked any human source in whose name he cast them out; whereas his disciples (authorized or unauthorized) cast them out in his name.

---

[17] Matt. 11: 27.

[18] Mark 2: 5, and parallels in the other synoptics; and Luke 7: 48. It should be noted, however, that John the Baptist's baptism was more generally 'for the forgiveness of sins'. But I argue later in this chapter that it did not involve the remission of the sins of particular individuals.

[19] John 20: 23.   [20] Mark 2: 27–8.   [21] Matt. 8: 22.

[22] E. P. Sanders, *Jesus and Judaism* (SCM Press, 1985), 267. I cite Sanders occasionally as an authority, both because of his eminence as a New Testament scholar and because he is a moderate liberal scholar who cannot be accused of giving much weight to any considerations arising from Christian doctrine.

I take most of the above items from the list in Raymond Brown's *The Death of the Messiah* of things which it is plausible to suppose that Jesus did in his lifetime which, taken together, would lead his opponents to consider him blasphemous.[23] The synoptists explicitly connect a comment by the scribes who heard Jesus' words of forgiveness to the paralytic man that 'It is blasphemy! Who can forgive sins, but God alone?'[24] Mark and Matthew report that the charge against Jesus before the Sanhedrin was 'blasphemy'.[25] There has been much discussion of what the Jewish leaders of Jesus' time would have thought of as constituting 'blasphemy'. The second-century AD Mishnah declared that 'the blasphemer is not guilty unless he pronounces the name',[26] that is, says aloud the Hebrew name Yahweh. But there are many other passages in the Septuagint (the second-century BC Greek translation of the Old Testament), and in the writings of Philo (50 BC) and Josephus (AD 90), where people are described as 'blaspheming' God where what the alleged 'blasphemers' have done is to abuse God or arrogantly to assume divine prerogatives.[27] Given the wider understanding of blasphemy to include the latter two actions as well as pronouncing the name of Yahweh, the only plausible way of understanding what Jesus' blasphemy was supposed to amount to, related to what is reported to have been said at the trial, is that Jesus arrogantly claimed for himself divine privileges. For the Gospel writers mention two issues raised at the trial: the accusation that Jesus announced that he would destroy the Temple and his reply to the question whether he was the Messiah.

Matthew and Mark state that the 'false testimony' which led to the condemnation included the charge that Jesus would or could destroy the (sanctuary of the) Temple and build it again in three days. As Sanders writes: 'It is hard to imagine a purely fictional origin for the accusation that he threatened to destroy the Temple.'[28] Mark described this accusation as 'false'. But probably Mark, and certainly Matthew, who has the same passage, believed that the Temple was destroyed; and, like other synoptists, Mark reports a further prediction by Jesus of its destruction.[29] So the falsity of the accusation (in

---

[23] (Doubleday, 1994), 545–7.   [24] Mark 2: 7.
[25] Mark 14: 64; Matt. 26: 65.   [26] *Sanhedrin* 7: 5.
[27] Brown, *The Death of the Messiah*, 523.
[28] Sanders, *Jesus and Judaism*, 72. The Gospel of Thomas 71 quotes the first part of the prophecy in the first person 'I will destroy this house,' but goes on 'and no one will be able to build it again'.   [29] Mark 13: 2 (Matt. 24: 2; Luke 21: 6).

their view) must lie in one of two things: Jesus did not threaten himself to destroy the Temple, but merely predicted that it would be destroyed; and/or he did not promise to build another in three days. But since both Mark and Matthew believed that he did build in three days something else which had been destroyed, 'not made with hands', which, when the Temple was destroyed, they came to regard as a replacement for it; the falsity in their view is more likely to consist in the fact that Jesus did not threaten to destroy the Temple but merely predicted that it would be destroyed. Luke describes Jesus as warning, at the time of the Passion, the 'daughters of Jerusalem' of a time of disaster;[30] and Mark, in the chapter preceding the Passion narrative, records Jesus as predicting the destruction of the Temple.[31] So Jesus indeed predicted the destruction of the Temple; but (maybe) by another rather than himself. John quotes Jesus as saying 'destroy this temple, and in three days I will raise it up'.[32] To replace the divinely instituted worship of the Temple with another kind of worship was clearly God's privilege; and Jesus is not reported as saying that God has commissioned him to do this—he is reported as saying that he would do it himself.

In all the synoptic Gospels, Jesus is asked by the high priest (or 'the elders of the people') if he is the Messiah, and he gives an answer in terms of 'the Son of Man' (fairly evidently himself) being seated at the right hand of God. This clearly refers to the one who in Daniel (7: 13–14) came 'with the clouds of heaven' and was presented to 'the Ancient One' and to whom was given an 'everlasting kingdom'. In John, on another occasion, he is asked by the Jews if he is the Messiah;[33] and in another passage he makes a claim somewhat similar to the synoptic claim.[34] In Mark he definitely accepts the title of Messiah. This might be a reading back of the later Christian view into the trial. However, in the centuries before AD 130 no other identifiable Jew was hailed as the Messiah; the title Christ (Messiah) stuck to Jesus very early in pre-Pauline confessions of faith. All of that gives some plausibility to the claim that Jesus allowed some of his followers to think of him as the Messiah,[35] and

---

[30] Luke 23: 27–31 (see also Luke 13: 35 (Matt. 23: 38) and 19: 44).
[31] Mark 13: 1–2.   [32] John 2: 19.   [33] John 10: 24.
[34] John 1: 51.
[35] Crucially relevant for the disciples' understanding of Jesus messianic status was the Transfiguration (Mark 9: 2–8). Jesus was transfigured before them so that his garments became gleaming white, while he talked with Moses and Elijah. God (represented by the

so to the plausibility that this issue was indeed raised at his Jewish trial. Now we have no reason to believe that claiming to be the Messiah would be blasphemous in itself. After all, many believed that God would indeed send a Messiah. But it is the response in terms of the Son of Man being seated at the right hand of God, cited in the synoptic Gospels, which leads to the high priest tearing his garments and saying, 'Why do we still need witnesses?'

Luke eliminates the blasphemy accusation from its place in the trial of Jesus in the Marcan narrative. Brown suggests that Luke's sense of propriety would not allow him to report that the highest authority of the Jewish people so directly insulted God's Son,[36] by accusing him of blasphemy. However, the same two issues—a threat to destroy the Temple and Jesus being at the right hand of God–are connected with blasphemy in Luke's account in Acts of the trial of Stephen. Stephen's accusers accused him of speaking 'blasphemous words against Moses and God', which they filled out by claiming that they had heard Stephen say that 'Jesus of Nazareth will destroy this place [presumably, the Temple sanctuary] and will change the customs which Moses handed on to us.'[37] But what led to his execution was his words 'Look, I see the heavens opened and the Son of Man standing at the right hand of God', which Luke glosses as seeing 'Jesus standing at the right hand of God'.[38] Clearly this text was seen as making greater than messianic claims by the Gospel writers, and their unanimity in reporting it in this context gives considerable plausibility to the view that Jesus was condemned for making this kind of eschatological claim about his authority.

John gives a very brief account of the trial of Jesus before the Jewish leaders, and it contains no statement of the charge against Jesus or of any guilty verdict. But I noted earlier that John has the habit of telling a story which is not meant to be historically accurate but captures what he regards as the essence of some aspect of the life of Jesus. In John 10 the Jews attempt to stone Jesus, saying 'It is not for a good work that we are going to stone you, but for blasphemy, because you, though only a human being, are making yourself God.' And Jesus responds with, 'Can you say that the one whom the Father

---

cloud) referred to Jesus as 'my Son, the Beloved' and told them to listen to him. But this expression here need not connote any status higher than that of Messiah.

[36] Brown, *The Death of the Messiah*, 520.

[37] Acts 6: 14.   [38] Acts 7: 55–6.

sanctified and sent into the world is blaspheming because I said "I am God's Son"?'[39] The essence of this passage is a charge of blasphemy and an attempt to administer the official penalty for blasphemy: stoning. Stephen was stoned for his blasphemy. Jesus was crucified, because that was the Roman penalty for making himself 'the King of the Jews'. There are various theories of why the Jews were able to stone Stephen but not able to execute Jesus without bringing in the Romans.[40] But the unanimous and lengthy testimony of the New Testament to the Crucifixion of Jesus leaves no doubt that Jesus was crucified by the Romans, on the instigation of Jews (see earlier). John saw the essence of the Jewish involvement as an attempt to administer the penalty for blasphemy. Earlier he records that 'the Jews were seeking all the more to kill [Jesus], because he was not only breaking the sabbath but was also calling God his own (ἴδιον) Father, making himself equal to God'.[41]

So the events at the trial of Jesus leading to his condemnation for blasphemy as well as his actions listed earlier were such as, he could foresee, would make it natural for the disciples after his Resurrection to attribute divinity to him. There are, however, two things which might seem to suggest to us, as to his immediate disciples, that he did not think of himself as divine. The most important is that he accepted John's baptism, which was, Mark tells us, 'for the forgiveness of sins'; those who came to be 'baptized' came 'confessing their sins'.[42] Does not Jesus being baptized imply that he believed himself inferior to the teacher who had baptized him, and a sinner, and so not one who had led the perfect life which I discussed in the last chapter, and so not God?

The baptism of Jesus certainly disturbed Christian writers, most of whom put a gloss on the event suggesting ways of interpreting it other than the obvious way, which seemed to carry these implications that he believed himself to be inferior to John or to have sinned. Matthew, for example, adds to the Marcan account by reporting John as attempting to reject Jesus' request for baptism with the words 'I need to be baptized by you, and do you come to me?' and Jesus replying, 'Let it be so now; for it is proper for us in this way to fulfil all righteousness.'[43] Now I do not think that Jesus

---

[39] John 10: 33–6.   [40] Brown, *The Death of the Messiah*, 369–71.
[41] John 5: 18.   [42] Mark 1: 4–5.
[43] Matt. 3: 14–15. For other early Christian glosses, see G. Thiessen and A. Merz, *The Historical Jesus: A Comprehensive Guide* (SCM Press, 1998), 207–8.

accepting John's baptism can be read as his considering himself inferior to John. For it was a central element of Jesus' teaching that
greatness, including his own greatness, belongs to people not
because they exercise authority, but because they serve.[44] But it
might well look as if his accepting baptism implied that he believed
himself to have sinned. If that implication is correct, then that would
rule out a unified incarnation, for on that view, if he was God, he
must have had true beliefs about everything including whether he
had sinned, and being God he could not have sinned. Given the
implication, a divided incarnation is still possible. For in a divided
incarnation he could at that point have acted in ignorance of his
divinity and so inferred that, like other humans, he must have
sinned at some time in his life. Like his cry of dereliction, it would
signify his believed separation from God at that moment, combined
in this case with a false belief about his past life. But although I have
argued that we have more reason to expect a divided than a unified
incarnation, I find it implausible to suppose that it would lead in
Jesus as far as to a false belief about whether he had sinned. He needs
that amount of knowledge in order to behave truthfully in his
symbolic acts, crucial for a perfect life.

However, I am most doubtful about the implication cited earlier:
that Jesus, accepting John's baptism implied that he believed himself
to have sinned. All depends on just what John's baptism amounted to.
Now certainly if those seeking John's baptism were required to state to
John or his disciples their own personal sins in detail (in the way that
an adult candidate for baptism in the Catholic or Orthodox Churches
is required to make a full detailed confession of past sins), if Jesus was
God, he could not do so unless he was ignorant of his sinlessness. But
there seem to me to be reasons for denying that implication. First, of
course, the impression in Mark of large numbers surging together for
baptism would leave little time for detailed confessions. Secondly,
there is Josephus' account of John's baptism:

[John] was a good man and had told the Jews to pursue righteousness and
to practise justice towards their fellows and piety towards God, and so to
join together (συνιέναι) in baptism. For he taught that baptism was
acceptable to God if people did not use it to gain pardon for their sins but
rather, their souls being thoroughly cleansed already by righteousness, for
the purification of their bodies.[45]

[44] Mark 10: 42–5.   [45] Josephus, *Antiquities* 18: 117.

This account seems to some extent implausible, for if John's baptism was mere body purification why was it performed only once? Now maybe Josephus wanted to make Jews seem more like Romans in seeking pardon via temple rites and righteous conduct rather than via something sacramental. Nevertheless, he is very explicit in denying that John's baptism was for the remission of individual sins; and this was a matter about which he would have received many eyewitness reports. On the other hand, since Christians basically approved of John the Baptist and so of his baptism, they might well read back into it aspects peculiar to Christian baptism, leading to their worry about why Jesus accepted baptism. Only Mark (and sources dependent on him) says that John's baptism was for 'the forgiveness of sins' and that people came 'confessing their sins'. No such phrases occur in the (Q) passages of Matthew and Luke not dependent on Mark. It is plausible to suppose that Josephus is not deceiving us totally, and so I suggest the following as an account of John's baptism which has the consequence that the accounts of all the various writers are largely correct. John was leading a national renewal movement into which people were incorporated by baptism. In being baptized they accepted membership of a purified community; confession there was, but it was not as individualistic a matter as a natural reading of Mark might suggest. Confession was in general terms for the sins of Israel and any involvement therein of the confessing person. The individual still had to perform deeds of righteousness in order to be right with God. This compromise account allows us to take account of the large numbers involved, and also of the use of Josephus of the word συνιέναι, which carries a suggestion of a mass baptism.

The comprehensibility of proxy baptism is brought out by the early practice, referred to by St Paul in 1 Corinthians, which no doubt soon died out, of baptism for others (namely, the dead).[46] St John's Gospel seems to endorse my account of what John's baptism amounted to where it has, in the place of a baptism of Jesus by John, John's statement about Jesus, 'Here is the lamb of God who takes away the sin of the world,'[47] implying that Jesus comes to John burdened with sin, but not his own sin. Given that it would not be wrong for Jesus to accept John's baptism, he had some reason to do so. He seeks to serve as an example to others; if he expects them to be baptized, he should be baptized himself.

---

[46] See 1 Cor. 15: 29.   [47] John 1: 29.

So I suggest that in accepting baptism Jesus did not need to confess sins of his own but merely to identify with Israel's need for repentance and forgiveness. I shall be arguing in the next chapter that Jesus was offering his life for the sins of humans. Hence, he was identifying with them and what they needed to do. They needed to repent and be baptized. So he would repent and be baptized on their behalf.

The second thing which might suggest, but much less seriously, that Jesus was unaware of his divinity are the temptations of Jesus (both the post-baptismal temptations[48] and the Agony in the Garden of Gethsemane[49]). I write 'much less seriously' because we can be tempted to do things to which there is not the slightest possibility of our yielding. One can still feel the frustration of a desire to yield. If Jesus was God, any temptation to do wrong must be of this kind. And the temptation to worship the Devil is clearly in that category. The other temptations were temptations to do less than the best: if Jesus had turned the stones into bread (for his own consumption or that of the people of Israel), or if he had not accepted crucifixion, no one would have been wronged. Hence, I argued in Chapter 2, God Incarnate could have yielded to a temptation not to do the best; and that is why his doing the best in these situations (if he did) is the work of supererogation which made available an atoning sacrifice for our salvation.

The Attitude of New Testament Writers to Jesus' Divinity

There is, further, quite a lot in the rest of the New Testament, from very different strands (some of them early), in which explicitly or implicitly the writers acknowledge Jesus' divinity, that it is natural to look for some source for this in the actions or teaching of Jesus. There is, of course, first, St John's Gospel: John 1: 1–14. And in the Johannine tradition, probably also 1 John 5: 20. In Revelation 1: 12–18 'one like the Son of Man' says, 'Do not be afraid; I am the first and the last, and the living one. I was dead, and see I am alive for ever and ever.' 'The first and the last' must be God; he who 'was dead and behold I am alive again' must be Jesus. The Epistle to the

---

[48] Mark 1: 12 and the fuller (Q) versions in Matt. 4: 1–11 and Luke 4: 1–13.

[49] Mark 14: 32–42 and partly similar passages in Matthew and Luke.

Hebrews (a quite different New Testament strand) is equally unambiguous: in Hebrews 1: 8 the author writes that God has addressed Jesus with words including 'O God', and he makes a contrast between the honour God pays to Jesus and the lesser honour due to angels. Then there are passages which imply Jesus' existence in at least a semi-divine state before his earthly existence. Most scholars hold that Philippians 2: 6–11 is a pre-Pauline hymn: it speaks of 'Christ Jesus who though he was in the form of God did not regard equality with God as something to be exploited (ἁρπαγμόν), but emptied himself, taking the form of a slave, being born in human likeness'. The majority interpretation of this hymn is that the author is saying that Jesus was equal to God, but 'emptied himself' (rather than that he resisted the temptation to become divine). In favour of the majority view is that St Paul writes in 2 Corinthians 8: 8 of Jesus, 'who though he was rich, yet for your sakes he became poor'. Paul writes in 1 Corinthians of Jesus Christ, 'through whom are all things and through whom we exist'.[50] The pre-Christian Wisdom Literature had come to speak of God's Wisdom as something like a person existing alongside God, and as his helper and agent in creation. In this passage Paul seems to be ascribing that sort of role to Jesus. Another relevant Pauline passage (also possibly a pre-Pauline hymn) is Colossians 1: 15–20, where the author speaks of the Son (that is, Jesus Christ) as 'the image of the invisible God, the firstborn of all creation', in whom and through whom 'all things in heaven and on earth were created', 'he himself is before all things, and in him all things hold together'. Then there is also 2 Corinthians 13: 14, when Paul puts Jesus alongside 'God' in a Trinitarian formula: 'The grace of the Lord Jesus Christ, the love of God, and the communion of the Holy Spirit be with all of you.'

And finally there are the infancy narratives in Matthew and Luke. Both writers tell us that Jesus was conceived without a human father through the operation of the Holy Spirit.[51] Even if they did not intend their stories of the birth of Jesus to be taken literally but intended them as myths to bring out the significance of Jesus, their stories show the very high status they supposed Jesus to have. They

---

[50] 1 Cor. 8: 6. See the discussion in Christopher Tuckett, *Christology and the New Testament* (Edinburgh University Press, 2001), 62–4.

[51] For arguments in favour of the majority view that the Lucan narrative does indeed claim a virginal conception, see Raymond Brown, *The Birth of the Messiah* (Geoffrey Chapman, 1977), 299–303.

bring this out by claiming (whether literally or metaphorically) that Jesus is different in nature from any other human in that the 'Holy Spirit' of God is the cause of a conception which would otherwise have needed a human father. Raymond Brown plausibly suggests that this theological message is a further stage in what he calls the 'backwards development' of Christology. What he means by this is that, as Christian theology developed, the New Testament writers claimed that Jesus acquired some status (e.g. as 'Son of God') at earlier and earlier moments of time. When did Jesus acquire his status as 'Son of God' (whatever exactly that means in the New Testament)? There are some early passages, which seem to imply that he became Son of God at his Resurrection.[52] Then there are the passages describing the baptism of Jesus by John which might be thought to imply that that was the moment at which Jesus became Son of God.[53] If we take the apparent implications of passages of either of these kinds seriously, they represent an adoptionist Christology: Jesus became Son of God at a certain period in his life. The infancy stories suggest otherwise: he always was Son of God throughout his earthly life. This 'conception Christology' (that Jesus was Son of God from his conception onwards) makes no claim that the Son of God had a previous existence, but it seems to me to be compatible with it. His being God at the beginning of his earthly life is compatible with his having been God before that. The conception Christology shares with the explicit 'pre-existence Christology' illustrated by the passages cited previously, the view that throughout his earthly existence Jesus always had a 'Son of God' status, and sees that as involving a difference in nature from ordinary humans. Note also that in St Matthew's infancy narrative the Magi 'worship' the infant Jesus.[54] The almost total independence from each other of the two infancy narratives, having in common only certain crucial features—including the overshadowing by the Holy Spirit, and the Virginal Conception—indicate that beliefs in these latter well antedate the composition of the two narratives, let alone of the whole

---

[52] An example of this is the (probably pre-Pauline) formula given in Rom. 1: 3–4, which describes God's son as 'descended from David according to the flesh; declared to be Son of God with power according to the spirit of holiness [Holy Spirit?] by resurrection from the dead'.

[53] Mark 1: 11 and the passages in Matt. and Luke dependent on it.

[54] This paragraph is entirely dependent on Brown, *The Birth of the Messiah*; see esp. p. 140–2.

Gospels. They form part of a general correction widespread in the New Testament to apparent adoptionism.

The apparent adoptionism in the form of passages seeming to imply that Jesus became Son of God at his Resurrection or his baptism may, however, be merely apparent. Passages quoted as favouring a 'Resurrection Christology' include Romans 1: 4, speaking of Jesus 'declared to be (ὁρισθέντος) Son of God with power', 'by resurrection from the dead'; Peter's speech in Acts 2 that God has made 'this Jesus whom you crucified' (2: 36), 'both Lord and Messiah'; and Paul's speech in Acts 13, Acts 13: 33 quoting, as a comment on the Resurrection Psalm 2: 7, 'today have I begotten you'. But these passages can be understood in more than one way e.g. 'begotten' as 'brought to life'; ὁρισθέντος as 'recognized as' rather than 'made'. And Peter cannot really have thought that Jesus was not the Messiah (Christ) when he was crucified, but became that afterwards. The passages in the three synoptic Gospels which might be thought to support a 'baptism Christology' are the descriptions of the baptism when a heavenly voice announces 'this is (or "you are") my Son'. But all of these passages, except that in Luke, seem to me equally well understood as public announcements of what was already the case. One disputed reading of Luke, however, represents the heavenly voice as saying 'you are my Son. Today I have begotten you', the same quotation of Psalm 2: 7 which Luke in Acts put into the mouth of Paul. This reading, unlike the alternative reading, seems to carry the implication that this is the day on which Jesus became Son of God. But writers can use quotations because of the aptness of some aspects thereof without endorsing every aspect thereof, which Luke cannot possibly be doing on both occasions when he uses the same quotation, for he would then be using it to support two incompatible Christologies. In any case his infancy narrative (a much more serious affirmation than the isolated use of a quotation) seems to commit Luke to the view that Jesus was Son of God throughout his life. and although the conception Christology of the infancy narratives says nothing about Jesus' pre-existence, it is, I have claimed, perfectly compatible with it. And as with the two passages from Luke and Acts, if any of the passages in St Paul's letters cited above are thought to imply that Jesus acquired his high status at the beginning or in the course of his earthly life, they are contemporary with other Pauline passages (e.g. 2 Cor. 8: 8, cited earlier) in which the author clearly expresses a different view. It might have taken some time before theological reflection on the life of Jesus clarified the difference between the two positions and led to the view that Jesus had his high status before his birth, as making best sense of what had happened, including the behaviour of Jesus in his life.

Unprecedented

It is indisputable that there was no Jewish expectation that God would become incarnate. Pagans believed that their 'gods' had taken human form from time to time; but their 'gods' were lesser gods with limited powers, not God, omnipotent and omniscient. There simply was no precedent, Jewish or pagan, for expecting an incarnation: God almighty truly taking a human nature. And that again is reason for supposing that the first Christians were not reading back into history something which they expected to occur.

The biblical writers who claimed fairly explicitly that Jesus was God Incarnate did not in general quote Scripture to prove that an incarnation was predicted. There was so little in Scripture that could be used with any plausibility for this purpose. The one author who attempted to marshal some quotations for this purpose was the author of the Epistle to the Hebrews. He interestingly uses the well-worn 'You are my Son; today I have begotten you'[55] to prove a sonship far higher and more explicit than the other writers I have cited. And he joins with it in addressing the 'Son' quotations from Psalms, in their original context clearly addressed to God himself.[56]

I conclude that there is evidence of Jesus acknowledging or letting others acknowledge his divinity (especially in accepting worship), his doing many actions in such a way as to carry some implication that his authority was God's authority, and implicit recognition of his divinity in various New Testament writers. There is also some evidence that the latter did not always recognize his divinity. I argued earlier that we would not expect Jesus to make an explicit claim to divinity (at any rate before his Resurrection), but that, if he was God Incarnate, we would expect him to leave a variety of clues

[55] Heb. 1: 5.
[56] Pss. 45: 6 and 102: 25–7, used in Heb. 1: 8 and 10–12.

to this on which his followers could meditate and which would lead them to recognize that divinity for themselves. What we find is the kind of thing we would expect to find, but, I am inclined to think, perhaps not as much of it or as powerful clues as we might expect to find.

7

Jesus Taught his Atonement

THE NEXT requirement for Jesus being God Incarnate is that he should state publicly that his life (culminating in his death) was a sacrifice for sin. Whether Jesus did this is, of course, controversial, and I must enter into the controversy. The notion of sacrifice to God in the Temple as the means of reconciliation and communion was central to the religion of first-century AD Judaism. It was central to the Torah; the Torah was the spiritual food of first-century Jews and the law by which many of them tried to live. There is no evidence that Jesus considered past observers of the sacrificial system to have been totally mistaken; and quite a bit of evidence to the contrary, e.g. his telling a leper to show himself 'to the priest, and offer the gift that Moses commanded'.[1] But then there is also evidence that he sought to reform, or more plausibly replace, the whole system of Temple sacrifice. He performed at Passover time (probably at the time of the Passover at which he was crucified; even though John seems to place it at an earlier Passover) the symbolic act recorded in all four Gospels of cleansing the Temple, expelling those who sold animals for sacrifice and overturning the tables of the money-changers. This is an event regarded by E. P. Sanders as 'certain',[2] but what did it mean? Mark (followed by Matthew and Luke) and John both seem to regard it as a demand for reform. Mark, for example, quotes Jesus as saying on this occasion, 'Is it not written "My house shall be called a house of prayer for all the nations", but you have made it a

---

[1] Matt. 8: 4. See also various references cited in Bruce Chilton, *The Temple of Jesus* (Pennsylvania State University Press, 1992), 110 n. 57, and the discussion on pp. 110–11. The early disciples centred their worship on the Temple (Acts 2: 46; 3: 1), though we have no reason to suppose that they offered sacrifice.

[2] *Jesus and Judaism* (SCM Press, 1985), 307.

den of robbers'. Sanders argues against this interpretation. He argues that there is no reason to suppose that the system of selling animals for sacrifice was being operated corruptly, and that animal sacrifice was so central to Temple worship that to abolish the former would be tantamount to abolishing the latter.[3]

The accusation against Jesus at his trial reported by Mark (and in abbreviated form by Matthew) was that he said, 'I will destroy this temple that is made with hands, and in three days I will build another, not made with hands.'[4] I argued in the last chapter for the genuineness of the saying by Jesus that the Temple would be destroyed (though perhaps not by himself). That leaves us with the second part of the saying which the accusers of Jesus, according to Matthew and Mark, attributed to him. Did the evangelists or early Christians put this accusation into the mouth of his accusers? St Mark and Christians after AD 70 (when the Temple was destroyed by the Romans) clearly understood the new Temple, since it was to be built 'in three days', to be the body of Jesus; and so Jesus to be in some sense a substitute for the Temple. But Mark wrote very close to the time of the destruction of the Temple, and he would not on the spur of the moment have put into the mouth of the accusers of Jesus such a deeply significant way of expressing the relation of the new religion to the old, unless he, or more widely the Christian community, had come through reflection to interpret the destruction of the Temple in this way—which would only happen after the Temple had been destroyed for a while. But since the sentence was known while the Temple was still standing, the early Christians who thought of it as genuine must have thought at an earlier stage that it said that the old Temple worship was to be replaced by the body of Jesus, whether or not that was Jesus' meaning. It is almost impossible to think that they would deliberately take over what might seem to be a false prophecy ('I will destroy this temple') by adding a further claim to it, unless it was indeed an original saying.[5] And all the different references to it considered in the last chapter support this.

---

[3] See e.g. E. P. Sanders, *The Historical Figure of Jesus* (Penguin Books, 1993), 252–62.

[4] Mark 14: 58.

[5] In the Gospel of Thomas 71, Jesus says 'I will destroy this house and no one will be able to rebuild it.' The form of this saying does suggest a date after AD 70, when the Temple lay in ruins, and is therefore less good evidence for the original saying than Mark's two versions. (Two versions, because the bystanders at the Cross (Mark 15: 29) repeat the saying without the words 'not made with hands'.)

But how much of the saying was original? 'I will build another' would by itself be a rather pointless claim: there would be no point in destroying the old Temple merely to replace it by a similar one. It must be a quite different kind of Temple. 'Not made with hands' suggests that.[6] This then makes the prophecy similar to prophecies of Jewish apocalyptic that God would bring down from Heaven a new and ready-made Temple.[7] But what of 'in three days'? Was this part of the original saying or inserted after the (believed) Resurrection? If the latter, it clearly involved the claim that Jesus' body was a substitute for the Temple. This latter claim is a sophisticated one, not naturally suggested by other parts of Jesus' teaching as recorded in the Gospels or the events of the Passion and Resurrection; but one which could have been added if the Church thought that Jesus had taught it separately, perhaps after his (believed) Resurrection. If, on the other hand, 'in three days' was part of the original saying, it need not have referred to the risen body of Jesus. Jesus might have been claiming that within three days of his trial God would bring down a heavenly Temple. But if so, it would have been a considerable coincidence that the period predicted turned out to be identical with the period before his (believed) Resurrection—unless he had information from God (or as God) that something was going to happen after three days. And in that case there is no reason to suppose that the information did not include information that what would happen would be his Resurrection (and, of course, St Mark's Gospel does claim that Jesus predicted his Resurrection on three separate occasions). So either way, whether one thinks that 'in three days' was or was not part of the original saying, it does rather look as if Jesus thought of his body as a substitute for the Temple. In that case he would hardly fail to think of his life and his (by this stage) largely foreseen death as a substitute for the sacrifice of the Temple; and so itself a greater and purer sacrifice. And that, of course, is what the

---

[6] Raymond Brown thinks that 'not made with hands' was not part of the original saying (*The Death of the Messiah* (Doubleday, 1994), 439). It appears only in the Marcan version, and not when the saying is repeated by the bystanders at the Cross (Mark 15: 29), and it is not easy for the experts to see how the contrast between 'made with hands' and 'not made with hands' could be made in Hebrew or Aramaic. The Epistle to the Hebrews, however, shows knowledge of this contrast when it says that 'Christ did not enter a sanctuary made by human hands' (9: 24), and it is not easy to see why it should have been inserted if it was not there in the first place. It is not so obviously appropriate to the use to which the saying was subsequently put—to refer to the body of the risen Jesus.

[7] See e.g. Sanders, *The Historical Figure of Jesus*, 261–2.

whole of the Epistle to the Hebrews teaches; and so we can explain this teaching without postulating excessive originality on the part of its author.

Then there is the Last Supper. St John's Gospel dates the Passion of Jesus on Friday Nisan 14, before the beginning of the Feast of the Passover at sundown. In that case, despite Mark's contrary affirmation (14: 12–16) taken up by Matthew and Luke, the Last Supper would not have been a Passover meal. In Chapter 4 I endorsed arguments in favour of John's chronology. For example, legal proceedings on Passover would be illegal; a Passover amnesty offered by Pilate would only make sense before Passover. And in the context of this chapter we should note that St Paul's affirmation 'Our paschal lamb, Christ, has been sacrificed'[8] fits his death occurring at the same time (afternoon before Passover) as the Passover lambs were being slaughtered in the Temple.[9] Passover would have formed the obvious occasion for Jesus to institute a solemn ceremony; and no doubt for that reason Mark dated the Last Supper as a Passover meal. But if Jesus held the solemn meal earlier, the obvious explanation of that was that he did not expect to be alive at Passover, and hence his words at the Last Supper must be understood as uttered in that context.

All the accounts of the Last Supper in the New Testament (Matthew, Mark, Luke, and Paul in 1 Corinthians[10]) although differing in detail, include Jesus uttering the words 'This is my body' over the bread, and either 'This is my blood of the covenant' (Matthew and Mark) or 'This cup is the new covenant in my blood' (Luke and Paul) over the cup (presumably, of wine). Joachim Jeremias in his classic study *The Eucharistic Words of Jesus*[11] claims that, among the forms cited in the New Testament, the Marcan form of these 'words of Institution' is the earliest of the forms recorded in the New Testament:

---

[8] 1 Cor. 5: 7.

[9] For other reasons in favour of John's chronology, see G. Thiessen and A. Merz, *The Historical Jesus: A Comprehensive Guide* (SCM Press, 1998), 426–7.

[10] Paul describes his account of the Last Supper as something which he 'received from the Lord' (1 Cor. 11: 23). It is not plausible to suppose that this means that he is describing the contents of a private vision. There would not have been the general agreement of his account with that in the three synoptic gospels without it having roots stronger and earlier than a Pauline vision. What he must mean by this phrase is that what he received was teaching, handed on through others, but deriving from Jesus' own teaching.

[11] Rev. edn. (SCM Press, 1966).

While they were eating, [Jesus] took a loaf of bread, and after blessing it he broke it, gave it to them, and said, 'Take; this is my body'. Then he took a cup, and after giving thanks he gave it to them, and all of them drank from it. He said unto them, 'This is my blood of the covenant, which is poured out for many'.[12]

Jeremias speculates that there may have been a pre-Marcan form without the words 'of the covenant which is poured out for many'. Nevertheless, he concludes that by the use of the words 'body' and 'blood', 'Jesus speaks of himself as a sacrifice'.[13] He predicts his own death, the vicarious death of the servant. If we accept Jeremias' understanding of the words of institution, there is no doubt that Jesus made a very solemn and public statement that his life was being offered as a sacrifice. It follows that subsequent Eucharists in which these words were uttered were in some sense memorials of that sacrificial life and death. And Paul described the celebration of the Eucharist as proclaiming 'The Lord's death until he comes'. It would be very difficult in view of the firm and detailed affirmation of the first three Gospels to deny that at the Last Supper Jesus himself used words of institution including 'my body' and 'my blood', with the inevitable connotations that his life was a sacrifice, but for the fact that St John's Gospel has no account of the supper, and the Didache, a Christian writing of perhaps the early second century, seems to contain quite different words to be said by the celebrant of a Eucharist over the bread and wine. So I need to show that the latter two phenomena are perfectibly compatible with the view that Jesus instituted the Eucharist as a re-presentation of his sacrificial life and death.

I think that a major part of the explanation of both these phenomena is the *disciplina arcani*, that is, the aim of keeping secret the formulae of ceremonies to guard the words of sacred rites from falling into wrong hands and to be subject to pagan mocking or misunderstanding as an act of cannibalism. Jeremias gives a long list of such practices of keeping words and ceremonies secret among the rabbis and the Essenes, and of New Testament circumlocution.[14] It is noteworthy that Hebrews 6: 1, listing 'the basic teaching about Christ' which the author wishes to pass beyond, includes baptism but not the Eucharist. The possibility of misunderstanding is

---

[12] Mark 14: 22–4.   [13] Ibid. 144.
[14] Jeremias, *The Eucharistic Words of Jesus*, 125–32.

brought out by the fact that the Christians who abjured their faith before Pliny, and explained to him what their custom had been, emphasized that the food which they took together was 'ordinary and harmless food'.[15] Often people do not take precautions against some danger until they have suffered the consequences of not doing so. Hence in the early period represented by the first three Gospels and St Paul's letters, written before the main Roman persecutions, Christians felt less need to keep secret details which might be so badly misunderstood as to increase the risk of persecution. St John's Gospel puts in the place in the Passion narrative occupied by the Last Supper in the other Gospels the washing of the disciples' feet.[16] However, St John, especially in chapter 6, shows very clear knowledge of the custom of celebrating the Eucharist with the traditional words; thus, 'Those who eat my flesh and drink my blood have eternal life and I will raise them up on the last day'.[17] A further reason, besides the *disciplina arcani*, why John might have substituted the washing of the feet for the Last Supper is that John knew that every reader knew the story of the Last Supper (since they were reminded of it at each weekly Eucharist), and so thought it better to put instead a parable which would show the meaning of that story, e.g. that Jesus giving his body and blood was a service like washing the disciples' feet by a master for his servant. I pointed out earlier (in Chapter 4) that it looks as if John on other occasions tells a fictional story to show the true meaning of what is happening.

The Didache seems to contain quite different words to be said at regular Eucharists over the bread and wine, which make no mention of 'body and blood'.[18] There has been much dispute about whether

---

[15] Pliny, *Ep. ad Traianum* 10. 96. 7.   [16] John 13: 2.   [17] John 6: 54.

[18] The text of Didache 9–10 is as follows: 'At the Eucharist, offer the eucharistic prayer in this way. Begin with the chalice: "We give thanks to thee, our Father, for the holy Vine of thy servant David, which thou hast made known to us through thy servant Jesus." "*Glory be to thee, world without end.*" Then over the particles of bread: "We give thanks to thee, our Father, for the life and knowledge thou hast made known to us through thy servant Jesus." "*Glory be to thee, world without end.*" "As this broken bread, once dispersed over the hills, was brought together and became one loaf, so may thy Church be brought together from the ends of the earth into thy kingdom." "*Thine is the glory and the power, through Jesus Christ, for ever and ever.*" No one is to eat or drink of your Eucharist but those who have been baptized in the Name of the Lord; for the Lord's own saying applies here, "Give not that which is holy unto dogs." When all have partaken sufficiently, give thanks in these words: "Thanks be to thee, holy Father, for thy sacred Name which thou hast caused to dwell in our hearts, and for the knowledge and faith and everlasting life which thou hast revealed to us through they servant Jesus." "*Glory be to thee for ever and ever.*" "Thou, O Almighty Lord, hast created all things for thine own Name's sake; to

the prayers recorded there were really prayers for a grace at the agape meal (that is, an ordinary fellowship meal before the Eucharist), or alternatively, Eucharistic prayers. But even if, in the Didache's churches, the words of consecration (of the elements) were not Christ's words about body and blood, the Didache still explicitly refers to the Eucharist as your 'sacrifice'.[19] The words of consecration can most plausibly be understood in that way if the 'Vine' and the 'life and knowledge' mentioned in it are thought of as the life of Jesus which is offered. But is is also noteworthy that this passage has a great deal of Johannine ideas and terminology: the notion of the vine, bread being connected to life and immortality, the gathering together of the scattered children of God,[20] etc.[21] The Johannine spirit may well have led to a suppression of the traditional words of institution. I conclude that the Johannine omission of the Last Supper and the Didache's alternative words for subsequent Eucharists do not count against the view that in the Last Supper Jesus showed that his life was being offered as a sacrifice.

For what was the sacrifice made? The Old Testament allows sacrifice either to seal a covenant or to atone for sin. As we have seen, all the New Testament accounts of the Last Supper connect it with 'covenant', Luke and 1 Corinthians with 'the new covenant in my blood', and it is hard to suppose that Matthew and Mark, who do not mention the newness of the covenant, can have supposed the covenant to be other than a new one. Whether or not Jesus used the words 'covenant' at that stage in the proceedings, he must have given them some understanding of what the sacrifice symbolized by the Last Supper meant, and this understanding of it as sealing a covenant is common to all the accounts. The 'new covenant' can be none other than that prophesied by Jeremiah:

all men thou hast given meat and drink to enjoy, that they may give thanks to thee, but to us thou hast graciously given spiritual meat and drink, together with life eternal, through thy Servant. Especially, and above all, do we give thanks to thee for the mightiness of thy power." "*Glory be to thee for ever and ever.*" "Be mindful of thy Church, O Lord; deliver it from all evil, perfect it in thy love, sanctify it, and gather it from the four winds into the kingdom which thou hast prepared for it." "*Thine is the power and the glory for ever and ever.*" "Let his Grace draw near, and let this present world pass away." "*Hosanna to the God of David.*" "Whosoever is holy, let him approach. Whoso is not, let him repent." "*O Lord, come quickly. Amen.*" (Charismatists, however, should be free to give thanks as they please)' (transl. M. Staniforth, *Early Christian Writings* (Penguin Books, 1968)).

[19] Did. 14. [20] John 11: 52.

[21] See Johannes Betz, 'The Eucharist in the Didache', in Jonathan A. Draper (ed.), *The Didache in Modern Research* (E. J. Brill, 1996), 255.

The days are surely coming, says the Lord, when I will make a new covenant with the house of Israel and the house of Judah. It will not be like the covenant that I made with their ancestors when I took them by the hand to bring them out of the land of Egypt—a covenant that they brake, though I was their husband, says the Lord. But this is the covenant that I will make with the house of Israel after those days, says the Lord: I will put my law within them and I will write it on their hearts; and I will be their God, and they shall be my people. No longer shall they teach one another, or say to each other, 'Know the Lord', for they shall all know me, from the least of them unto the greatest, says the Lord: for I will forgive their iniquity, and remember their sin no more.[22]

Note that this new covenant is connected by Jeremiah with forgiveness of sins.[23] Matthew adds to the descriptions in Mark and Luke of the blood as 'poured out' 'for many' or 'for you', 'for the forgiveness of sins'. And the Epistle to the Hebrews combines in one verse the ideas of Christ as 'the mediator of a new covenant' and 'a death has occurred that redeems them from the transgressions under the first covenant'.[24]

Whether or not the connection of the sacrifice of Christ with atonement for sin was made clear by Jesus in the words of institution of the Last Supper, it was certainly pervasive and early in the Christian understanding of the (life and) death of Jesus. That 'Christ died for our sins' was part of the pre-Pauline creed which Paul reports that he has received.[25] Other pre-Pauline formulae containing the same idea are Romans 5: 8, 14: 15; 1 Corinthians 8: 11; 1 Thessalonians 5: 10; Romans 8: 32 speaks of God, who 'gave up [his own Son] for all of us'; Galatians 1: 4 speaks of Christ, 'who gave himself for our sins'; and Galatians 2: 20 of the Son of God, who 'gave himself up for me'. 1 Corinthians 5: 7 claims that 'our paschal lamb, Christ, has been sacrificed'. Most significantly, Paul reminds his readers in Romans,[26] as something which they could certainly be expected to know ('Do you not know that . . . ?')[27] that 'all of us who have been baptized into Christ Jesus were baptized into his death'. John's baptism was 'for the forgiveness of sins', but it soon became important that it was insufficient for Christians. Those baptized only

---

[22] Jer. 31: 31–4.

[23] When Hezekiah resolved to make a covenant with God, according to 2 Chr. 29: 10, he first cleansed the Temple and made a sin offering (29: 24), before other 'sacrifices and thank offerings' could be made (29: 31).

[24] Heb. 9: 15.

[25] 1 Cor. 15: 2.

[26] Rom. 6: 3–4.

[27] Rom. 6: 3.

with John's baptism had to be rebaptized, according to Acts 19: 3–5. A plausible explanation of why that was necessary is that only through such a baptism could the benefits of Christ's death be received; and Paul makes the connection in Romans two verses after 6: 3–4 of the death of Christ with the doing away of sin. So, through baptism, Christians receive the benefit of the doing away of sin achieved through the death of Christ. And such a way of doing away with sin is inevitably a substitute for the old way of Temple sacrifice.

If we turn to the Johannine literature, 1 John 1: 7 writes that 'the blood of Jesus . . . cleanses us from all sin', and John's Gospel is just full of the notion of the blood of Christ availing for us. In St Matthew's infancy narrative the angel tells Joseph in his dream that Jesus 'will save his people from their sins'.[28] And finally, there is the saying of Jesus, reported by Mark,[29] that 'the Son of Man came . . . to give his life a ransom for many'. As an isolated saying, its genuineness might be questioned. But the pervasiveness throughout the New Testament of the idea of the atoning power of Christ, together with the evidence of the Temple saying and the Last Supper, suggest a common origin for the idea of the atoning power of Christ in the teaching of Jesus. The Marcan saying is not far away in spirit from the notion of the death of Christ as a sacrifice—unless, that is, we start asking those awkward questions which later generations asked, such to 'To whom was the ransom paid?' and 'Why did it need to be paid?' There is no sign of these questions being around in the Gospels, and so the notion of 'ransom' needs be understood as no more than 'offering freely given'. I conclude that the evidence of the Last Supper and the pervasiveness of atonement teaching in the various different strands of the New Testament is the kind of evidence to be expected if Jesus taught that his life and death constituted an atonement for human sin.

Once again here is something which the Jews did not expect of their Messiah or Messiah-like figure; and so the Gospels and Epistles are not open to the charge of reading back into the life of Jesus an understanding of his role derived from contemporary Jewish understanding of what the messianic role should be. The contemporary Jewish literature certainly often expected a priest–Messiah as well as a King–Messiah.[30] But the role of the priest was to offer a sacrifice of

---

[28] Matt. 1: 21.　　　　　　　　　　　　　　　　　[29] Mark 10: 45.

[30] See e.g. J. H. Charlesworth, 'From Messianology to Christology', in J. Neusner, W. S. Green and E. S. Frerichs (eds.), *Judaisms and their Messiahs at the Turn of the Christian Era* (Cambridge University Press, 1987), 230–1, on the two Messiahs in the Qumran literature.

other things in a purified cult, not of himself. Certainly for a Messiah-like atoner (unlike for a Messiah-like God Incarnate) there were Old Testament passages which talk of a person or people who suffers on behalf of others, and notably the servant songs of Isaiah. Here there is the idea of suffering and death as a role of the divine agent on whom 'the Lord has laid . . . the iniquity of us all'.[31] But it is generally agreed that, as depicted in Isaiah, the 'servant' is Israel itself, not some one person. Only when Jesus had been crucified were these texts seen as prophetic of the role of an individual,[32] as I mentioned in Chapter 4. It needed the stranger on the Emmaus road after the Resurrection to explain to the puzzled disciples, 'Was it not necessary that the Messiah should suffer these things and then enter into his glory?'[33]

[31] Isa. 53: 6.

[32] In the sermons of Peter, recorded in Acts and purportedly delivered within months of the Resurrection, Jesus is referred to more than once as God's 'servant' (παῖς). This expression is never used of him in the Gospels. The one reference in the Gospels to the prophecies of Isaiah is Matt. 8: 17, a comment of the Gospel writer on what was happening then, not a comment attributed to any participant in the events of the life of Jesus.

[33] Luke 24: 26.

8

Jesus Founded a Church

To Continue after his Death

MY FINAL prior requirement for Jesus being God Incarnate is that he should found a church which would provide God's forgiveness to repentant sinners and which would hand on his teaching, including his teaching about his own atoning work and what he implied about his divinity. He might for this purpose, if the leaders of the old Israel had agreed to this, have reconstituted the old Israel and given it a new gospel and a new role. But since the leaders did not recognize Jesus' authority, he had to found a new body, perhaps hoping that it would become Israel, absorbing the old system. But, however he viewed its ultimate relation to the old Israel, it is necessary that he should have founded a church; and my claim is that he did. That 'Jesus called disciples and spoke of there being twelve' is one of E. P. Sanders's almost indisputable facts.[1] To form a community based on twelve leaders (parallel to the twelve founders of the twelve tribes of the old Israel) could hardly be understood in first-century Palestine other than as a foundation of a new Israel. Sanders writes that the use by Jesus 'of the conception "twelve" points towards his understanding of his own mission. He was engaged in a task which would include the restoration of Israel.'[2] Although the Gospels are not always in agreement as to who those twelve were, and which of them participated in which subsequent events, that there were twelve founders is often mentioned in the New Testament.

But his commissioning of the Twelve would have been compatible with Jesus holding that their ministry would be confined to his life-time, during which God's rule on Earth would be established. And it

---

[1] *Jesus and Judaism* (SCM Press, 1985), 11.   [2] Ibid. 106.

would have been compatible also with the Church founded on the Twelve being concerned with Israel alone and not having a world-wide mission. It needs to be shown that the Church of the twelve apostles was intended for all generations and cultures. Let us begin by considering whether Jesus intended to found a church which would continue in time after his death.

I argue for Jesus (publicly) intending his Church to continue after his death from his institution of the Eucharist at the Last Supper in which the Twelve were formally involved. Mark and Matthew report that the Twelve participated in the Last Supper, and in Jesus' address to his 'apostles' at the Last Supper in Luke he appoints them 'to eat and drink at my table in my kingdom, and you will sit on thrones judging the twelve tribes of Israel'.[3]

Within a few years of the Passion, churches had been set up in various places in the Middle East; we do not know of any Christian community which lacked the practice of celebrating a Eucharist. St Paul reports as among the things he 'received from the Lord' (i.e. as part of the primitive tradition of the early Church) that the ceremony of the Last Supper was to be repeated by the Church.[4] And the synoptic writers must surely have had the same understanding; for if they had not, they would have felt the need to distance themselves in their account of the Last Supper from the current practice of repeating the ceremony. I argue from these facts of the universal practice and the Pauline and synoptic accounts of the supper to the intention of Jesus that the ceremony of the Last Supper was to be celebrated regularly.

It was, I argued in the last chapter, intended by Jesus to be cele-brated as a sacrificial meal of memorial of Christ's sacrifice. This ceremony is the commemoration of a sacrifice in which the partici-pants eat the 'body' and drink the 'blood' of the victim. Sacrifice in the ancient world is traditionally associated with a meal. For the Israelites of old offering sacrifice often involved participating in a meal in which you consumed some parts of the sacrifice. And that conception had not died away by the time of Christ. St Paul comments: 'Consider the people of Israel; are not those who eat the sacrifices partners in the altar?'[5] But to offer sacrifice, you must come in the right spirit. Before you offer your gift at the altar, you must be reconciled to your brother.[6] So, St Paul tells the Corinthians, they

---

[3] Matt. 26: 20; Mark 14: 17; Luke 22: 30.   [4] 1 Cor. 11: 23–6.
[5] 1 Cor. 10: 18.   [6] Matt. 5: 23–4.

have to examine themselves lest they eat and drink the body and blood of Christ unworthily.[7] In eating and drinking the commemorative elements, the participants are clearly identifying themselves with the sacrifice; it becomes theirs as well as that of Jesus. I noted in the last chapter the connection made between the sacrifice of Jesus and the sealing of the 'new covenant', made by accounts of the Last Supper. The covenant was clearly a covenant with an Israel, but it was certainly not a covenant with an old Israel whose official representatives were hostile to what Jesus represented, and so it must be a covenant with a new Israel, and those present at the Last Supper represent that.

I argued in the last chapter that the Last Supper was not a Passover meal, and that a very obvious reason why Jesus held a meal of enormous new-Israel significance which was not a Passover meal was that he did not expect to be around at Passover. That he expected arrest and possible crucifixion is shown further by the considerable secrecy with which the arrangements for the Last Supper were made. Two of the disciples were sent to meet a man to be identified by his carrying 'a jar of water'; the other disciples were kept away from the preparation.[8] Hence, I argue that the ceremony which Jesus instituted was one which he expected to be celebrated after his death, should he die; and so that he intended the community of 'the Twelve' who participated in it, and to whom any instruction to continue the ceremony would have been given—his Church on Earth—to continue after his death, should he die.

The other ceremony which continued was, of course, baptism. John baptized 'for the remission of sins', and the symbolism of washing so evidently represents that. I argued in Chapter 6 that those who received John's baptism identified themselves with a national renewal movement rather than receiving forgiveness on an individual basis. Jesus almost certainly baptized or encouraged his disciples to do so on his behalf.[9] There is no direct evidence from his life that Jesus intended baptism, whatever its other significance, to become the admission ceremony for a body which would continue after his death, the Church. But it clearly did become that within three or four years of the (supposed) Resurrection. Even if the baptism of

---

[7] 1 Cor. 11: 27–8.

[8] Mark 14: 12–17. Mark of course, I have argued, erroneously identifies this meal with the Passover.

[9] John 3: 22, 26; 4: 1–2.

those who 'welcomed his message' delivered by Peter in his Pentecost sermon[10] was 'read back' by Luke into history as an event which must have happened, the main other references, especially in Acts, to early baptisms (including that of Paul himself[11]) clearly indicate that it acquired this role very quickly. That may be some indirect indication that Jesus so intended it during his lifetime; but it is in the institution of the Eucharist that his intentions to constitute the Twelve as a body to continue after his death are most evident.

The other event, apart from the Last Supper, with which the 'Twelve' (or, as almost all the writers put it more carefully, the 'Eleven') are associated was the Resurrection. They are the 'witnesses' to the event: Matthew (28: 16), the longer ending of Mark (16: 14), Luke (24: 33), John (20: 24), Paul (1 Cor. 15: 5) all associate the event with the Twelve and their witness. The Church, these writers taught (and their unanimity leads me to suppose that they thought that Jesus taught'), was a community not merely to commemorate his death but to witness to his Resurrection. That provides reason to suppose that, if the Resurrection occurred, these writers taught this because Jesus taught this. Having noted the involvement of the Twelve as witnesses to the Resurrection, I leave it aside now and return to it in Part III.

To found an earthly church involves *not* assuming an immediate end of the world; and since Jesus must have thought his teaching was important, he must have intended this Church to continue his teaching. There is evidence of his commissioning disciples to represent him; e.g. 'He that heareth you heareth me',[12] and the authority given to Peter to 'bind and loose'.[13] He may originally only have intended this authority to last for short-term missions during his lifetime. But, given his later view that the Church was to continue after his death, he must be seen as viewing it as having his authority (including authority to teach) then.

For Whom?

Was the Church founded by Jesus intended only for Israel? It is clear

---

[10] Acts 2: 41.   [11] Acts 9: 18.   [12] Luke 10: 16.
[13] Matt. 16: 19. See the references in Christopher Rowland, *Christian Origins* (SPCK, 1985), 153, to evidence of the Semitic origin of this saying.

that Jesus himself deliberately confined his own mission to Israel; he sought to convert Israel. 'I was sent only to the lost sheep of the house of Israel.'[14] The Gospels do contain a few stories of Jesus helping Gentiles,[15] but these are clearly exceptional. However, the more progressive thought of pre-Christian Israel for the previous 400 years looked forward to the conversion of Gentiles to Israel, and various books of the late Old Testament look forward to and encourage that. The book of Jonah where Jonah (a Jew) was sent to preach to Nineveh (a Gentile city) is but one example. And Jesus certainly allied himself on other issues with the more progressive thought (e.g. in affirming life after death). The Gospels contain sayings of Jesus which look forward to wide conversion: 'There will be weeping and gnashing of teeth when you see Abraham and Isaac and Jacob and all the prophets in the kingdom of God and you yourself thrown out. Then people will come from east and west, from the north and south, and will eat in the kingdom of God'.[16] The latter group of people, being contrasted with 'you yourselves', are more naturally to be thought of as Gentiles rather than Jews of the Diaspora.

So why did not Jesus himself initiate this work? To that there is an obvious answer. This was the task of Israel, as the later Old Testament writings which Jesus would have absorbed made clear. But in this, as in other respects, the old Israel had failed. Jesus tried to convert it to fulfil its role, which would include converting the Gentiles; but it rejected him. Only the new Israel centred on the Twelve consecrated at the Last Supper accepted him; and so he would think that they should undertake this task. The very expression 'I was sent only . . .' carries the implication of a particular task which Jesus was given, and suggests that others might be sent to convert the Gentiles. This is borne out forcibly by the even more exclusive command which Jesus issued to the disciples sent out on a short mission during Jesus' ministry: 'Go nowhere among the Gentiles, and enter no town of the Samaritans, but go rather to the lost sheep of the House of Israel.'[17] The Samaritans were the remains of the lost ten tribes of Israel, and it was a wide Jewish hope and

---

[14] Matt. 15: 24.   [15] e.g. Matt. 15: 21–8.

[16] Luke 13: 28–9. And see the similar saying in Mark 13: 27: 'Then [the Son of Man] . . . will gather his elect from the four winds, from the ends of the earth to the ends of heaven.'

[17] Matt. 10: 5–6.

belief that the lost tribes (or at least the faithful among them) would be restored to Israel. Jesus shared that belief, as can be seen by his saying to the disciples: 'you who have followed me will also sit on twelve thrones, judging the twelve tribes of Israel'.[18] (Since the Twelve included Judas, this saying is not very likely to have arisen after Jesus' death.) So Jesus believed that a group (the Samaritans) could be included in the new Israel, and yet commanded the disciples not to preach to that group. Hence his failure to preach to Gentiles in no way indicates that he did not believe that this was a task to be done in future. Jesus must during his lifetime have expressed to the Twelve some view about the situation of Gentiles with respect of the kingdom. And if it had been in any way hostile to their incorporation, the early Church would certainly not have sought to convert them as readily as it did.

Though Samaritans[19] and proselytes[20] seem to have been readily incorporated into the Church without controversy, it took the early Church two or three years and some heart-searching before it began a Gentile mission. The heart-searching, however, as recorded in Acts 8: 15, turned on whether Gentiles who converted should be circumcised—not on whether circumcised Gentiles should be admitted to the Church (about which there would presumably be no problem, since Gentiles who converted by circumcision were recognized as Jews)—and on whether there should be an active mission to the Gentiles. Why the delay before this mission, if Jesus had expressed an opinion favourable to it? The very early Church would have hoped that the (believed) Resurrection of Jesus would lead to the conversion of the old Israel for which Jesus worked, for here was something new which might finally persuade it; and then the old Israel (absorbed by the new Israel) could fulfil its vocation. There would than be no need for the separation of the new Israel from the old, which a Gentile mission with baptism without circumcision would involve. Acts 1–8 records the attempts of that very early Church to convert the old Israel, ending with the failure symbolized by the stoning of Stephen accused of saying that Jesus would 'change the customs that Moses handed on to us'.[21] I conclude that Jesus founded a church for all peoples.

---

[18] Matt. 19: 28.   [19] Acts 8: 14.   [20] Acts 6: 5.   [21] Acts 6: 14.

For How Long?

The Church which derives from the twelve apostles has lasted 2,000 years and articulated doctrines which at best were present only in embryo in the teaching of Jesus. But did Jesus intend to found a church for all times? I think that there can be no doubt that he intended his Church to last until his second coming (or Parousia, as it is often called), when he would establish his rule finally on Earth. But he may well have expected that that would be a fairly short interval, and certainly the early Church thought that the Parousia would occur very soon indeed. But, though he may have so believed, did he explicitly teach this? If so, this would cast doubt on whether any church deriving from the Twelve was the Church which he founded, for its commission from Jesus would have expired. I suggest (on balance) that there is no evidence that makes it probable that he did so teach.

Jesus' preaching was concerned with the Kingdom of God. This was an already existing reality in Heaven, and the good would go there when they die. Jesus taught that this kingdom would be realized on Earth also. Indeed, Jesus taught that the kingdom was already present in his work (see Chapter 5) and in those who allied themselves with that work. That Jesus taught all this would be agreed by most scholars.[22] He also certainly claimed that there would be a cosmic event which would finally usher in that kingdom upon Earth in an unmistakably obvious way. The prevalence of sayings to this effect in the synoptic Gospels and generally in the New Testament would be extremely hard to explain except on the supposition that they originated from the teaching of Jesus.[23] But Jesus may also have predicted other important things which may have got confused with

[22] For one presentation of all these points, see E. P. Sanders, *The Historical Figure of Jesus* (Penguin Books, 1993), 169–76.

[23] One interesting piece of evidence of this, among much other evidence, is the detailed verbal parallels to which Sanders has drawn attention (ibid. 181) in the accounts of the Parousia between what St Paul wrote in his earliest letter (1 Thess.; about AD 50) and two passages in St Matthew's Gospel. Even by the time of 1 Thess. the fact that Jesus taught this would have been slightly awkward—for the event had not yet happened; even more so by the time of the writing of St Matthew's Gospel. And so the detailed verbal similarities can only be explained by this really being the teaching of Jesus, which as such was all-authoritative. The sentence 'Truly I tell you, there are some standing here who will not taste death before they see the Son of Man coming in his Kingdom' (Matt. 16: 28) has, however, no parallel in 1 Thess. and is taken from Mark 9: 1; I discuss this sentence below.

his predictions of the Parousia. Mark, for example, claims that Jesus three times predicted his Resurrection. And it may be that, especially in his early ministry, Jesus often predicted that God would be publicly victorious, without saying or even having a clear belief as to how he would be victorious. His central early teaching was that the kingdom has 'drawn near',[24] but its manifestation might as easily turn out to involve the Resurrection as the Parousia. There is, too, Mark 9: 1: 'Truly I tell you, there are some standing here who will not taste death until they see that the Kingdom of God has come with power.' But again, the power could as easily be the power of the risen Christ in the Church as the Parousia. (Mark 9: 1 is followed immediately by Mark's account of the Transfiguration, plausibly a prefiguring of the Resurrection.) Others who thought naturally in apocalyptic terms may have filled this out in terms of a Parousia, whereas Jesus may have later come to understand the Resurrection as this victory. But it is clear that Christians after the (believed) Resurrection who thought that the Resurrection constituted something all-important did not understand that as sufficient to fulfil all Jesus' predictions about God's future intervention in history. Jesus certainly led them to expect a Parousia of a sort which would not be constituted by the Resurrection, but it may be that he would have regarded some of his predictions of God's victory as fulfilled by his Resurrection—and these may include those predicting an immediate victory.

So did Jesus teach that the Parousia would occur very soon? One thing which is evident is that he never predicted an exact date. He is recorded by Mark as saying, 'about that day or hour no one knows, neither the angels in Heaven, nor the Son, but only the Father'.[25] A saying in which Jesus reported his own ignorance (presumably referring to himself as 'the Son' but in any case certainly not as the one individual who did know the date, 'the Father') would never have been incorporated into the Gospel unless it had been genuine. This saying would have been an embarrassment to Christians and is not taken up in Matthew or Luke. Acts, however, has a post-Resurrection saying similar to Mark's saying in that in it Jesus refuses to name the time or even the 'period' in which Parousia-type events will occur, and says that these matters lie within the Father's authority. In answer to the apostles' question 'Lord, is this the time when you will

---

[24] ἤγγικεν (Mark 1: 15).   [25] Mark 13: 32.

restore the kingdom to Israel?', Jesus replied, 'It is not for you to know times or periods which the Father has set by his own authority.'[26]

However, a refusal to name an exact date is compatible with Jesus' having given a rough indication of when the Parousia would take place. And there are two sayings which can be interpreted as saying that it will take place in the lifetime of those alive with Jesus. The first is Mark 9: 1, cited above; but, as we have seen, it is not clear that the Parousia is being referred to. The other is Mark 13: 30: 'Truly I tell you, this generation will not pass away until all these things have taken place.' If the saying were in its original context, 'all these things' would refer to the whole succession of events eventually culminating in the Parousia described in Mark 13. It is generally supposed that this was originally an isolated saying; but, while agreeing with that, Werner Kummel claims that the literal and most likely reference of 'all these things' is to the totality of eschatological events,[27] which would include the Parousia. That does not seem to me obvious. Mark 13: 1–23 describes a long succession of events before the Parousia. 13: 24–7 describing the Parousia seems to be a separate passage inserted after 1–23. Its introductory phrase seems to suggest an interpolation, and this impression is reinforced by the fact that the 'they' of 'they will see' in verse 26 has no very obvious earlier reference in the preceding passage. (The 'elect' of verse 20 is a long way back.) So it looks as if there were separate sections in circulation, including Mark 13: 1–23, describing pre-Parousia events which did not include the Parousia, and so 13: 30 might refer to them. This would also be the case if 13: 30 was not originally an isolated saying, but belonged to a section into which 24–7 was interpolated. And then 'all these things' would have the same reference as 'all these things' (13: 4), which refers to the destruction of the Temple. And if it did not originally belong to that context at all, it could be an earlier saying of Jesus referring in a vague way to his victory, without giving any detailed indication of what that might consist in.

Indeed, the long series of pre-Parousia events described in Mark 13: 1–23 seems to me to count against the supposition that Jesus

---

[26] Acts 1: 6–7.
[27] Werner G. Kummel, 'Eschatological Expectation in the Proclamation of Jesus', in B. Chilton (ed.), *The Kingdom of God in the Teaching of Jesus* (SPCK, 1984), 40.

explicitly taught that the Parousia would occur within the lifetime of those alive with him. For it is implausible to suppose that the whole of 13: 1–23 (a fairly integrated passage) was invented by Mark or anyone else and put into the mouth of Jesus, in view of the general fidelity of Mark in recording incidents (e.g. the baptism of Jesus; see Chapter 5) or teaching of Jesus (see above) which would be unwelcome to Christians. The section includes 13: 10: 'the good news must first be proclaimed to all nations'—a human endeavour (not a miraculous divine intervention) which was clearly going to take a long time. This verse may be an interpolation, but it was known to Matthew since he transferred it to Matthew 24: 14, using it with the same meaning. (Luke omits it.) If that verse is original to Jesus, it reinforces the view that he did not himself predict that the Parousia would occur within his lifetime. And Matthew 28: 19 does also have Jesus' (believed) command to make disciples of all nations, and even if the nations were to accept the Gospel, time would be needed to achieve that goal.

Matthew 10: 23 suggests that the Son of Man will come before the disciples have fled to or perhaps finished evangelizing every city in Israel, but there is no need to think of that as concerned especially with disciples then living (especially if, as Kummel argues, 'You will not have gone through the towns of Israel' is to be understood as 'You will not have accomplished your mission to Israel'[28]). And once again the 'coming of the Son of Man' might be a vague claim about Jesus' victorious return to Earth, which Jesus himself might have come to see as fulfilled in the Resurrection. Anyone who doubts that Jesus might have understood some such claims as fulfilled by the Resurrection should bear in mind that there is no evidence whatever of any claims about an immediate Parousia being made at the Last Supper, when Jesus formally commissioned his Church for its future work, or thereafter, including after his (believed) Resurrection. Here at the Church's commissioning and after Jesus' (believed) Resurrection, where it was important that clear instruction be given, there is no talk of immediate return, but rather of a worldwide task to be performed.[29]

But if Jesus did not teach that the Parousia would occur within

---

[28] Kummel, 'Eschatological Expectation in the Proclamation of Jesus', 43.

[29] Matt. 28: 19; Luke 24: 47; Acts 1: 6–7. And note too that the prediction of woes to the 'daughters of Jerusalem' on the way to the Crucifixion (Luke 23: 27–31) had no mention of a Parousia-like ending.

his lifetime, why did early Christians expect that it would (as can be seen from many things in the New Testament, including the placing by Mark of 13: 30 after the description of the Parousia)?[30] It is clear from many passages that Jesus warned his followers to be on their guard since the Day might come any time.[31] The servants must be ever on watch, for they do not know when the master of the house may return.[32] People who take such advice seriously are inclined to believe that the event for which they must watch will happen 'soon'; it is difficult to stay up watching if you do not think the event for which you are watching is going to happen at all soon. 'It may happen any time' tends to become 'it must happen soon'. But if the parable of the barren fig tree threatened with destruction by the owner of the vineyard but given another year's grace in which to yield figs at the pleading of the vinedresser is original to Jesus, Jesus implies that an impatient God may nevertheless delay.[33]

So, I conclude that the evidence we have is not too unexpected if, at any rate by the time he commissioned his Church at the Last Supper, Jesus conceived of it as a church for all peoples and times without any commitment to the length of the times.

The Teaching and Practice of the Later Church

It would have been pointless for God to set his sign of approval on Jesus' teaching and atoning life, and on his act of founding a church, with the aim of providing us with knowledge of that teaching and a means for us to associate ourselves with that life, unless he took some steps to ensure that the Church's teaching coincided on the whole with that of Jesus. For otherwise he would have failed through Jesus to provide teaching and ways of associating with that life for other cultures and generations. If God was incarnate in Christ, he must be deemed to intend to achieve this. So he must be construed as giving his signature of approval to the central elements of the Church's subsequent teaching and practice (in the sense of means of making available the benefits of that life and death to subsequent

---

[30] When writing his earliest extant letter, 1 Thess. (*c.*AD 49), St Paul seems to have expected that he himself would be alive when the Parousia arrived. In describing it, he refers to '*we* who are alive, who are left until the coming of the Lord' (4: 15; my emphasis; see also 4: 17).

[31] See e.g. Mark 13: 33–7.   [32] Matt. 24: 42–4.   [33] Luke 13: 6–9.

generations). If it were to turn out that the Church which developed from the Church of the Twelve did not teach the central elements of Jesus' teaching or provide suitable means to make available his benefits, then that would be strong reason to suppose that God had not made provision through Jesus for the benefits of his life and teaching to be available to future generations, and that in turn would cast doubt on Jesus being God Incarnate risen from the dead. I have written only that God must ensure the correctness of the 'central elements' of the Church's teaching and practice, for the reason given in Chapter 2, that one might expect God to leave us to work out some things for ourselves. I have argued that we need a lot more material for this purpose than natural reason alone can provide; hence the need for revealed teaching. The need to work things out for ourselves could, however, still be adequately provided by our having to sort out the lesser discrepancies in Church teaching.[34]

Although different communities derived from the Church of the Twelve have had in detail somewhat different developed versions of Christian teaching and practice, there is so much central in common to almost all those communities—Catholic, Orthodox, and Protestant as well as Oriental Orthodox (those Christians, mainly in Egypt, Ethiopia, and some other parts of the Middle East, who, while not wishing to deny the divinity of Christ, did not accept the formula of the Council of Chalcedon as to how it should be expressed). In all these traditions there are the sacraments of baptism and Eucharist, understood as in some way proclaiming or making available to us the benefits of the life (and death) of Christ. And they have all taught in some form the doctrines of the Atonement and the Incarnation. Likewise, they have all taught that the life of Jesus was a holy life, and that his moral teaching as contained in the Gospels is true, although they have differed somewhat over exactly what he taught (how the parables were to be interpreted; whether some injunctions applied only to his immediate hearers or whether they applied to all humans on Earth, however far in the future). Given my claim in Chapter 5 that in general the Gospel accounts of what Jesus taught are basically correct, it follows that in these various respects the teaching and practice of the Church of the Twelve were continued in almost all Church communities derivative from them.

---

[34] I discuss in my book *Revelation: From Metaphor to Analogy* (Clarendon Press, 1992) what are the right ways to do this.

Those communities have taught as central elements of their creeds also things additional to those mentioned above; and if it were to be shown that some element taken as central subsequently by almost all communities was contrary to the explicit teaching of Jesus, then that would be reason for supposing that the Church founded by Jesus was not God's Church, which again would lead to serious doubt as to whether Jesus was God Incarnate risen from the dead. I do not believe that this can be shown.

The other central doctrine of Christianity besides the Atonement and the Incarnation is the doctrine of the Trinity—that God is in some way triune; Father, Son, and Holy Spirit. This is contained, in essence, together with the other two doctrines, in the Nicene Creed, the creed approved by the Council of Constantinople in AD 381. If, as I have argued, it would have been almost impossible for Jesus to convey the doctrine of the Incarnation by saying too explicitly 'I am God', it would have been totally impossible for him to teach explicitly the doctrine of the Trinity—that God was in some way triune— Father, Son, and Holy Spirit. But if he implied that he was divine, he also distinguished himself sharply from God the Father in so much of his teaching recorded in all the Gospels: he constantly addressed the Father as another, often, as I noted in Chapter 6, by the term Abba. There is also a great deal in all the Gospels and the Acts of the Apostles about the Holy Spirit. He is represented as active in the events of the life of Jesus: in his conception (in the very different accounts given by Matthew and Luke[35]), descending on Jesus at the time of his baptism (in all four Gospels[36]), and driving him into the wilderness (in the three synoptic Gospels[37]). Matthew's Gospel ends with the command to baptize 'in the name of the Father and of the Son and of the Holy Spirit'.[38] Acts records the descent of the Spirit on to the Church after the Resurrection,[39] and Acts and some of Paul's Epistles have much about the gift of the Spirit being given to

[35] Matt. 1: 18; Luke 1: 35.
[36] Matt. 3: 16; Mark 1: 10; Luke 3: 22; John 1: 32. John does not explicitly describe the baptism of Jesus. I argue, however, in Ch. 4 that he shows knowledge of it by mentioning the incident (closely connected by the other Gospels with the baptism of Jesus) of the descent of the Spirit on Jesus when Jesus at the beginning of his ministry came to John while he was baptizing.
[37] Matt. 4: 1; Mark 1: 12; Luke 1: 4. Matthew and Luke have a source independent of Mark for their subsequent accounts of the Temptations in the Wilderness to which Jesus is driven by the Spirit.
[38] Matt. 28: 19.   [39] Acts 2: 4.

Christians by baptism and/or the laying on of hands.[40] John's Gospel
contains a very lengthy passage of teaching attributed to Jesus, about
the work which the Holy Spirit, whom he called 'the Advocate' will
do in the Church after Jesus is no longer among the disciples in a
bodily form.[41] And there is much else in the New Testament about
the Spirit. It seems implausible to suppose that all of the reports and
teaching about the activity of the Spirit would be in the New Testament unless Jesus had given some teaching about the Spirit. But
there are various different ways in which one could extrapolate from
New Testament verses doctrinal systems in which the Spirit plays a
role but which would differ by underplaying the significance of
some verses and emphasizing that of others. It would not be too
obviously incompatible with some passages concerned with the
Spirit to suppose talk of the Spirit to be just talk about the Father
acting by inspiring. But it would be implausible to deny that the
doctrine of the Trinity, as formulated in the Nicene Creed, has roots
in teaching attributable to Jesus; and it would be implausible to
affirm that it contradicts what we know of that teaching. Hence, the
fact that the Church taught this doctrine does not count against its
being founded by God Incarnate for the purpose of preaching his
message to future generations.

Conclusion of Part II

I have argued in Part II that the data we have about the life and
teaching of Jesus are such as it is not too improbable that we would
find if Jesus was God Incarnate, and had become incarnate for all the
reasons considered in Chapter 2. The probability is far greater that
Jesus was God Incarnate than is the probability on available data
concerning any of the other prophets of human history that any of
them was God Incarnate. Of course, we would like a lot more data
about Jesus, not just about exactly what Jesus said and did but about
his inner life; but what we have is not inconsiderable. Some of our
data, I suggest, is very much what we would expect to find if Jesus
was God Incarnate; for example, the evidence of his way of life and
general moral teaching. So too, I suggest, is the evidence of his teaching that he was atoning for human sins and founding a church

---

[40] Acts 2: 38; 6: 17; and other passages.   [41] John 14: 25–16: 15.

(which taught his Atonement and divinity). The evidence is not, however, exactly what we would expect to find, I acknowledge, when we come to his implying his divinity and his intending the Church to continue for a long time. But it is not too distant from what we would expect. And we shall see, when we come to the concluding chapter (and the Appendix to the book), that what is crucial for the probability of the Resurrection is that the probability of finding the kinds of evidence we do should be far greater for Jesus than for any other prophet; and that there should be a modest probability (maybe much less than ½) that we should find the kind of evidence in connection with Jesus that we do. Jesus satisfies not too badly and far better than any other known figure in history the prior historical criteria for being God Incarnate, and so for being the person on whose life and teaching God would put his signature in the form of a super-miracle. I pointed out in an earlier chapter that, if the Resurrection happened in anything like the way traditionally believed, it would constitute such a super-miracle. So I turn in Part III to consider the detailed historical evidence relevant to the occurrence of the Resurrection, and to its having the significance which I am ascribing to it.

PART III

POSTERIOR HISTORICAL EVIDENCE

9

The Appearances of the Risen Jesus

IF JESUS rose bodily from the dead and wished his Church to know about it, two things are to be expected: first, that it would seem to his Church (which meant paradigmatically the Eleven remaining from the Twelve after the betrayal by Judas) that they saw and talked to him; and secondly, that the tomb should be empty. (I shall consider in due course the issue of why no one apart from his disciples seemed to see and talk to him.) In this chapter I shall consider whether the reports of the appearances were such as would be expected if there were real appearances. By the principles of Chapter 1, appearances and reports of appearances should be supposed veridical in the absence of counter-evidence such as major discrepancies in the reports. In Chapter 10 I shall consider whether the evidence is such as would be expected if the tomb was indeed empty, and I shall devote much of that chapter to an important neglected piece of evidence about when the women and the disciples discovered the empty tomb. If Jesus did not rise bodily, some rival account of what happened to the body must be correct, and in Chapter 11 I shall consider the probabilities of these rival accounts. In the final chapter of Part III I shall consider whether the significance which the disciples attributed to the Resurrection was of the kind that I claimed in Chapter 3 that a super-miracle must have.

The New Testament is full of statements in books of all its different genres that Christ rose from the dead, or that God raised him from the dead (using, apparently equivalently, the verbs ἐγείρω and ἀνίστημι for 'raise'). Many of these statements look like credal formulae (e.g. from the New Testament book generally agreed to be the earliest complete book, 1 Thessalonians, written about AD 49:

Jesus 'died and rose again').[1] Nor is there any passage where doubt is cast on there having been a 'resurrection' of Jesus. The formulae would have been taught to Christian converts, and clearly required expansion and justification, which would have been provided in their instruction and generally in the preaching of the Gospel. The speeches of Peter in Acts (which are somewhat different stylistically from the main text, and may well derive from earlier memories) stress that 'we' the apostles are 'witnesses' of 'these things' (namely, the death and Resurrection of Jesus).[2]

The most explicit grounds for believing in Jesus' Resurrection, where these are given in the New Testament, are that he 'appeared to' or 'was seen by' (ὤφθη) many.[3] (In discussing, for the rest of this chapter, issues of when and to whom Jesus 'appeared', I am understanding by an appearance of Jesus that it seemed to someone that he was present—I am leaving aside for the moment the issue of whether the appearance was veridical, that is whether he really did appear.) This was clearly a central element of Christian teaching before any of the books of the New Testament had been written. The various accounts in the New Testament of the appearances of Jesus do, however, differ in respect of to whom Jesus appeared and where. I noted in Chapter 4 that, while a very short statement of the central elements of the Christian message (the deeds and words of Jesus) and their grounds would have been transmitted accurately from one Christian community to another, details of the grounds for belief in those elements would not have been transmitted so accurately, or remembered so well, as they would have been by direct witnesses. So, when the deeds and words of Jesus were recorded in writing, discrepancies were bound to appear in different accounts. So, while the fact that the universal agreement on the fact of Jesus' Resurrection, and that there were many witnesses thereof, is good evidence of its truth, the existence of somewhat different versions of to whom he appeared, and when, do little to lessen the force of that evidence unless they are too much at odds with each other. The band of followers of Jesus, routed by his Crucifixion, had become enthusiastic missionaries for a Gospel centred on the Resurrection of Jesus. This requires explanation. We can, I suggest, rule out deliberate deceit by the inner circle of Jesus' followers. So many of the inner circle of disciples were prepared to die for their beliefs, while

---

[1] Thess. 4: 14.   [2] Acts 2: 32, 4: 33, 5: 32.   [3] e.g. Acts 13: 31.

acknowledging that at the beginning some doubted.[4] Clearly (rightly or wrongly) on the whole the disciples believed that Jesus was risen because many had seen him, and that at his appearances he had given them a gospel to proclaim. It is significant that among those who recognized the Resurrection were 'James, the Lord's brother' (described as an 'apostle' in Galatians 1: 19); Jesus' family are pictured as being somewhat hostile to his work before the Passion. The issue which we must consider is whether the discrepancies between the different accounts are so great that, although Jesus' followers believed that he had appeared to many, we are not justified in doing so.

There is just one formal credal-type statement of to whom Jesus appeared in the New Testament, which is contained in 1 Corinthians 15: 1–8. St Paul repeats it to the Corinthians as what he had told them previously, and what he himself had 'received' (apart, that is, presumably, from Christ's appearance to himself[5]). This was that Jesus appeared first to Peter, then to the Twelve, then to the 'above five hundred brothers and sisters at one time, most of whom are still alive, though some have died',[6] then to James, and then to all the apostles, and finally to Paul himself 'as to one untimely born'. The implication of the later phrase is that the appearance to Paul was much later than the other appearances. The 'thens' imply an explicit commitment to a temporal sequence of appearances. Paul tells us in Galatians that he spent fifteen days with Peter in Jerusalem, where he also met 'James, the Lord's brother', and where he must have heard what Peter and James had to say about the basis of this central Christian message; what he records in 1 Corinthians must have been sensitive to those conversations. Both Galatians and 1 Corinthians are letters universally agreed to have been written by Paul; Paul dates this visit to Jerusalem some three or four years after his conversion, perhaps some six years after the Crucifixion. The formal character of 1 Corinthians 15 and the knowledge possessed by its author must give it the greatest authority in comparison with all other accounts of what happened when. The context of 1 Corinthians 15 makes it unequivocally clear that Paul is purporting to give a literally true account of meetings with the risen Jesus; for he writes it to assure

---

[4] Matt. 28: 17.   [5] 1 Cor. 15: 8.

[6] The New Standard Revised Version translates ἀδελφοῖς as 'brothers and sisters', but the Greek carries no implication either that women were or that they were not involved on this occasion.

the Corinthians that 'resurrection of the dead' is possible, since Christ is already risen.[7] In talking about the former he is talking about a *future* event, because it will happen to those who have died;[8] and so must involve a literal coming to life again (as well, of course, as a lot more), and so its justification must involve Christ having already literally come to life again.

And there is the additional reason for giving this account of the Resurrection by far the greatest authority, and that is the character of the author. I urged earlier that Paul is different from any other person who appears on the pages of the New Testament in that we can judge his character as a witness for ourselves by reading those of his letters that are without dispute genuine, and he comes over as a totally honest person. If Paul endorses a credal formula, above all on this all-important matter, he believes it. And since he believes it after talking to Peter and James about these matters, he believes that they believe it. If they seemed to doubt it, he could not but share their doubts.

The other detailed accounts we have of the Resurrection appearances are not in the form of an official credal statement; they are all written down much later as parts of a Gospel narrative. I made the point earlier that the very passage of time weakens the force of an oral tradition, and that the length of time needed for communication between Christian groups having the consequence that it was difficult for a group to check its account where there was doubt would almost inevitably lead to some divergence in the accounts of the Resurrection appearances. We do, of course, find that. But is it any more divergent than accounts of much else in the life and Passion of Jesus, which is rightly not felt to cast serious doubt on the occurrence of the main incidents and kinds of incident and teaching recorded in all the Gospels? I don't think so. The divergencies in the Resurrection accounts, I shall suggest, can easily be accounted for by one or other author doing a little 'theologizing' (putting his own gloss on a common historical core), or having a source whose memory was not totally accurate. The differences are certainly not substantial enough to cast doubt on the basic story.

The other detailed accounts of the Resurrection appearances do not give the same list of persons or groups appeared to as does 1 Corinthians, nor the same lists as each other; and they disagree

---

[7] 1 Cor. 15: 12–13.   [8] 1 Cor. 15: 18.

among themselves as to where the appearances took place. (1 Corinthians has nothing to say about the latter.) There are seven other sources. Matthew reports appearances to Mary Magdalene and to 'the other Mary' (in Jerusalem) and to 'the eleven disciples' (in Galilee). Mark (in the original text, which ended at 16: 8) records no Resurrection appearances, but does contain predictions of appearances to 'the disciples and Peter' in Galilee, which the author surely believed to have been fulfilled.[9] There are also the three predictions by Jesus in Mark of his Resurrection. Then there is the longer Marcan appendix; that is, Mark 16: 9–20, as printed in most Bibles, added at a later date to St Mark's Gospel, which looks unfinished, ending at 16: 8 in a somewhat ungrammatical way in what looks like the middle of a narrative. This appendix reports appearances to Mary Magdalene, to 'two of them, as they were walking into the country', and 'to the eleven as they were sitting at the table'. No location is given. Luke reports appearances to 'two of them' including Cleopas walking to Emmaus, to Peter, to 'the eleven', and then— perhaps separately, but probably part of the same appearance—at an Ascension before 'them'. All of these are located in the region of Jerusalem. John 20 reports appearances to Mary Magdalene (and probably to others with her; see 20: 2: 'we'), to the 'disciples' without Thomas ('one of the twelve'), and to the disciples with Thomas. At least the first two of these are located in the region of Jerusalem. John 21 (a separate chapter attached subsequently to the rest of the Gospel) reports an appearance to seven disciples (including Peter, James, and John) in Galilee. I argued in Chapter 4 in favour of taking John as a serious witness on historical matters when dealing with the central events of the life of Jesus recorded in the other Gospels, and especially events around the time of the Passion. And finally Acts (1: 3) records that Jesus showed himself to the 'apostles' by many proofs over forty days; and then records an Ascension before them at the Mount of Olives. And in an early speech of Paul reported in Acts (13: 31) the claim is repeated that 'for many days [Jesus] appeared to those who came up with him from Galilee to Jerusalem, and they are now his witnesses to the people'.

Now 1 Corinthians does not rule out others than those mentioned having observed the risen Christ. All those Paul mentions are individual apostles, or groups which must include

---

[9] Mark 16: 7, picking up 14: 28.

apostles, in that fairly narrow sense of 'apostle', which is a little wider than the Twelve. For Paul regarded himself as an apostle,[10] and, in view of the respect which he pays to James 'the Lord's brother', must have thought of this James also as one—presumably the James who has a significant Church role later in Acts.[11] The 'five hundred brothers and sisters' must have been an official Church assembly and must therefore have included apostles. I stress this because at the beginning of Acts Peter asks the 'believers' to help to choose one of those who had been part of the group from the time of 'the baptism of John' until 'the day when [the Lord Jesus] was taken up from us', to become 'a witness with us of [Jesus'] resurrection'.[12] The implication is that Peter is asking the brethren to choose from among those who in some sense (directly or by being told by someone else) were 'witnesses' of the Ascension and so of the Resurrection, to become a 'witness' in a narrower and more formal sense—as a member of the Twelve, and thus an apostle. So the existence of this more formal sense of 'witness' means that the fact that Paul mentions only apostles in what is a formal credal statement certainly does not rule out others from having seen the risen Jesus, and Acts 1: 22 does carry the implication that there were witnesses other than official witnesses.

The other sources mention two appearances which are clearly appearances to non-apostles, and their omission from Paul's list may be due simply to this fact. One is the appearance of Jesus to the disciples on the road to Emmaus involving a long conversation with them (Luke 24: 13–32; clearly the same as the two disciples in the Marcan appendix 16: 12). There are two ready explanations for that omission. The first is that the appearance to the disciples together (in Luke 24: 36) included the walkers on the road to Emmaus. So the appearance on the Emmaus road can be regarded simply as an early part of the appearance to the Twelve listed by Paul, and not worth a separate mention. And the other possible explanation for Paul not listing this appearance is simply that it was to non-apostles. The two who walked to Emmaus were not important enough to be official witnesses. Cleopas plays no significant part elsewhere in the New Testament; and the other disciple was so unimportant as to have no name. (Maybe it was Cleopas' wife, apparently mentioned in John 19: 25 as being at the foot of the Cross.)

The other appearance omitted from Paul's list is an appearance to

---

[10] See e.g. 1 Cor. 1: 1.   [11] Acts 12: 17, 15: 13.   [12] Acts 1: 22.

Mary Magdalene at or near the tomb on the Easter Sunday morning (mentioned by Matthew, the Marcan appendix, and John). (Matthew describes the appearance as being also to the other Mary.)The well-known point that in Jewish law women were not fully qualified as witnesses[13] can readily account for the omission of Mary from the formula endorsed by Paul (as also from the account in Luke); the early Church did not want its account to depend on witnesses who would be regarded, at any rate by many hearers, as of doubtful status. And the same reason may account for Luke not mentioning this appearance. The Church needed important figures as its official witnesses. So we can certainly add the first of these appearances to Paul's list, but there is a problem about the appearance to Mary Magdalene.

Mark 16: 1–8 records the visit by 'Mary Magdalene, and Mary the mother of James, and Salome' to the tomb on the Sunday morning, their finding it empty, and their being told by a young man in white that Jesus is risen and that they are to tell 'his disciples and Peter that he is going ahead of you to Galilee; there you will see him just as he told you'. They then fled the tomb and 'said nothing to anyone, for they were afraid'. And that is where the original text of Mark ends (16: 8). Its apparent implication is that the women did not see Jesus at the tomb, or anywhere near it very soon, nor did they tell the disciples that the tomb was empty; and that the first appearances at any rate were all in Galilee, as the previous verse predicts. It is not merely that no appearance to Mary Magdalane or other women is mentioned, but there is an apparent implication that there was no such appearance.

In discussing this problem, I am going to assume for the present that Mark is correct in telling us that there was a visit by women to the tomb on the Sunday morning. This testimony, like all testimony, is to be believed, in the absence of counter-evidence. But some have put forward arguments denying that the tomb was empty, from which it would follow that the women could not have found it so; and I shall discuss these arguments in Chapter 10. So, given that women did find the tomb empty on the Sunday morning, if then

---

[13] Josephus, *Antiquities* 4. 219, states that Moses prohibited recognizing women as witnesses. The fact that several of the women who accompanied Jesus and the disciples during his ministry were ones who 'had been cured of evil spirits and infirmities' (Luke 8: 2) might be thought to make them particularly ill suited as witnesses, being open to the charge of being still under the influence of these spirits, or (by the more secularly minded) of being liable to fantasize.

there was no appearance to Mary Magdalene, it would be very surprising indeed that Matthew, the Marcan appendix, and John should all claim that there was. This would be very surprising in view of the fact that the obvious honour of being the first witness (or one of the first two witnesses, as Matthew claims) to the risen Jesus would not have been attributed to Mary Magdalene, a woman and not Jesus' mother, but one 'from whom seven demons had gone out',[14] rather than to Peter or the Eleven, the official Church leaders, unless her claim had been staked pretty soon before the other appearances were well known. If Mary really 'said nothing to anyone' for some weeks, that claim is very unlikely to have been accepted. And 'said nothing to anyone' seems inconsistent with three sources: Matthew, Luke, and John (none of whom show any textual dependence on each other), who claim that the women conveyed immediately to the disciples the information that the tomb was empty. For these two reasons—that Mary's claim to have been the first to have seen the risen Jesus must have been staked early, and the strong agreement of the other sources that the women immediately told the apostles that the tomb was empty—it looks as if, either accidentally or intentionally, Mark (16: 8) is misleading.

Given that Mark (16: 8) is misleading, the arguments for supposing that St Mark's Gospel did not end at (16: 8) but that there is a lost ending must be very strong. There are to my mind two powerful such arguments. The first is that it is very improbable that a book would end as 16: 8 does, with the connective γὰρ, with which no Greek sentence, let alone book, would normally end. And the second argument is that Mark certainly believed that there were Resurrection appearances: he records Jesus as having during his earthly ministry prophesied his Resurrection, and in (16: 8) he records the young man in white prophesying an appearance in Galilee; and so to have reported one or more appearances would have been to have given the proof of Jesus' Resurrection which was the culmination of the work begun in his life and Passion. However, many twentieth-century scholars have claimed that Mark intended to end his Gospel with the empty tomb, so as to leave room for each of us to choose how to react to the uncertainty as to what had happened to Jesus.[15]

---

[14] Luke 8: 2.

[15] For a statement of the arguments of others for supposing that Mark's Gospel had a lost ending, and argument in favour of the view that the author intended it to end at 16: 8, see Morna Hooker, *The Gospel According to St. Mark* (A. & C. Black, 1991), 391–4.

True, Mark claims that in his earthly life Jesus kept things secret—above all he kept it secret that he was the Messiah—leaving such things to his disciples to discover for themselves, until they were publicly revealed. But Mark does in the end show how things were made public, or at least made evident to the disciples. Above all he surely would have intended to record the manifestation of the Resurrection. Enigmatic twentieth-century plays might end with deliberate uncertainty, but it seems to be most implausible that a Gospel ('good news', as Mark described his own work) would have ended this way. Given that, the phrase 'said nothing to anyone' might have meant simply 'said nothing to the authorities', that is, 'did not report the theft of the body to the Jewish or Roman authorities'; and the Gospel might have gone on to recount the women telling the disciples. Or, if 'anyone' includes the disciples, the Gospel might well have gone on to fill out which women did not tell the disciples, and for how long. For obviously Mark believed that at some time the women did tell their experiences to disciples, otherwise he would not have known of them. The only issue concerns how soon any of them told anything to others. The Gospel might have been going on to say something like 'Although all the women fled, after a few hours one of them pulled herself together and told the disciples.'

One solution is suggested by John (20: 2). This verse seems to tell us that, although there was more than one woman who saw the empty tomb—Mary's message to Peter and 'the other disciple' refers to 'we' not knowing where the body was—only Mary Magdalene told the disciples. And the other women having fled would explain further why Mary was found by Jesus alone when she revisited the tomb in John 20: 11–18. This would also explain why the two disciples on the road to Emmaus told the unrecognized Jesus only that the women had found the tomb empty and had seen a vision of angels, and then other disciples had found the tomb empty 'but they did not see him'.[16] No appearance to Mary is mentioned by the two disciples, for the reason that it happened after they had checked the story of the empty tomb and before Mary had reported to the disciples Jesus' appearance to her. By the time that she did report this the two disciples had already departed for Emmaus and so did not mention to Jesus the appearance to Mary Magdalene.

This solution does, however, clash with three very minor Gospel

[16] Luke 24: 24.

claims. Matthew reports 'the other Mary' as having seen Jesus at the same time as Mary Magdalene.[17] Luke claims that all the women, not just Mary Magdalene, told the apostles what had happened. And John reports the vision of the angels as seen by Mary Magdalene on her second, rather than on her first, visit to the tomb.[18] But these are all very small confusions easily likely to occur in the course of decades of oral transmission or fading memory. If 'the other Mary' (and perhaps other women as well) were with Mary Magdalene when she saw the empty tomb, and then Jesus appeared to Mary Magdalene, oral transmission could very easily lead to a version in which Jesus appeared simultaneously to two Marys. And if several women saw the empty tomb, and Mary Magdalene alone reported this to the disciples, oral transmission could very easily lead to a version in which all of them reported to the apostles. And when John is recording not what he saw but what Mary reported having seen, the memory of an old man may err on a tiny detail after many decades, even if he recalled the central events with crystal clarity.

Exactly who found the tomb empty or who saw a vision of angels and when were, from the early Church's point of view, minor matters in comparison with who saw Jesus first. And I repeat my view that it is very unlikely that this honour would have been attributed to Mary Magdalene unless she had staked her claim early. The supposition of three very minor errors in oral transmission and memory must take precedence over a supposition that there was no early general belief in a first appearance to Mary Magdalene at the tomb. If Mark's Gospel was read in the first century as denying such an appearance (either because it ended at 16: 8 or because its continuation denied it), neither Matthew nor the Marcan appendix would have included an appearance (since they both knew Mark) unless they had very strong evidence to the contrary, for they had a strong motive for attributing the first appearance to Peter or the apostles. And in view of its great significance John's Gospel would certainly not have included it if, as I have argued, its author was a reliable

[17] Matt. 28: 9–10.

[18] John 20: 12–13. A vision of one or more angels was reported as having been seen by more than one woman in Matthew, Mark, and Luke. Mark reports a 'young man' rather than angels, but a young man in a white robe who inspired terror. Luke at first (Luke 24: 4) describes the women as seeing 'two men in dazzling clothes', but later reports the walkers on the road to Emmaus as reporting that the women had seen 'a vision of angels' (Luke 24: 23).

witness of the central events of the Passion and Resurrection—
unless he believed it to be a historical fact. However Mark's Gospel
did end, we should not let the apparent denial of an appearance to
Mary, or the apparent denial that Mary was the source of information for other disciples that the tomb was empty, overrule the strong
contrary evidence in favour of these occurrences.

So, on the assumption that the apparent implication of Mark 16:
1–8 in respect of no appearance to Mary Magdalene on the Sunday
should not be drawn, we can proceed further. The omissions of
some of the appearances listed by Paul from the other accounts can
in general be attributed either to the author's ignorance of the
details of appearances, or simply to his intention to report only
representative appearances. And some of the sources clearly imply
that the authors knew of other appearances than the ones they
recorded. Given that Luke–Acts is basically one work, the allusion in
Acts to Jesus showing himself alive by 'many convincing proofs
appearing to them during forty days, and speaking about the Kingdom of God'[19] implies that not all the appearances known to Luke
were recorded in Luke 24. John 20: 30 claims that 'Jesus did many
other signs in the presence of his disciples which are not written in
this book'; and since this occurs immediately after the reports of the
appearances, it may plausibly be thought to allow that not all
appearances were recorded. John 21 is normally regarded as a separate pericope, written separately before being added to the main
account, not intended to list everything; and in that case 21: 14 (stating that the incident related in John 21 was 'the third' of Jesus'
appearances) can only be regarded as a connecting verse added very
late, and not part of the original tradition. Mark 16: 1–8 did not get
as far as appearances, and (as I mentioned earlier) the Marcan
appendix is clearly simply a brief summary of the tradition from
other sources to make up for the obvious deficiency of a Gospel
ending at 16: 8.

Then there is the problem, on which I have already touched, of the
location of the appearances. There is a strong tradition (Mark's
predictions, 16: 7 and 14: 28; Matthew; and John 21) of appearances
in Galilee, which cannot be ignored. In order to reconcile Mark with
accounts of appearances in Jerusalem, we shall need to regard the
predictions (16: 7 and 14: 28) as not ruling out other appearances but

---

[19] Acts 1: 3.

as saying where the main appearance to all disciples together would take place—in Galilee. There seems little difficulty in reconciling appearances in Galilee with John 20, for there is no implication there that the appearance to the disciples with Thomas (which might itself be in Galilee, eight days journey from Jerusalem) was the last. The Marcan appendix is late, and in any case gives no location for its final appearance. The problem is that Luke's Gospel seems to imply that all the appearances took place on one day in Jerusalem. But since Acts asserts that they took place over forty days, either Luke is simply juxtaposing two obviously inconsistent accounts, which is not too plausible, or he is using one or other of these accounts to make a theological point by redescribing what he regarded as the bare historical facts—but without seeking to deceive us, since he sets out the plain history in the other account. In view of the tradition in all the other accounts of a lengthier period of Resurrection appearances, we must treat Luke 24 as making a theological point—perhaps the point that the preaching of the Gospel takes off from the Resurrection of Jesus in Jerusalem.[20] Given a forty-day interval between the Resurrection and Jesus' last appearance, there is time for a journey to Galilee and back again. But why 'back again'? Matthew 28 puts a blessing of the Eleven by Jesus on a mountain in Galilee; and it looks like an Ascension story. It does not, however, state that it was Jesus' final appearance, nor does it record an ascension. Clearly many of the disciples did return to Jerusalem. Even if Luke's story of Pentecost is regarded as myth, there are just too many details of too many disciples being in Jerusalem in the opening chapters of Acts.

So, without too much difficulty, there is beginning to emerge one way to reconcile the various accounts. There was first an appearance to Mary Magdalene at or near the tomb (Matthew, Marcan appendix, John 20), then to the disciples on the road to Emmaus (Luke), then to Peter (Luke and 1 Corinthians), and then to the 'eleven' (in 1 Corinthians Paul must mean 'the eleven' when he writes the 'Twelve'; Luke, and John 20's 'the disciples')—all of these in Jerusalem, on Easter Sunday itself. I do not think that we need suppose all the Eleven to have been present on this occasion, but at any rate a representative sample. We must doubt whether they were all present, first because of the tradition that after the Betrayal 'all of them deserted him and fled'.[21] People fleeing tend to flee in different directions,

---

[20] Luke 24: 47–9; Acts 1: 4.   [21] Mark 14: 50.

TABLE 9.1. *Table of appearances*

1 Corinthians	Matthew	Mark	Longer Marcan appendix	Luke	Acts	John	John 21
	1. Mary Magdalene and 'the other Mary', Jerusalem		1. Mary Magdalene			1. Mary Magdalene, Jerusalem	
			2. 'two of them'	2. Cleopas and another, Jerusalem	['appearing to—the apostles whom he had chosen—during forty days']		
3. Peter				3. Peter			
4. 'the Twelve'						4. 'the disciples' (minus Thomas), Jerusalem	
5. 'five hundred brothers and sisters at one time'	5. the Eleven, Galilee	5. Galilee, appearances to 'the disciples and Peter' predicted			['appear for many days']	5a. 'the disciples' (including Thomas) ['many other signs']	5b. seven disciples, Galilee
6. James							
7. 'all the apostles'			7. 'the eleven' + Ascension	7. 'the eleven' + Ascension, Jerusalem	7. Ascension, Jerusalem		
8. Paul					8. Paul		

Note: This table lists all the appearances of Jesus mentioned in the New Testament, listing them under each New Testament source in the order in which the source seems to claim that they occurred (apart from the two general references to 'appearances' in Acts, where there is no claim about historical sequence). I put on the same numbered historical line those which, I argue in the text, are plausibly the same appearances. (5b) and possibly (5a) are Galilee appearances which may be distinct from (5).

and some of them may not have gone very far. But the Twelve had all come from Galilee, and a very natural reaction for many of them, when things went wrong, would have been to return there very quickly. Secondly, of course, John records that Thomas was absent. And thirdly, a subsequent move of the others to Galilee may readily be explained by a desire to find the lost sheep and reincorporate them into the Eleven. No doubt many of Jesus' disciples had remained in Galilee when Jesus and the Twelve had come up to Jerusalem. And so the appearance to the 500 can plausibly be located in Galilee as an appearance to the whole Church assembly; which is why Mark referred specially to Galilee as the place where Jesus would meet his disciples. The appearances to James mentioned in 1 Corinthians and to the Eleven including Thomas in John 20, as well as the appearances explicitly stated to have occurred in Galilee—the appearance by the lake in John 21, and the appearance to the Eleven in Matthew—can also therefore naturally be located in Galilee. (No doubt some of these stories concern the same appearance.) Then, after a return to Jerusalem, a final appearance to 'all the apostles' (1 Corinthians, and the Ascension as recorded in the Marcan appendix, Luke, and Acts). The appearance to the Eleven in the Marcan appendix is perhaps an amalgam of post-Emmaus appearances. Why did they return to Jerusalem, if that is what happened? Perhaps because they believed that Jesus had told them to do so, because it was from Jerusalem that the preaching of the Gospels to all nations must begin, as Luke claims. Or perhaps in order to check that the tomb really was empty, that what they believed that they had experienced was no apparition.

One remaining problem is that, if there was indeed an appearance to 'five hundred brothers and sisters at one time', it is surprising that none of the Gospel writers draws attention to the large numbers involved. I can only suppose that their interest was in apostolic witness (and so only mentioned the apostles involved in this); and some of them knew of the details of no more than two or three paradigm appearances. Luke may have failed to mention it because, being set by Paul in the middle of the list of appearances, it was probably a Galilean appearance and he was only interested in Jerusalem appearances. Or, just possibly, he substituted for it his Pentecost story. But this is speculative. There is a difficulty; but it is not one to be solved by denying the historicity of the 500 brethren, for Paul and his source would never have asserted it unless there were plenty of people around who had participated in it.

I do not deny that my way of reconciling the various accounts of the Resurrection appearances does involve attributing minor errors to some of the writers and some very minor theologizing (Luke locating all the appearances in Jerusalem). But minor errors and a very small amount of theologizing are to be expected in first-century AD accounts of any historical event believed to have deep theological importance, transmitted by oral testimony by evangelists at the end of long journeys. I suggest that my proposed reconciliation does not make any very implausible suppositions. It has the kind of historical error and theologizing which remains basically sensitive to the main (believed) historical fact that we would expect.

Of what kind were these appearances? Various. Some were to individuals, some to groups. The appearance to Paul was unique as far as we know, in that although it happened to an individual when he was with others, the others did not see the risen Jesus. Acts 9 states that both Paul and the others saw a light and heard a voice, but implies that none of them saw the speaker. The parallel account in Acts 22 states that Paul's companions did not hear the voice. Yet 1 Corinthians says that Christ 'appeared' to Paul (ὤφθη, 'was seen' by him). Jesus was not always recognized immediately (Mary Magdalene in John 20: 14; the disciples on the Emmaus road; John 21: 4). He could appear and disappear at will. Yet Luke is keen to stress his embodiedness ('touch me', 24: 39; Jesus ate fish, 24: 23); John (20: 27) implies that Thomas could have put his fingers in Jesus' side. Matthew too reports the women taking hold of Jesus.[22] (Yet in John, Mary Magdalene is told not to hold on to Jesus, 'because I have not yet ascended to the Father'.[23] However, perhaps that too implies that Mary could touch Jesus and so he was embodied, but that she must not do so.) And the various references to Jesus being involved in a meal with his disciples after his Resurrection, to which I will come in due course in more detail, do suggest that Jesus himself ate (as Luke states explicitly[24]). So there is quite a tradition of Jesus being embodied in the normal way for a little of the time, although in that embodied state possessing extraordinary powers.

---

[22] Matt. 28: 9.   [23] John 20: 17.   [24] Luke 24: 43.

10

The Empty Tomb and the
Observance of Sunday

The Empty Tomb

NOW, EVEN if Jesus appeared to his disciples in an embodied form, he could have been embodied in a new body, having no connection with the body which lay in the tomb. But clearly the four Gospels wished to claim that Jesus was risen in his old body, transformed. They all begin their accounts of the Resurrection with the story of an initial visit by women on Easter Sunday morning to the tomb and their finding it empty; and Luke has Peter, and John has Peter and the disciple 'whom Jesus loved', confirm that the tomb was indeed empty. I assumed earlier that there was no reason to deny the testimony that these visits to the tomb really occurred. There used, however, to be a theory fashionable among scholars that these stories were a later addition inserted to make sense of the appearances. And perhaps the main reason for this theory was that Paul nowhere, and above all not in 1 Corinthians, mentions an empty tomb.

But if the Gospel writers felt this need, presumably it was because they felt that appearances of a ghost of Jesus were not nearly as worth having as appearances of Jesus embodied. Luke's claim that Jesus ate fish in front of them[1] to demonstrate that he was no ghost shows that an embodied Jesus alone would have given them the joy of the Resurrection. And although Jesus might have been embodied in a new body, this was not a possibility that would readily have occurred to first-century Jews; they would have expected his embodiment to go with an empty tomb. But if the Gospel writers felt that a

[1] Luke 24: 37–43.

Resurrection required an empty tomb, presumably Christians of a decade or two earlier would have felt the same—St Paul would have felt that. So if there was a belief held by anyone in the Church or outside it that the body of Jesus still lay in its tomb, surely St Paul would have felt the need to explain how really the fact that the body was still in the tomb made no difference to Resurrection faith. Those whom he is addressing in 1 Corinthians who held that 'there is no resurrection of the dead'[2] would have had an argument to support them—even Christ's body was still in the tomb—which would need to be answered. But of course there is none of that in 1 Corinthians or anywhere else in the New Testament (and no evidence of later deletions of any such passages). And the reason is clearly that St Paul assumed that the Resurrection of Christ entailed the emptiness of the tomb. It was part of the tradition which St Paul mentions, that immediately precedes the claim that he rose, that Christ was buried. Peter's Pentecost speech in Acts contrasts the patriarch David, who was also buried, 'and his tomb is with us to this day', with David's prophecy, which Paul interprets as referring to Christ, that 'his flesh' did not 'experience corruption'.[3]

Two passages which are cited to suggest that belief in Resurrection does not require an empty tomb are Mark 6: 14–16 and 12: 18–27. In the first passage Herod Antipas, hearing of Jesus, fears that he is John the Baptist who 'has been raised' from the dead, yet he is not reported as making an effort to check the tomb. This is supposed to show that whether their body is still in their tomb is irrelevant to whether someone has been raised. However, the passage recounts just the wild musing of one guilt-ridden man; others had other views of who Jesus was. It was not greatly important for Herod whether his musing was correct; what mattered to him is that he was guilty in respect of John the Baptist's death, and that someone else was uncannily like him. Herod may well have checked the tomb (if he knew where it was), but Mark may not have known of it; nor would it have been greatly important for his story if he had.

The second passage looks more significant. It tells of the Sadducees' question to Jesus about whose wife would a seven-times widow be in the Resurrection (that is, the General Resurrection on 'the last day'). Jesus claims that the dead are 'raised', but that they do not marry. He quotes in support of the claim that the dead are

---

[2] 1 Cor. 15: 12.   [3] Acts 2: 29–31.

'raised' (ἐγείρονται, present tense) God's words to Moses, 'I am the God of Abraham, the God of Isaac, and the God of Jacob,'[4] and claims that God is the God of the living. Yet the tombs of the patriarchs were being venerated without people supposing them to be empty. So, the argument goes, 'resurrection' does not entail empty tomb. But the Sadducees' question concerns whose wife 'will' the widow be 'in the Resurrection', clearly one future event in which all would be involved and which had not yet happened. It is the Sadducees' denial that there will be such an event which Jesus is opposing. So what does Jesus mean by the claim that God is the God of the 'living', Abraham, Isaac, and Jacob; and what is its relevance to the argument? There seem three possibilities. First, the patriarchs are now alive; this means they have already risen; this is reason to suppose that other dead people will also rise. Secondly, the patriarchs are now alive (but without their bodies); this is evidence that God will complete the process by raising them in future (giving them back their bodies) and so raising other people as well. Thirdly, the patriarchs are only temporarily dead (asleep); their status is basically a living one, and so God will bring them (and so others) to life by raising them in future. I don't see much in the text to choose between these interpretations, but it is only the first which has the consequence that resurrection does not entail an empty tomb. And if the first were correct, and was the kind of resurrection which early Christians affirmed of Jesus, then one would expect them to have venerated the tomb of Jesus containing his corpse (as people venerated the tombs of the patriarchs) or maybe the ossuary in which the bones were subsequently put; but there is not the slightest evidence to suppose that they did. (See again the contrast with David in Acts 2: 29.)

So I stick with what all the other evidence suggests, that the disciples' belief in the Resurrection involved a belief in an empty tomb. Given that, it beggars belief that the disciples could have affirmed the Resurrection of Jesus without checking the tomb as soon as they could (and if they were in Galilee, they would have needed to return to Jerusalem). They must have believed very early that the tomb was empty. (There may be mundane explanations of why it was empty, or why they falsely believed that it was empty; and I will come to those in due course). Hence it is highly plausible to suppose what

---

[4] Exod. 3: 6.

the Gospels tell us about why they came to hold this belief; namely, that the women found the tomb empty and (whether immediately or rather later) told the disciples this. They would not otherwise have had the prominence in the tradition which they have. And again it beggars belief to suppose that the disciples would have taken the word of the women for this; they, too, would have wanted to check it for themselves.

Sunday

But then when did the checking by the women take place? When did anyone first believe that the body was not in the tomb? All four Gospels tell us that it happened on the Sunday morning, the morning of 'the third day'. And 'on the third day' is a phrase frequently associated with the Resurrection itself. No one seems to allow for the possibility that the Resurrection took place on the Saturday, and was only discovered on the Sunday. We will need to consider possible explanations for that shortly.

There is a very important piece of evidence relevant to when the checking of the empty tomb took place, which must now be brought into the equation.[5] Christian communities spread out from Jerusalem very quickly—within three or four years of the events of the Passion. Acts 8: 1 records that after the death of Stephen there was a great persecution against the Church which led to Christians (apart from the 'apostles') being 'scattered throughout the countryside of Judaea and Samaria'. (And there is no reason to suppose that separate communities were not set up in other places even earlier.) They took with them their customs, including the custom of celebrating a Eucharist; and all the evidence we have (described below) suggests that there was a universal custom of celebrating the Eucharist on a Sunday, the first day of the week. This must have antedated the scattering; otherwise we would have heard of disputes about when to celebrate, and some instructions being given from on high (analogous to the way in which disputes about circumcision

---

[5] Much of the next few paragraphs consists in rearranging the evidence assembled in W. Rordorf's *Sunday* (SCM Press, 1968), ch. 4, on the origin of the Christian Sunday, into the form of evidence for the Resurrection. Note that I am not concerned with the issue of when or why Sunday became the Christian sabbath, only with the origin of the custom of celebrating the Eucharist on Sunday.

and eating sacrificial meat were purportedly resolved by the 'Council of Jerusalem' described in Acts 15).

First, there is New Testament evidence of the significance of Sunday in Christian thinking. Acts 20: 7 is in one of the 'we' passages in Acts. These are the passages in which Paul's journeys are described in terms of what 'we' did and what happened to 'us'; and so probably reflect the participation of the author of Acts (Luke) or his immediate source. Acts 20: 7 records for a 'first day of the week' the breaking of bread. κλᾶν ἄρτον ('to break bread') was the expression used by St Paul (1 Cor.) and the synoptic Gospels for what Jesus did at the Last Supper,[6] and was always used later as a description of the common Christian meal which included the Eucharist. This passage is the only New Testament passage which tells us the day of a post-Ascension celebration of the Eucharist. 1 Corinthians 16: 2 says that each Church member should lay aside a certain sum each 'first day of the week'. Gentile Christians were presumably not normally paid on a weekly basis; and so the 'first day' must be mentioned at least because it has significance in theological terms; that is, when Christians made up their accounts before God. Although commentators say that there is no implication in this passage that Christians met together on the 'first day', I think that there is. For Paul goes on to say that the purpose of people laying aside a sum each first day is 'so that collections need not be taken when I come'. But if the money was laid aside in each Christian's home, it would still have to be collected when Paul came, from each Christian publicly; and that is what Paul wished to avoid. That would only be avoided if, as well as being put aside, it was also brought to church regularly, and if this regular bringing was to take place on any day other than Sunday it would be natural for Paul to say when. For it being brought to church regularly, rather than it being laid aside regularly was what Paul wished to achieve. In Revelation 1: 10 John tells us that he had his vision on 'the Lord's Day' (ἡ κυριακὴ ἡμέρα),[7] giving Sunday

---

[6] The other uses of κλᾶν ἄρτον in the New Testament (e.g. Acts 2: 46) are also all plausibly taken as referring to a Eucharist, with the exception of Acts 27: 35. It would be a mistake to think that early Christians made no sharp distinction between Eucharists and other communal meals. 1 Cor. 10: 21 and 11: 28–30 already give a 'real presence' significance to the 'bread' and the 'cup' of the Lord (the bread and wine of the Eucharist being more than mere symbols of the body and blood of Christ). Those who eat the bread and drink the cup unworthily, writes Paul, 'will be answerable for the body and the blood of the Lord'.

[7] For the argument that the 'Lord's Day' is Sunday, and not Easter Day, see R. J.

the name which it has retained in Greek ever since, and showing that it had immense theological significance. When we come to post-New Testament evidence, all references in early literature to when the Eucharist was celebrated refer to a weekly Sunday celebration; see the *Didache* (14) and Justin's *First Apology* (65–7). Eusebius records, of one of the two groups of Ebionites (a Jewish Christian sect who separated from mainstream Christianity in the reign of Trajan), that they 'celebrate the Lord's day very much like us in commemoration of his Resurrection'.[8] A group so dedicated to Jewish discipline would not have preserved the custom of Sunday worship if they had regarded it of non-Palestinian origin.

There are other days on which it might have been more natural for Christians to celebrate the Eucharist (e.g. on the day of the original Last Supper—probably a Thursday and certainly not a Sunday—or annually rather than weekly). No such are known. There is no plausible origin of the sacredness of Sunday from outside Christianity.[9] There is only one simple explanation of this universal custom, which, I argued, must derive at the latest from the first two or three post-Resurrection years. The Eucharist was celebrated on a Sunday (and Sunday had theological significance) from the first years of Christianity because Christians believed that the central Christian event of the Resurrection occurred on a Sunday. Yet such early practice would have included that of the Eleven themselves, and so could only go with a belief of theirs that Christians had seen either the empty tomb or the risen Jesus on the first Easter Sunday. This shows that the visit to the tomb on Easter Sunday was not a late invention read back into history to make sense of the appearances but a separately authenticated incident.

One reason why people have believed the 'third day' tradition to be late is that they have reasonably supposed that the early Christians searched the Old Testament to find possible predictions of the Resurrection, and finding Hosea 6: 2, 'After two days he will revive us: on the third day he will raise us up, that we may live before

Bauckham, 'The Lord's Day', in D. A. Carson (ed.), *From Sabbath to Lord's Day* (Zondervan, 1982), 230–2.

[8] Eusebius, *Ecclesiastical History* 3: 27.

[9] See Rordorf, *Sunday*, 280–93.

[10] This version of Hosea 6: 2 is that translated from the Hebrew and it talks of 'us' being raised. The Resurrection here predicted concerns a community not an individual; the Greek of the Septuagint (which might have been more familiar to many hearers of the Gospel) translates 'on the third day we shall be raised up'.

him,'[10] they attributed the Resurrection to the third day. The evidence of early Sunday Eucharistic celebration counts massively against the suggestion that the 'third day' tradition is late. Certainly early Christians searched the Old Testament for all they could find by way of types or possible predictions of New Testament events, and they had much success. Both 1 Corinthians 15: 4 and Luke 24: 46 claim that 'on the third day' was a scriptural prediction, and it is probably the case that these writers have Hosea 6: 2 in mind here. However, it is quoted nowhere in the New Testament as a prediction of the Resurrection. (Indeed, the first text we have, in which Hosea 6: 2 is applied to the Resurrection, is by Tertullian.[11]) Nevertheless, it does seem the obvious source of the claim in Luke and 1 Corinthians that 'the third day' was a scriptural prediction. However, in the three predictions of the Passion in Mark,[12] the prediction is that Jesus will rise 'after (μετὰ) three days'; and in the saying about the Temple in Mark,[13] (repeated by Matthew) the prediction is that Jesus will build it again 'in (διὰ) three days'. So Mark does not quote the phrase from Hosea. Matthew and Luke both replace the phrase 'after three days' of the Marcan Passion prediction by 'on the third day'. (Luke does not contain a detailed second prediction.) This could be either because it fitted the believed facts better or because it fitted Hosea 6: 2 better. But Matthew gives elsewhere a quite different Old Testament text (the one text actually quoted for this purpose in the New Testament) in order to justify the day of the Resurrection as the third day. 'Jonah was in the belly of the fish three days and three nights.'[14] Matthew has Jesus say, 'As Jonah was three days and three nights in the belly of the sea monster, so for three days and three nights the Son of Man will be in the heart of the Earth.'[15] It would have fitted the one text we do know that Matthew had in mind as a prediction of the Resurrection better to leave the Marcan expression ('after') as it stood. So even if Matthew thought of Hosea 6: 2 as a prediction of the Resurrection (of which we have no direct evidence), he had a rival text (which he actually cites) suggesting a different day for the Resurrection, and there is no reason why he should change 'after three days' merely to fit Hosea. He must have made the change in order to fit what (he believed to be) the facts.

---

[11] *Adversus Iudaeos* 13.   [12] Mark 8: 31, 9: 31, and 10: 34.
[13] Mark 14: 58.   [14] As reported in Jonah 1: 17.
[15] Matt. 12: 40.

For applying the quotation from Jonah literally would mean that Jesus was raised on the Monday (after three days *and* three nights). Yet, of course, Matthew thought that Jesus was raised on the Sunday morning,[16] after only two nights 'in the heart of the Earth'. And indeed his quoting the text from Jonah, an extremely inaccurate prediction of what he believed to be the day of the Resurrection, casts considerable doubt on whether he even thought of the text from Hosea as a prediction of the Resurrection. I conclude that neither Mark nor Matthew can be accused of claiming that the Resurrection occurred on the third day merely in order to fit Hosea 6: 2. Of course, earlier Christians might have made the claim in order to do so, but in that case it is surprising that Matthew quoted Jonah, and no writer quoted Hosea 6: 2. And, as I have already noted, 1 Corinthians 15: 4 appears to be part of an early creed cited by Paul; and one which he cited having discussed what happened with Peter and James within a very few years indeed of the events in question. All of that makes it likely that even if 'on the third day' is an (unacknowledged) citation of Hosea 6: 2, it was cited because it fitted the facts believed to be such for other reasons.

Many rabbinic passages of the third century AD associate Hosea 6: 2 with the resurrection of the dead, and with the idea that God will not allow the righteous to remain in distress for more than three days.[17] But note that this association is made in a general context where exact prediction is not at stake, and that the text from Jonah is also quoted in several of these passages. So if this association was already there early in the first century, this general idea could have been extrapolated as easily to yield a Monday resurrection as a Sunday resurrection. But in all four Gospels that the tomb was discovered to be empty on the first day of the week is central to those stories. I conclude that there is no reason to suppose that the 'third day' tradition was derived from Old Testament texts rather than the latter being found as (somewhat weak, in the case of Jonah) predictions of what was believed on other grounds.

Given that the Eucharist was celebrated on a Sunday in commemoration of the Resurrection, a further interesting question then arises: who in those very early days decided that the Eucharist was to

---

[16] Matt. 28: 1.

[17] See H. K. MacArthur, 'On the Third Day', *New Testament Studies*, 18 (1971–2), 81–6.

be celebrated on a Sunday? One obvious explanation is that some very early gathering of apostles decided, in view of what they believed to have happened on a Sunday, that Sunday would be the most appropriate day on which to hold regular worship in the form in which Jesus instituted it at the Last Supper. But we find no hint in the New Testament of such a decision being taken,[18] analogous to the reported decisions of the apostles about the conditions under which Gentiles were to be admitted to the Church.

The New Testament contains quite a number of hints in favour of a different answer to the 'who decided?' question. A number of the Resurrection appearances of Jesus to disciples together are associated with a meal at which Jesus presided or was present.[19] The descriptions of these occasions have associated with them the Eucharistic phrases which St Paul and the synoptic Gospel writers record in their accounts of the institution in 1 Corinthians 11 and Luke 22; Luke 24: 43 speaks of Jesus 'breaking bread' and Luke 24: 35 of his being 'known' in 'the breaking of bread'. Luke 24: 43 speaks of Jesus 'taking' the fish; John 21: 13 speaks of Jesus 'taking' and 'giving' the bread and 'giving' it to his disciples and doing 'the same with' the fish. (Literally, he gave the fish 'in a like way' (ὁμοίως); see Luke 22: 20: ὡσαύτως.) Although only John 21 (and not John 20) mentions a meal, the author of the main body of the fourth Gospel (including John 20) was unwilling to record the Eucharistic details of the Last Supper although the wealth of Eucharistic references earlier in the Gospel shows his clear knowledge of them. As I argued in Chapter 7, St John's unwillingness in his chapter 13 to record the details of the original Last Supper may be attributed to his awareness that this Christian readers would already know the details of the rite by heart, and to his desire that non-Christians should not be given details which would allow them to parody the sacred rite—*disciplina arcani*; and consequently his preference for telling a story that showed the 'true meaning' of the Eucharist. Hence it is not to be expected that he would mention a Sunday meal of Eucharistic character explicitly.

[18] It was not, for example, a matter that concerned the 'Council of Jerusalem' of Acts 15.

[19] On particular occasions, see Mark 16: 14; Luke 24: 30, 35, 43; John 21: 13; and in general, see Acts 10: 41. O. Cullmann (*Essays on the Lord's Supper* (Lutterworth Press, 1958), 11–12) understands Acts 1: 4, speaking of Jesus 'staying' with his apostles, συναλι-ζόμε υος, as 'taking salt' with them, and so referring to a meal.

But note that the two appearances which St John records, to the disciples as a group, are both Sunday appearances.[20] All of this suggests an explanation of the universality of the tradition of Sunday celebration—not merely in the belief that Jesus rose on Sunday, but in the beliefs of the apostles (true or false) that they had joined with Jesus in post-Resurrection Eucharists, which he led them to understand should continue on Sundays because he had risen on a Sunday.[21] It would also explain their conviction not merely that the tomb was empty on the Sunday, but that the Resurrection had occurred then and not on the Saturday.[22]

So there is some reason to suppose that the universal custom of Sunday Eucharist derives from (what seemed to the disciples to be) the immediate post-Resurrection practice and command of Jesus himself. But whichever detailed account of the early origin of the Sunday Eucharist is accepted, it constitutes one further piece of

[20] St Matthew's account of post-Resurrection events, of course, does not include even the hint of a meal, but there is some reason to think that even he was aware of a post-Resurrection Eucharist. The three synoptic Gospels and 1 Cor. contain accounts of the institution at the Last Supper so similar in words to each other that it is reasonable to suppose that they were used at subsequent celebrations. The three Gospels all include the words of Jesus to the effect that he will not 'drink again of the fruit of the vine until the kingdom of God comes'. These words would not have been preserved as part of Eucharistic celebration unless some common meaning or other was attached to them by the Christian communities which used them. Now the Lucan tradition mentioned earlier records that Jesus did eat and drink (Acts 10: 41) with the disciples after the Resurrection (and I have given reasons for thinking of such meals as Eucharists). Hence Luke must have thought of those as occasions when Jesus drank again of the fruit of the vine. True, the vast majority of commentators interpret Jesus as vowing to abstain from the fruit of the vine until some final, more distant establishment of his kingdom. But whatever Jesus may have meant by his words, it is hard to suppose that St Luke could have so understood them unless he also supposed that no wine was drunk by Jesus on any of the occasions when Jesus ate and drank after his Resurrection. But it is not plausible to suppose that St Luke did suppose that: wine was an ordinary enough drink, and above all to be drunk on an occasion of a new meal with old friends; and, further, I have given some reason to suppose that he thought of some of these meals as Eucharists. So the post-Resurrection meals must be what the phrase 'until the kingdom of God comes' was seen by St Luke as referring to. And, though I admit to some hesitation about this, it seems plausible to suppose that St Matthew would have attributed the same meaning to his similar phrase and seen it as referring to a post-Resurrection meal (and, since the 'vow of abstinence' was made in a Eucharistic context, to a Eucharist).

[21] It is true that if there had been one formal Eucharist at which all eleven disciples were present on the first Easter evening, most of the Gospels would inevitably have mentioned it. (See the objection in Bauckham, 'The Lord's Day', 235.) But this is reason merely for supposing that the first post-Resurrection Eucharists did not involve all the disciples and were occasions somewhat unexpected for their participants—both points made in the Gospels (see both the road to Emmaus, and John 21).

[22] I give an additional explanation of this conviction in Ch. 11.

evidence, either that witnesses found the tomb empty on the first Easter Sunday, or that witnesses believed that they had seen, and probably eaten and drunk with, Jesus on or shortly after that day; and hence constitutes further evidence for the Resurrection itself.

The Unexpectedness of the Resurrection

The Resurrection, like other features of the life and death of Jesus, was unexpected. The disciples did not expect that Jesus would rise from the dead.[23] That comes over clearly from so much in the New Testament. It may or may not be the case that, as Mark claims, during his ministry (before its last week) Jesus predicted his Passion and his Resurrection; but if so, the latter part of the prediction fell on deaf ears. The women went to the tomb to anoint the body of Jesus, not to check whether he was risen. And the others did not visit the tomb at least until the women told them that it was empty. The message of the angels at the tomb was good news, and, all the accounts agree, highly unexpected. The disciples at first did not believe the women's report: their words appeared as idle talk and 'they did not believe them',[24] and they still 'were disbelieving in their joy'[25] when, it seemed to them, they saw him. John tells how Thomas did not believe that the 'other disciples' had seen Jesus;[26] and in this story Thomas may represent further disciples as well. The Marcan appendix reports similar disbelief.[27] Although subsequently the disciples discovered that the Resurrection had significance, and had been predicted (they thought) by the Old Testament, they had not understood the Old Testament to make such a prediction before it happened. Jesus needed to explain these things to the disciples on the road to Emmaus. 'Oh, how foolish you are and slow of heart to believe all that the prophets have declared,' was the rebuke of Jesus to the disciples who expressed their amazement at the empty tomb. 'Was it not necessary that the Messiah should suffer these things and then enter into his glory?' Then beginning with Moses and all the prophets he interpreted to them the things about himself in all the

---

[23] '[Jesus'] disciples did not expect him to arise from the dead any more than their contemporaries expected the Messiah to do so' (Geza Vermes, *Jesus and Jew* (SCM Press, 1994), 20).

[24] Luke 24: 11.   [25] Luke 24: 41.

[26] John 20: 25.   [27] Mark 16: 11, 13.

Scriptures.[28] And speaking afterwards to the Eleven, Jesus claimed to have done this explaining before the Crucifixion; but he went on to do it again: 'Then he opened their minds to understand the scriptures; and he said to them, "Thus it is written that the Messiah is to suffer and rise from the dead on the third day" '.[29] John also comments that, when the disciples saw the empty tomb, 'as yet they did not understand the scripture, that he must rise from the dead'.[30]

All of which powerfully indicates that the disciples did not force themselves to believe in the Resurrection because they expected it. (If they had expected it, they would have given themselves credit for doing so.) And very few passages in the Old Testament are naturally interpreted as predicting a resurrection, which is why no one else predicted it. 'All the prophets testify about him,'[31] declared Peter in a sermon in Acts. And, as I have claimed earlier, there are Old Testament passages which it is not unnatural to think of as predicting, or at any rate as describing 'types', of a Messiah (or other similar figure) who taught and suffered. But rose from the dead? The few passages quoted in the New Testament include Jonah liberated from the whale after three days.[32] And, as I noted earlier, there does seem to be an implicit reference to the passage in Hosea 'after two days he will revive us; and on the third day he will raise us up, that we may live before him'[33] in one or two places, including, for example, by Jesus in his instructions, according to Luke, to the disciples after his Resurrection.[34] Then there is Psalm 16, 'You will not abandon my soul to Hades, or let your Holy One experience corruption,' which Peter quoted in his sermon in Acts.[35] Then there are quotations emphasizing the victory of a holy one after defeat or rejection, especially Psalm 118's 'the stone which the builders rejected is become the head of the corner';[36] but no one previously had interpreted any of these passages to predict the Resurrection from the dead of a man executed for a crime. When the disciples believed it had happened, they searched the Old Testament for proof texts and they believed that Jesus himself helped them to do so.[37]

---

[28] Luke 24: 25–7.
[29] Luke 24: 44–6.
[30] John 20: 9.
[31] Acts 10: 43.
[32] Jonah 1: 17. For discussion of this passage, see pp. 166–7.
[33] Hosea 6: 2. See my discussion of this in pp. 165–7.
[34] Luke 24: 46.
[35] Ps. 16: 10, as quoted in Acts 2: 27.
[36] Ps. 118: 22, quoted in various places including Acts 4: 11, immediately after a statement that God raised Jesus from the dead.
[37] Luke 24: 45.

Whether or not individual Old Testament texts predicted the Resurrection, the first Christians found significance in it *after* they had come to believe that it had happened, as I shall bring out in Chapter 12.

Not Evident to All

Jesus did not present himself after his Resurrection to Caiaphas or Pilate or 'to all the people, but to us who were chosen by God as witnesses, and who ate and drank with him after he rose from the dead', claimed Peter in Acts.[38] There is a contrast between the (purported) Resurrection, of which the sole public evidence was the absence of a body, which, the Jews claimed, had a non-miraculous explanation; and the miracle done immediately after the Resurrection by Peter, of making the man 'lame from birth' to walk and indeed leap.[39] With regard to the letter, 'it is obvious to all who live in Jerusalem that a notable sign has been done through [Peter and John]; we cannot deny it', complained the council of 'rulers, elders and scribes' including Caiaphas.[40]

That Jesus did not appear to everybody is a common objection to the Resurrection. If he really wanted to convince people, why didn't he set about it seriously? To answer that question we must return to the point made in Chapter 2 about the whole point of the human drama on Earth itself: to enable us 'to choose over a significant period of time the kind of people we are to be . . . and to choose how to influence the kind of other people there are to be . . . and the kind of world in which we are to live'. For this purpose, we saw that God must put a certain 'epistemic distance' between himself and human beings. He must not make his presence and his intentions for us too obvious. The point of his intervention in human history was to help us to make the right choices by making available atonement and teaching; to encourage us, but not to overwhelm us so that we have no options left. Otherwise, he would have abandoned his method for dealing with humanity evident in the pre-Christian era. So it must not be too obvious, at any rate to most people, that he has intervened. But there must be evidence of it which can help us; and it is good that some should have access to that evidence and then be able

---

[38] Acts 10: 41.　　[39] Acts 3: 1–10.　　[40] Acts 4: 5–6.

(if they so choose) to help others to know about God's intervention. If God made his intervention equally evident to all, then none would be able to help others to learn about it. And it is surely a good thing that they can. If he shows himself only to chosen witnesses, then they can tell others about it. As a result, others will have quite a bit of evidence of what God has done and taught, which they can utilize to make themselves fitted for God's friendship; but they will still not have the overwhelming evidence that would make free choice impossible.

11

Rival Theories of what Happened

IF JESUS was not raised bodily from the tomb, and yet, as I have argued, the disciples in general believed that he was, what did happen to the body? What alternatives are there and how plausible are they? The possible alternatives can be divided exhaustively into five. I take them in order of (what I judge to be) decreasing improbability.

1. *Jesus did not die on the Cross*. He was only half-dead when taken down from the Cross, and he revived in the cool of the tomb. Mark tells us of Pilate's surprise that Jesus had died after a mere six hours on the Cross.[1]

This theory has very large difficulties. First, of course, the soldiers and those who buried Jesus would have taken some care to see that he was dead. Secondly, how did Jesus escape from the linen cloth in which he was wound and push away the stone from the tomb, being so enfeebled? He must have needed help, and that entails deceit by some of the disciples. (For difficulties with that suggestion, see below.) Thirdly, he could not have been responsible for the Resurrection appearances. His enfeeblement would be obvious, and he could not then (being but an ordinary human) have appeared to vanish, pass through doors, etc. So the Resurrection appearances would be mass illusions. (For difficulties with that suggestion, see also below.) And finally, what then happened to Jesus? If he died fairly immediately, again more deception would have been required by those who knew that he had escaped the empty tomb, to bury the body. If he continued to live, is it really plausible to suppose that he would have taken no further interest in the mushrooming move-

---

[1] Mark 15: 43–5.

ment which his Passion and apparent Resurrection had inspired? Would he (in view of what we know about him from the Gospels) really have colluded with such massive deception? Now it is certainly logically possible that this theory is true, but the improbabilities required in the light of the four difficulties are so large that the total improbability is enormous.

2. *The body remained in the tomb*, but the disciples misidentified the tomb. There was an empty tomb, which gave rise to the legend of the Resurrection, but it was not the tomb of Jesus. (None of the Eleven nor any of the women who were the first to find the empty tomb themselves buried Jesus.)

The three synoptic Gospels agree that Joseph of Arimathea (no doubt with some help) buried Jesus; John states that Joseph buried Jesus with the help of Nicodemus. Matthew describes Joseph as 'rich' and 'a disciple'; Mark as 'a respected member of the council, who was also waiting himself expectantly for the kingdom of God'. Luke echoes Mark, adding that Joseph 'had not agreed to [the Jews'] plan and action'; and John describes him as a secret disciple. Matthew and Mark describe the tomb as 'hewn in the rock'; Luke and John as a 'new tomb'; Matthew describes it as Joseph's 'own new tomb'. In total opposition to this unanimous tradition Lüdemann has suggested that in fact Jesus may have had a quite different kind of burial—a 'dishonourable' one.[2] His sole ground for this suggestion, as far as I can see, is that the Johannine account of the burial seems to contain an inconsistency. John 19: 31 reports that 'the Jews' asked Pilate that the legs of Jesus and the two criminals be broken, so that, being dead, the three might be taken away. And, of course, the soldiers commissioned to perform this task found Jesus dead already. John 19: 38 then, seems to start all over again: Joseph of Arimathea 'asked Pilate to let him take away the body of Jesus. Pilate gave him permission.' 'The incompatibility of the two accounts cannot be denied.'[3] Hence Lüdemann suggests, in view of the (to him) clear genuineness of the first account, the invented nature of the second. However, it seems to me quite unobvious that there is an incompatibility here at all. The first request is for the Crucifixion to be brought to a quick end, a request which John needs to include in

---

[2] 'There are indications that Mark was confronted with the tradition of a dishonourable burial and reinterpreted this' (G. Lüdemann with A. Ozen, *What Really Happened to Jesus* (SCM Press, 1995), 20).

[3] Ibid. 23.

order to introduce the event of the blood and water streaming from the pierced side of Jesus.[4] This is an event which John thinks enormously important, and so his great emphasis on the eyewitness testimony to it.[5] The second request concerns what shall happen to the body, a quite different issue. Because of the enormous theological significance which John attributes to the consequences of the first request, I would urge that if (which I don't accept) there is any incompatibility between the two accounts, it is the first one which, containing much peculiar to John, should be dismissed, as a device introduced merely in order to explain why Jesus' side was pierced. Anyway, it seems very odd that a scholar such as Lüdemann should give such significance to a possible incompatibility in a detail of the Johannine account when none such is found in the earlier synoptic accounts. (John, as we saw in Chapter 4, is traditionally regarded by more liberal scholars as an unreliable historical source in comparison with the synoptics.) However, Mark certainly suggests two stages in the process of the request. First Joseph asks for the body.[6] Then the centurion is asked if Jesus is already dead (and most probably this involved the centurion being summoned from the scene), and then the body is handed over.[7] No incompatibility here, but a clear basis for two stages.

The synoptic Gospels have, of course, an implicit answer to the accusation that the location of the tomb was misidentified. They all claim that several women watched the Crucifixion and the burial from a distance, and deliberately noted the place.[8] This claim may well have been included in the Gospels for apologetic purposes—to rebut such an accusation. But that is little ground for supposing it to be false, and it is extremely probable that women would have noted the burial place. The male disciples clearly feared arrest. They all fled at the arrest of Jesus, according to the synoptists;[9] and even if Peter or one or two of the others tried to follow some of the events, they would have kept a very low profile. The women were clearly far less liable to be arrested, and equally clearly were devoted to Jesus. Of course, they would have wanted to follow the events and note where he was buried.

It is of course just possible, nevertheless, that they all misremembered exactly which of several similar tombs was that of Jesus. But

---

[4] John 19: 34.   [5] John 19: 35.   [6] Mark 15: 43.
[7] Mark 15: 45.   [8] Matt. 27: 61; Mark 15: 47; Luke 23: 55.
[9] Matt. 26: 56; Mark 14: 50.

then the disciples would certainly have made their own independent inquiries if there were any other tombs which might conceivably be confused with the tomb of Jesus. And above all Joseph, who at any rate had the use of the tomb and may have owned it (and his helpers, including perhaps Nicodemus), would not just have left the real tomb (whose identity they certainly knew) uninspected for the next thirty years, when he heard rumours of the Resurrection. Of course, Joseph might at that stage have been party to a deception, but that would be an additional improbability (of which see below) to the improbability of misidentification of the location both by the women and by the disciples who checked their report. And all of that on top of the Resurrection appearances. So I find it immensely improbable that the whole legend of the Resurrection arose from a misidentification of the tomb.

It is sometimes pointed out that there is no evidence, at any rate a few decades later, that there was a cult of the tomb of Jesus; and that has suggested to some that people then did not know where it was. By contrast, Hegesippus (c. AD 180) records that James, the Lord's brother, was buried 'on the spot where his tombstone is still remaining, by the Temple'.[10] There may have been a cult at this latter place, but there is no evidence of it. The obvious traditional explanation of the absence of a cult of the tomb of Jesus is that the very early Christians thought that Jesus was risen, and so no special significance would attach to a tomb. Tombs are only venerated because of what they contain (bones). If the situation in the AD 80s had been that Christians appeared uncertain about where Jesus had been buried, there would have been no need for the Jewish enemies to circulate the story that the disciples had stolen the body (as Matthew 28: 15 records that they did); it would have been sufficient to refer to the obviously confused character of the Christian story.

Finally, it is worth mentioning in this connection the story in St Matthew of Pilate approving a Jewish request to send soldiers to guard the tomb—soldiers who did guard the tomb, but fled when something happened late on the Saturday or early on the Sunday (and here Matthew inserts his account of the Resurrection), and told the chief priests what had happened.[11] Most commentators treat this

---

[10] Cited in Eusebius, *Ecclesiastical History* 2. 23.
[11] Matt. 27: 62–6 and 28: 11–15, between which Matthew inserts his account of the Resurrection.

story as having no historical basis. For myself, I find it quite probable that it has the historical core that Pilate sanctioned a guard and
the guard fled when something happened. My reason is that Pilate
had very good reason to do just this. Jesus had been crucified on a
charge of treason. Pilate may well have thought of the charge as
trumped up and that Jesus' 'kingship' was not a threat to Roman
power; still, it would be a bad example to others to show compassion
by handing over the body to Jesus' family for a normal burial, let
alone handing it over to Jesus disciples, who might use it to
strengthen a cult (which would lead to further trouble with the
Jewish leaders). Roman governors tended to treat the bodies of those
crucified for treason differently from the bodies of those executed on
other charges.[12] There is, therefore, some reason to suppose that the
body would not have been handed over to Jesus' family or disciples
for a normal burial; handing it over to a significant Jew who was
probably not a disciple of Jesus[13] was as far as Pilate was prepared to
go. There was, therefore, a danger that the body might be stolen by
the family or disciples and given a normal burial, and even used to
strengthen a cult. And also, the Jewish leaders might well have
reminded Pilate that Jesus at his trial had threatened to come 'on the
clouds of heaven'. So a guard to prevent the body from being stolen
would seem a natural precaution. There was no point in handing it
over to Joseph of Arimathea if it was going to be handed over immediately to extremists. But, of course, Roman manpower was scarce,[14]
and a guard could only be posted for a limited period. Yet clearly the
burial of Jesus by Joseph was a hurried one (in order to complete it
before the sabbath), and a more permanent arrangement may well
have been envisaged, dependent upon whether there were signs of
trouble from Jesus followers; meanwhile, a guard might seem appropriate.

Part of the reluctance of commentators to accept this story arises,
I suspect, from their reluctance to accept some of the more miraculous details in Matthew's account of what, it is implied, the guard
saw (an earthquake, an angel rolling away the stone and speaking)
and reported. But, given that Matthew 28: 1–10 (Matthew's account
of the Resurrection) has been interpolated into the story of the

---

[12] See Raymond E. Brown, *The Death of the Messiah* (Doubleday, 1994), 1207–9.

[13] See ibid. 1121–41.

[14] For argument that, if this story is basically true, the guard which Pilate authorized
was a guard of Roman soldiers, not a guard of Jewish troops, see ibid. 1294–6.

guard,[15] there is no need to suppose that the original story is telling us that the guard saw, let alone reported to the chief priests, everything recorded in Matthew 28: 1–10. An earthquake (Matt. 28: 2) would have been quite sufficient to get them to flee,[16] or they might, indeed, simply have been asleep and, waking to find the corpse gone, have run away.

Brown sees it as 'a major argument' against the historicity of the guard story that 'the evangelists would have had to explain how the women hoped to get into the tomb if there was a guard placed there possibly to prevent entry'.[17] But, if Mark is to be believed, they were concerned about getting entry anyway, asking themselves 'who will roll away the stone for us from the entrance of the tomb?'[18] They may not have known that there was a guard, but if they had known, that would probably not have deterred them. They might very well have believed that they could persuade the guard to help them to roll away the stone and let them anoint the body. The purpose of the guard was surely not to 'prevent entry' but to prevent the corpse from being removed. (Many other women in history have believed that they could persuade guards of various kinds to allow them to do various things, legal or not quite legal.)

If there is the minimal historical content to the story of the guard which I have suggested, it will be yet further evidence against the suggestion that the tomb was misidentified: the guard would have been taken by the Jews to the right tomb and checked that the right corpse was in it before they guarded it. Or, at any rate, this would have happened barring considerable improbable coincidences. However, the case against misidentification is, I suggest, very strong, even without bringing in the story of the guard. This minimal historical content would also provide a further explanation for the disciples' conviction that the Resurrection occurred on the Sunday morning, rather than at some time on the Saturday, for it was on the Sunday that something happened (probably an earthquake) to make the guards flee. The disciples could have known that, and plausibly attributed the Resurrection to the time at which the 'something happened'. But, as I argued in the last chapter, they probably had as

---

[15] See ibid. 1301–4.

[16] Earthquakes were well known in that region, and an earlier earthquake on the Friday is recorded separately by Matt. 27: 51–2.

[17] Brown, *The Death of the Messiah*, 1311.

[18] Mark 16: 3.

well a quite different reason for claiming that the Resurrection occurred on the Sunday morning.

If Jesus really died, and the tomb was correctly identified by some of his disciples, and the disciples in general believed that Jesus was risen, the only alternative to their view is that the body of Jesus was removed from the tomb (in a way unknown to many of the disciples) soon after its burial. If the traditional Christian account is false, this seems to me the most likely alternative. Under this heading there are three possibilities: that it was removed by enemies of Jesus, by grave-robbers, or by some friends of Jesus.[19]

3. *The body was stolen by enemies of Jesus.* Presumably these would have been Jewish enemies, and their motive would have been to prevent an honourable burial and to prevent a cult from building up around the corpse. The overwhelming difficulty of this hypothesis is that, once the Christian movement got going, as clearly it did within a year or so, proclaiming that Jesus was 'risen', the enemies would have produced the body to show that he was not risen. They did not do so. If they had forgotten where they had put it, or were unable to recover it (not very likely within a year), at least they would have told their story. But they did not do so. The enemies' version was that the disciples had stolen the body,[20] which it would not have been if they could have produced witnesses[21] who claimed to have stolen the body, or even, if they were unwilling to produce

[19] Relevant to the suggestion that the body was removed without the permission either of the Roman authorities or of Jesus' family, and so unlawfully, is the inscription found at Nazareth, issued by a Caesar, declaring that graves should remain in perpetuity. Those who violate burials, it declares, include both those who cast out bodies and/or 'with malicious deception' transfer them to other places; and it threatens capital punishment for this crime. This inscription has been the subject of a large number of articles in view of the fact that it was found at Nazareth (though not necessarily originating there), and that it might be thought to be prompted by the disappearance of the body of Jesus. (On this, see Brown, *The Death of the Messiah*, 1293–4. The latest article discussing it is A. Giovanni and M. Hirt, 'Inscription de Nazareth: Nouvelle interpretation', *Zeitschrift für Papyrologie und Epigraphie*, 124 (1999), 107–32.) Majority opinion among experts seems, however, to be that this inscription has no connection with Jesus, and indeed that the Caesar concerned was Augustus, and so the inscription is to be dated well before the time of the Crucifixion. It does, however, indicate that removing bodies was prevalent (though I remain puzzled about why this would normally involve 'malicious deception'), and also that it was a very dangerous thing to do.

[20] Matt. 28: 15.

[21] The Roman authorities would surely have pardoned such witnesses from any penalty for their crime, in view of the fact that their testimony would put an end to an unwanted cult; and the Jewish authorities would have been only too keen to negotiate such a deal.

the thieves, produced witnesses who could testify that that was what happened. If the thieves felt strongly enough about the danger of a cult of Jesus to steal the body, they would have taken some steps to proclaim a minimally authenticable account of what happened, instead of circulating an uncheckable rumour that the disciples had stolen the body.

Further, if enemies had stolen the body, there is no remaining reason to doubt the Gospel story of a visit by the women to the tomb on the Sunday morning when they found it empty. They would have reported it. As I mentioned earlier, I find it implausible to take Mark's comment that the women 'told nothing to anyone' to imply that they didn't tell *any*one at all that the grave was empty for weeks. And even if they didn't, someone (one of the disciples at least, or Joseph of Arimathea) would have sought to visit the tomb soon enough and found it empty. If the disciples suspected that enemies had taken the body (which they would have done but for the appearances occurring very soon indeed), they would have asked Joseph of Arimathea what had happened, and he would have complained to Pilate, since Pilate's instructions on the disposal of the body would have been violated, in the hope of securing the body. Whatever the cause of the absence of the body, the story of the empty tomb would have circulated quickly round Jerusalem. Unless the disciples had claimed (however hesitantly) within a month or so that Jesus was risen (because they had seen him), their enemies could have said later, 'That's not what you thought at first.' But again, there is not the slightest trace of scope for this kind of accusation: all the Gospel accounts indicate an immediacy between the discovery of the empty tomb and enough of the miraculous to convince some that Jesus was risen. But then my suggestion above that enough time might have elapsed for thieves to forget where they had put the body is overgenerous. Rumours of Resurrection could have been defeated very quickly by producing the body if enemies had stolen it; and that would have been the end of the Christian movement. A further piece of evidence against this suggestion is the assertion that, at a very early stage before the martyrdom of Stephen, 'a great company of the priests were obedient to the faith'.[22] If the body had been stolen by the enemies of Jesus, the Temple priests would be the people most likely to know about it.

---

[22] Acts 6: 7.

4. *The body was stolen by grave-robbers.* Grave-robbing was certainly common in the ancient world. But the normal motive for it was to steal the valuables buried with the body, often valuables which the deceased had used in life. Hence, while robbing the tombs of the Pharaohs was very common, robbing the tombs of ordinary Egyptian people was much less common, for their 'valuables' were far less valuable. But it is extremely unlikely that there were any valuables at all in this tomb. Jews did not normally bury valuables; and this was a hurried burial of a crucified criminal, buried by a stranger who would not have had access to such associated valuables. And if there were such valuables, it would have been they, not the body, which would have been stolen. The body would probably not even have been anointed.[23] The synoptists all imply a hurried burial, and Mark and Luke plausibly explain the women going to the tomb on the Sunday morning by their intention to anoint the body. Mark reports Jesus as saying of the woman who poured costly ointment over him in Bethany two or three days before the Crucifixion that 'she has anointed my body aforehand for the burying'.[24] It was merely wrapped hurriedly in a burial cloth. John claims that Joseph and Nicodemus did anoint the body before its burial. But I read the balance of evidence on this against John, leading to a suspicion of misremembering. True, if grave-robbers in search of more valuable things had broken into the tomb, they might have wanted the burial cloth. But then they would have unwound it, probably on the spot or at any rate not far away, and then the naked body would have been found. Those who found it would have had no motive for keeping it secret unless they were enemies or disciples. If they were the former, they would have revealed their knowledge at a later date. If they were disciples, the situation is tantamount to the suggestion to be discussed below that some of the disciples stole the body.

This fourth hypothesis is automatically ruled out if we accept St John's account that the grave clothes were found in the tomb, an account which seems detailed and so more likely to be historical in including the detail that 'the napkin that was upon [Jesus'] head' was 'not lying with the linen clothes, but rolled up in a place by itself'.[25] Now John may be theologizing here; his telling us that the grave clothes remained in the tomb may be his way of contrasting the

---

[23] For arguments on this, see Brown, *The Death of the Messiah*, 1242–79.
[24] Mark 14: 8.   [25] John 20: 7.

Resurrection of Jesus, where Jesus body acquired new powers, being able to pass through grave clothes, with the resuscitation of Lazarus,[26] where he remained bound by the grave clothes from which he had to be freed. Believing that the risen Jesus had supernatural powers, he may have symbolized it by inserting this detail for which he had no direct historical evidence of witnesses. Maybe. But it is difficult to see the theological significance of the napkin being rolled up separately, and that suggests a historical origin for the whole story which in no way contradicts anything in the synoptists. However, I would not put too much weight on this piece of evidence since John's details *may* have had a deep theological significance for him which it is not now possible to discern, though recent majority opinion holds that the similar verse in Luke[27] stating that the grave clothes remained in the tomb is original to Luke and hence an independent tradition on this matter.

5. *The body was stolen by friends of Jesus*, who concealed their act from most of the disciples. Barring the traditional account, this seems to me by far the most probable account. By far the most plausible way of filling this account out would be that the women, early at the tomb on the Sunday morning according to all four Gospels, removed the body, and then told the other disciples that the tomb was empty. That disciples removed the body was the official Jewish version of what happened. What motive could the women have had? They obviously all had a deep personal devotion to Jesus, and might have wanted to have his body near to them. Above all, they might have considered that he ought to have a proper burial in the family vault in Nazareth. They might have suspected that the burial by Joseph was only a temporary arrangement, and the Jewish and Roman authorities might do worse things to the body, e.g. throw it in some common criminal grave.

But, while they had good motives for removing the body, they

---

[26] John 11: 44.

[27] Luke 24: 12 records that Peter saw the linen cloths in the tomb. This verse (along with a number of other verses in chs. 22 and 24, known as the 'Western non-interpolations') is not found in the Western family of texts. It is, with the others, however, found in the recently discovered P[75]. The most recent textual commentary on the New Testament states that 'a majority of the Committee regarded [Luke 24: 12] as a natural antecedent to ver. 24, and was inclined to explain the similarity with the verses in John as due to the likelihood that both evangelists had drawn upon a common tradition' (B. M. Metzger (ed.), *A Textual Commentary on the Greek New Testament*, 2nd edn. (United Bible Societies, 1994)).

had no motive for keeping their actions secret from the other disciples. They too had great devotion to Jesus, and the women would surely have wanted Jesus to receive their devotion. Any burial in a family vault would be public knowledge. But even if they had other plans in order to keep a new burial secret from the Jews, how could they have wanted, or thought it right, to keep the location of the body secret from the family and especially from James, the Lord's brother, who is among the leaders of the Christian community who confessed the Resurrection and with whom Paul talked at length?

And even if they had tried to keep the theft secret from the other disciples, it is most unlikely that they would have succeeded. A body is a large item. Houses in which disciples were likely to be lodged temporarily were tiny—far too tiny to conceal a body. And if they were trying to give the body an honourable burial, they wouldn't have hidden it in places too easy of access where others might disturb it. Any tomb would either be easy of access (and so no place for them to hide it), or difficult of access for three women without help (they would have both to open and to shut such a tomb). And that, of course, raises the problem of how they could have got into the original tomb in the first place, in view of the large stone which all the Gospels agree was rolled in front of the tomb. Maybe, as I suggested above, there was an earthquake; and maybe the earthquake disturbed the stone (and if there were guards, made the guards flee). Or perhaps they sought help from some passer-by; but if they were planning to steal the body, that would have been dangerous. And if they took the risk of asking help, they would have been lucky if their secret did not become known.

Further, the highly plausible unanimous Gospel tradition is that many of the disciples did not at first believe the story of the women. Now, of course, the most natural ground for the suspicion would have been that the women had themselves been misled in some way. But if they had had the slightest grounds for suspecting deceit by the women, e.g. from their past attitude to Jesus or any apparent secret visits to unknown locations, they would surely have investigated that possibility further. And finally, it would be most unlikely that the women would have removed the grave clothes when taking away the body; and if there is any reason to believe the Johannine account of their discovery (not by the women, but by Peter and John), then that counts yet further against this fifth theory.

Conclusion

I have been arguing that on each of these five alternatives to the traditional account by themselves—neglecting background evidence about how likely God is to intervene in history and so neglecting also the prior historical evidence, and neglecting also the evidence of the appearances—it is improbable that we would have the evidence we do. Thus, to take two of the less improbable alternatives, if enemies had stolen the body, it is most improbable that the Jews would claim that the disciples had stolen it, instead of producing evidence that their own friends had done so. If Mary Magdalene and the other women had stolen the body, it would have been most improbable that James, the Lord's brother, would have been a leader of the movement affirming the Resurrection. And so on in more detail. There is also no reason to expect appearances. Psychologists, of course, have told us that people do sometimes seem to see newly departed loved ones; but visions shared by a number of witnesses are very hard indeed to document. In their simplest versions, each of these alternative 'explanatory' hypotheses fail to make the evidence probable. However, each of the alternative hypotheses could have added to it all sorts of further hypotheses: we could tell a very detailed story of how Mary Magdalene and the other women managed to steal the body, concealed it from the other disciples, led them to believe that they had not stolen the body; how some impostor dressed up to look like Jesus led various people and groups (including 'five hundred brothers and sisters at one time') to think that they saw Jesus and that he said things to them, etc. But such a story, even if it is made so elaborate as to make the evidence probable, becomes thereby highly complicated and so highly improbable a priori. Only if any other hypothesis were even more improbable should we adopt this one.

The traditional account does not have these disadvantages of complexity. If Jesus did indeed rise, then this one action would lead us to expect to find the data which I have been discussing in Part III—with no very great improbability. If the traditional account is improbable overall, that is because of its prior improbability, involving a massive violation of laws of nature, and just how improbable that makes it depends on the worth of natural theology; and on whether a Resurrection would be the sort of culmination we would expect for a life characterized by the 'prior requirements' discussed in Part II. I come in the next chapter to the issue of whether the Resurrection has this requisite significance.

12

The Significance of the Resurrection

The Concept of a Miracle Available to Other Cultures

THE RESURRECTION of Jesus, if it occurred, would constitute a massive violation of natural laws. The coming to full bodily life again of a human dead by normal criteria in such a way as to be able to appear and disappear would clearly be a violation of natural laws which only God could bring about. It is sometimes objected that the concept of a violation of a law of nature and so of a miracle as an act of God bringing about such a violation is a post-seventeenth-century concept. Hence, the argument goes, people would not have been able to recognize the Resurrection as an intervention into the natural order of things which God alone could bring about, and so the Resurrection would not have provided this kind of evidence of the Incarnation for the first sixteen centuries of Christianity. I believe this objection to be mistaken.

It is true that only since the seventeenth century has the natural order of things been seen as behaviour in accord with natural laws, and so a divine intervention upsetting that natural order would constitute a 'violation' of natural laws. But corresponding concepts existed in earlier times with different conceptual systems, concepts of states of affairs which mere natural processes could not bring about, and for which (if they occurred) a supernatural intervention would be required. The difference brought about by the introduction of the concept of law of nature lies rather in that in earlier times there were degrees of the supernatural. There were kinds of abnormal events such that if they occurred powerful magicians, or angels, or demons (or God) would have been needed to bring them about; and other kinds of events which God alone could bring about.

The picture of the natural world provided in Greek and medieval Western philosophical tradition was one in which, instead of laws of nature, there were individual things (substances) with their powers and liabilities. Instead of it being a law of nature that 'all copper expands when heated' which, as it were, operates on bits of copper to force them, when heated, to expand; it was, rather, that each bit of copper had its powers, including the power to expand, and its liabilities, including the liability to exercise that particular power when heated. Human beings, as well as natural objects, had powers (of limited kinds) to produce effects; though, as free agents, they could often choose whether or not to exercise some power. In a wide sense, Aquinas holds, a miracle is any event which is brought about by a rational agent in virtue of powers greater than the normal human ones, for example, an event brought about by demons or angels.[1] But strictly speaking, he claims, 'a miracle is that which occurs beyond the whole realm of created nature';[2] it is that which no other agent except God has the power to bring about. He lists as examples 'the Sun reverse its course'; 'the sea open up and offer a way through which people may pass'; 'to see after becoming blind'; 'to walk after paralysis of the limbs'.[3] Aquinas is aware that, through ignorance of science (of natural and human powers), we may sometimes falsely suppose events to be miraculous when they are not; he mentions a magnet attracting iron and an eclipse of the sun[4] as events which may seem falsely to the ignorant not to occur through natural causes, that is, not through the powers of natural objects. But, given that angels or demons may produce effects which the normal human cannot, I cannot see that Aquinas has any precise criterion for judging which events God alone can produce. How does he know that a powerful demon cannot make the sun reverse its course? However, the more an event beyond the powers of natural objects or humans to produce differs from events produced by the latter and has religious significance, the more he feels that one is justified in attributing it to the direct action of God; and anyway, clearly demons and

---

[1] 'Something is, however, said to be a miracle in a wide sense [*large*], if it exceeds human capability and consideration' (*Summa Theologiae* 1a.114.4).

[2] Ibid. 1a.114.4.

[3] *Summa contra Gentiles* 3.2.101.2 and 3.   [4] Ibid. 3.2.101.1 and 102.3.

angels can exert their supernatural powers only with God's consent. The resurrection of the dead is for him paradigmatically a divine intervention in the natural order.[5]

Likewise, for the writers of the New Testament, there were some supernatural events which not merely natural causes but, as far as they could judge, powerful magicians or angels could not bring about, because never before had they done so; and these agents were often at work directly producing effects. These events were, as far as they could judge, directly produced by God. Or at any rate, the more the events exceeded the powers of natural causes or ordinary human agents to produce, the more evident was God's direct action or explicit connivance involved. Thus in St John's Gospel the man born blind whose sight Jesus had restored comments, 'Never since the world began has it been heard that anyone opened the eyes of a person born blind. If this man were not from God, he could do nothing.'[6] Throughout the Gospels the healings and other good[7] events apparently beyond human powers to produce were seen as evidence of God's action through Jesus. The far more extraordinary Resurrection of Jesus would seem to his contemporaries a paradigmatic case of divine intervention into the natural order of things.

A mere revival of the soul—the soul or essential part of Jesus continuing to live and indeed manifest its presence to disciples after his death—would not serve this function. Coming to life again in a body after being dead for thirty-six hours clearly violates the laws of physiology (or constitutes an event beyond the natural powers of created things or agents). But there are no known laws about what happens to souls after death, and so we do not know whether their continuing existence or manifestation to others would violate any laws. And certainly the contemporaries of Jesus were familiar with ghosts who appeared to others. The manifestation of the presence of a person's soul would not, they would judge, necessarily constitute a divine intervention into the natural order. This sort of thing happened a lot, they might think.

---

[5] Ibid. 3.2.101.3.　　　　　　　　　　　　　　　　　　[6] John 9: 32–3.

[7] It was not merely the supernatural power involved in Jesus casting out demons, but its goodness (anti-Satanic character) which was seen as evidence that God was at work here through Jesus; see Luke 11: 14–20.

The Resurrection as God's Signature

The bodily Resurrection of Jesus (if it occurred) would be manifestly a violation of natural laws, requiring the action (or permission) of God to bring it about; and so in my terminology it would be a super-miracle; and, I have just argued, it would seem to the contemporaries of Jesus, as to the medieval Western philosophical tradition exemplified by Aquinas, to have the same kind of status, albeit differently expressed. But while the bodily Resurrection of Jesus would (if it occurred) be a super-miracle, is it the kind of super-miracle which would constitute God's authenticating signature on the life of Jesus, showing it to have fulfilled the purposes which I have described? I argue that it is. I have argued that a major reason for God to become incarnate was to provide a perfect life which would serve as an atonement for our sins. On the sacrifice model of the atonement, the sacrifice of Jesus would be Jesus giving the most valuable thing he has—his life; both a lived perfect human life, and a life laid down on the Cross—as a present to God. A recipient accepts a gift if he uses it and allows it to flourish. God accepts a life offered for us if he brings it to life again and allows it to benefit us. Our human life is an embodied life; God would accept the gift of the embodied life of Jesus by bringing him to life again in his body, that is, by bodily resurrecting him. God would accept the sacrifice by taking it away (not leaving the body in the tomb) to be (apparently) with himself, and by allowing us to plead that sacrifice in atonement for our sins. But if God is to do this, Jesus must make it clear to us that he is making available his life as a sacrifice.

On the model of the life and death of Christ as a 'penal substitute' for the punishment which was rightfully ours, or the ransom model whereby God gives Christ's life as a ransom to the Devil, the Resurrection constitutes God's signature that the penalty or ransom has been paid, in the way that the authorities let someone out of prison when his sentence has been served. On all these theories the Resurrection is not merely a *demonstration* to us that Christ has made available atonement for our sins, but it *constitutes* God's acceptance that the task has been completed.

If, further, God's purpose of identifying with our suffering and providing an example and instruction of how to live is to be fulfilled, he must show us that he is doing this. For God to bring to life someone condemned for certain teaching would be to express his approval of that teaching. And since belief in the Resurrection (and so, if it occurred, its cause—the Resurrection itself) was clearly the force which led to the spread of the Gospel throughout so much of the world, if God brought this about, his doing this constituted an intervention in history to make the life of Jesus successful. If God raised Jesus and thus gave impetus to the Church which centrally thereafter taught that Jesus was God Incarnate (which there are also independent grounds for supposing Jesus to have implied), he showed that it was God himself who had identified with our suffering. While the Resurrection would vindicate that and all the other teaching of Jesus, since a crucial element of that teaching concerned the availability for us ordinary humans of life after death, it would provide the first example of that to which it witnessed. Jesus was the forerunner. If God raised Jesus from the dead, he accepted his sacrifice and vindicated his teaching.

But, as with the Resurrection being a miracle, so with it being the kind of miracle which would constitute God's authenticating signature on the life and teaching of Jesus, the question arises that, while we can perhaps see that if it had occurred in our generation and culture, it would have constituted such a signature, could it and would it have been so recognized in earlier centuries and other cultures? I shall argue that it could be and was so recognized in first-century AD Jewish culture. And that, of course, is the crucial culture. For what constitutes a signature depends on the conventions of the time at which it is made, of what constitutes someone's unique mark of approval of something. The New Testament writers wrote down their understanding of the significance of the Resurrection, and later Christian generations accepted this from them as part of revealed truth. And while there was a tendency for later writers simply to write down phrases from the New Testament verbatim as argument for the significance of the Resurrection, some of them at least did argue for much of that significance in terms of their own thought.

I start with New Testament writers. They are very concerned to explain the significance of the Resurrection—more so than later generations. The contemporaries of Jesus had the relevant concepts to understand the Resurrection as having the kind of significance which I have ascribed to it, and they largely did so understand it. I have argued that the Resurrection would constitute God's acceptance of the perfect life of Jesus, as something which we could offer in atonement for our sins. The notion of someone making satisfaction for sin is the notion of their offering a sacrifice for sin. It is in terms of the model of sacrifice that the doctrine of the Atonement is worked out in the Epistle to the Hebrews, and is, I think, the way of expressing the doctrine which has the widest base in the New Testament. In the most primitive way of thinking about sacrifice lying behind Old Testament thought, a sacrifice is the giving of something valuable to a God who consumes it in part (by inhaling the smoke) and often gives back some of it to be consumed by the worshippers (who eat the roasted flesh).[8] The Old Testament itself does not in general think of God as literally inhaling the smoke; but the idea is there that God takes something valuable as a gift of reconciliation whose benefits he will often share with the worshippers—like, to use a humble modern analogy, the box of chocolates which one gives to one's host, who then offers one in return a choice from the box.[9] Bringing to life the crucified Jesus, showing him to humans for a short time and then taking him away, could be doing just that, paradigmatically accepting and distributing the sacrifice. But providing a continuing availability of the sacrifice would be doing it more abundantly; and the Church, in continuing to give the 'body' and 'blood' of Jesus to its members, would think of itself as doing just that. In the more general terms which I used earlier, a recipient accepts a gift if he uses it and allows it to flourish. God accepts a life if he brings it to life again and allows it to benefit as.

In the Old Testament way of thinking, the genuineness of a

---

[8] See e.g. J. Pedersen, *Israel, its Life and Culture*, rev. edn. (Oxford University Press, 1959), 299–575 (see esp. p. 359).

[9] That this understanding of sacrifice was common also in New Testament times is shown by a remark of St Paul about Temple sacrifices: 'Are not those who eat the sacrifices partners (κοινωνοί) in the altar?' (1 Cor. 10: 18). In his commentary on 1 Cor. ((A. & C. Black, 1968), 235) C. K. Barrett comments on this verse that in a sacrifice the worshippers jointly participated 'in the benefits arising from the altar; in addition, the worshippers naturally share in the spiritual benefits that the sacrifice made available. This, needless to say, was the rationale of sacrifice: those who shared in the act shared in its benefits. As Paul says, they were *partners in the altar*. To this expression there is a striking parallel (discussed by S. Aalen, "Das Abendmahl als Opfermahl im Neuen Testament", in *Novum Testamentum* vi (1963), pp. 128–52; see p. 137) in Philo (*De Specialibus Legibus* i. 221), who says that he to whom sacrifice has been offered makes the group of worshippers "partners in the altar, and of one table (with it)"—(κοινωνὸν . . . τοῦ βωμοῦ καὶ ὁμοτράπεζον). The meaning of this passage, however, appears to be that God the bountiful benefactor shares with his worshippers the good gift that they have offered him, by inviting them, as it were, to sit down at table with him. They thus have fellowship with him, and derive benefit from their meal.'

prophet (so long as he speaks in the name of the Lord[10]) is shown by his predictions being fulfilled or, more generally, his claims being shown true. Thus Deuteronomy: 'If a prophet speaks in the name of the Lord, but the thing does not take place or prove true, it is a word that the Lord has not spoken. The prophet has spoken it presumptuously; do not be frightened by it.'[11] This verse occurs at the end of a section in which Moses declares to Israel that 'the Lord your God will raise up for you a prophet like me from among your own people; you shall heed such a prophet',[12] a verse which Peter cites in reference to Jesus;[13] and it is a verse which Stephen quotes in his long speech.[14] Peter and Stephen thus see this reference to a prophet who would be shown to be one by his successful prophecy as fulfilled in Jesus.[15]

In two respects the Resurrection would indeed vindicate Jesus' teaching. First, and more obviously, it would vindicate his teaching that we all would be raised from the dead, by showing manifestly that resurrection is possible and so could happen to us. Secondly, the Resurrection of Jesus was a resurrection in which Jesus had supernatural powers (to pass through doors etc.). Now we saw in Chapter 6 that the words of Jesus at the trial cited in the three synoptic Gospels, 'You will see the Son of Man seated at the right hand of the Power, and coming with the clouds of Heaven,' which led to the high priest finding him guilty of blasphemy, have echoes elsewhere in the New Testament, indicating their genuineness. In bringing to life Jesus executed for uttering these words, with supernatural powers, God would be halfway to vindicating this eschatological status for Jesus. In vindicating some of Jesus' teaching that there is resurrection, and that the status of Jesus is a supernatural one, the Resurrection would thereby be telling us to believe the rest of his teaching. On the Old Testament understanding, it would show Jesus to be a real prophet whose message was from God. The Resurrection would

---

[10] Deut. 13: 1–3.

[11] Deut. 18: 22. Jeremiah cites the test of whether the prophecy comes to pass, to show whether it is he or Hananiah who is the true prophet (Jeremiah 28: 9).

[12] Deut. 18: 15.   [13] Acts 3: 22.   [14] Acts 7: 37.

[15] Of course, it may very well be that Jesus predicted both his Passion and his Resurrection. Mark tells us that he did so three times. But putting explicit predictions of the subsequent fate of heroes into their mouths or the mouths of others was a habit of ancient writers; and so many modern critics doubt the genuineness of those attributed to Jesus. But in so far as the evidence suggests that these predictions were really made, that would constitute further grounds for believing other claims which Jesus made.

show that God did not allow the efforts of those who killed Jesus for teaching certain things to be successful in eliminating the source of that teaching. Rather, if the Resurrection was the source of the movement which evangelized so much of the world, it would show the teaching of Jesus to be true.

So the Jewish culture nurtured on the Old Testament had the categories to recognize the Resurrection of Jesus as God's accepting an atonement and vindicating a teaching. And in fact they did (after the event) recognize it as doing just that. By Paul, by speeches of Peter in Acts, and elsewhere in the New Testament, the occurrence of the Resurrection is connected closely with forgiveness of sins which would not be available without it. In the passage where he discusses the Resurrection and its point most explicitly, St Paul writes, 'If Christ has not been raised, your faith is futile and you are still in your sins.'[16] And in a sermon reported in Acts, Paul goes on immediately after saying that Jesus had been raised, 'Let it be known to you therefore, my brothers, that through this man forgiveness of sins is proclaimed to you; by this Jesus everyone who believes is set free from all those sins from which you could not be freed by the law of Moses.'[17] Peter is quoted in a speech in Acts as saying that 'The God of our ancestors raised up Jesus, whom you had killed by hanging him on a tree. God exalted him at his right hand as Leader and Saviour that he might give repentance to Israel and forgiveness of sins.'[18] In another speech of Peter's, in Acts, immediately after his saying that Jesus had been raised, he states that, through the name of Jesus, 'everyone who believes in him receives forgiveness of sins'.[19] And in a post-Resurrection speech in Luke, Jesus himself moves quickly from 'it is written that the Messiah is to suffer and rise from the dead the third day' to 'and that repentance and remission of sins is to be proclaimed in his name'.[20] But it is not made clear in these passages how the Resurrection is connected with forgiveness of sins. For the connection we need to go to the two theological works in the New Testament which reflect on the significance of the death of Christ: St Paul's Epistle to the Romans, and the Epistle to the Hebrews.

Paul's argument in the Epistle to the Romans depends on his belief that the fact that humans die is due to the fact that they are in

---

[16] 1 Cor. 15: 17.   [17] Acts 13: 38–9.   [18] Acts 5: 30–1.
[19] Acts 10: 43.   [20] Luke 24: 46–7.

bondage to sin: they have inherited at least Adam's proneness to sin and so have sinned.[21] Hence the Resurrection of Jesus, being the overcoming of death, means that sin had lost its power. God accepted the 'sacrifice of atonement' for sin[22] made by Jesus in his death. This benefit comes to us through our baptism, whereby we are incorporated into Christ. 'All of us who have been baptized into Christ Jesus were baptized into his death',[23] in order that we shall 'no longer be enslaved to sin'.[24] But 'Christ, being raised from the dead ... death no longer has dominion over him'.[25] This means that we too who are baptized will live after our death: 'If we have died with Christ, we believe that we will also live with him'.[26] The Resurrection shows that sin has been conquered, but it effects the conquest of death; these benefits are ours through incorporation into Christ.

This argument is only going to appeal to someone who already accepts Paul's belief that death is the result of sin (and no doubt many Jews would have accepted that belief deriving from Genesis).[27] The argument of the Epistle to the Hebrews is to my mind more satisfactory in not relying on the connection, and explaining the connection explicitly in terms of the sacrifice model. Christ sacrificed himself,[28] but for us 'to bear the sins of many'.[29] The author stresses that Jesus does not go on like earthly priests offering more sacrifices, but 'when Christ had offered for all time a single sacrifice for sins, he sat down on the right hand of God'.[30] To achieve the sacrifice, Christ had to enter not into 'a sanctuary made by human hands', but 'into heaven itself, now to appear in the presence of God on our behalf'.[31] So Christ's exaltation is necessary for completion of the sacrifice. As in the old Jewish model, the sacrifice must reach God himself. In my earlier way of expressing it, the present must be

---

[21] Rom. 5: 12–14. Although many have read the whole passage (5: 12–21) of which these are the opening verses as claiming that we are guilty in the respect of the sin of Adam and we die in consequences of that guilt, I do not think that Paul is saying that. Our death is due to our sin: 'death spread to all because all have sinned' (5: 12); and hence guilt belongs to us because of our sin. See my fuller discussion in my *Responsibility and Atonement* (Clarendon Press, 1989), 206–7 n. 8.

[22] Rom. 3: 25.   [23] Rom. 6: 3.   [24] Rom. 6: 6.

[25] Rom. 6: 9.   [26] Rom. 6: 8.

[27] Gen. 2: 17 records that the Lord God told Adam: 'Of the tree of the knowledge of good and evil, you shall not eat, for in the day that you eat of it you shall die.' But Gen. 3 records that Adam and Eve ate from the tree, and hence it was part of God's sentence on Adam: 'You are dust, and to dust you shall return' (Gen. 3: 19).

[28] Heb. 9: 26.   [29] Heb. 9: 28.

[30] Heb. 10: 12.   [31] Heb. 9: 24.

received by God. We see that Christ has been exalted because the 'God of peace ... brought back from the dead our Lord Jesus, the great shepherd of the sheep, by the blood of the eternal covenant'.[32] The Resurrection shows that Jesus is exalted, no doubt in virtue of the superhuman powers which he then manifested, and his then not dying again but ceasing to live on Earth. Hence God must have accepted the sacrifice ('of the eternal covenant') and no more sacrifices are needed.

The New Testament writers also recognized that the Resurrection vindicated Jesus' teaching. It did that, in their view, because it showed that he already had (or because God then gave him) a supernatural status, as 'Son of God', however exactly that is interpreted. He was 'declared to be the Son of God ... by resurrection from the dead'.[33] It was 'impossible' for Jesus 'to be held' by death, claimed Peter in his Pentecost speech in Acts.[34] In this context of saying that Jesus had been raised, Peter goes on to say that 'God has made him both Lord and Messiah.'[35] And in the Epistle to the Philippians Paul, probably citing some earlier hymn, writes of Jesus being exalted, 'that at the name of Jesus every knee should bend, in heaven and on earth and under the earth'.[36] Just why the Resurrection showed that Jesus had this supernatural status is not spelled out, but I suppose the thinking is that in raising Jesus, when he had never raised anyone else from the dead to a life when they would not die again, God does a unique exalting act; and so recognizes a unique and exalted status. One with such a God-approved supernatural status clearly has authority in his teaching. God would not have conferred such status on someone whose teaching was badly in error. So Paul regarded a 'command' from 'the Lord'[37] as uniquely authoritative.

And, of course, the New Testament writers recognized that the very occurrence of the Resurrection confirmed a particular aspect of Jesus' teaching. Jesus shows that resurrection is possible and so offers us and others now dead the possibility thereof. Being raised, he has become 'the first fruits of those who have died'.[38] He is the 'firstborn of the dead',[39] and has 'the keys of death and of Hades'.[40]

---

[32] Heb. 13: 20.

[33] Rom. 1: 4. For discussion of whether the Greek should be translated as 'declared to be' rather than 'made to be', see p. 114.

[34] Acts 2: 24.   [35] Acts 2: 36.

[36] Phil. 2: 9–10.   [37] e.g. 1 Cor. 7: 10; contrast 7: 25.

[38] 1 Cor. 15: 20.   [39] Rev. 1: 5; Col. 1: 18.   [40] Rev. 1: 18.

I conclude that the New Testament writers had the concepts to recognize and did recognize the Resurrection of Jesus as putting God's signature on his life and death—as accepting his sacrifice and authenticating his teaching; and that, of course, will include any teaching about who he was and who had identified with our suffering.[41] Later cultures certainly recognized that the Resurrection of Jesus was evidence of his supernatural status (which they came to understand as his divinity). Thus Athanasius: '[The Greeks] were unable to forge the resurrection of their idols ... In this respect ... they have conceded the strength to Christ, so that by this also he is known by all to be the Son of God.'[42] And he sees the Resurrection as evidence that death has been destroyed: 'How would death be shown to have been destroyed unless the Lord's body had arisen?'[43] To move on some 800 years, Aquinas claims that God brings about our own resurrection and our newness of life through Christ's Resurrection[44]—that was his chosen appropriate method. And he gives two further evidential reasons for God having brought about Christ's Resurrection: 'to increase our knowledge in faith. For our faith is confirmed with regard to Christ's divinity,' and 'to increase our hope. For when we see the Christ who is our Head is risen, we hope that we too will rise again.'[45] He claims that the proofs (of his appearances including his eating with disciples) 'offered by Christ [were] sufficient both to show the truth of his Resurrection and also his glorious state',[46] adding that, while 'the individual arguments', that is, particular appearances, 'are not sufficient to show Christ's Resurrection, taken together they show it perfectly'.[47] Aquinas thus seems to be affirming that we learn about the Resurrection by normal historical means.

[41] John Barton discusses the significance of the Resurrection in his 'Why does the Resurrection of Christ Matter?', in S. Barton and G. Stanton (eds.) *Resurrection* (SPCK, 1994). He thinks that the most 'persuasive' theory about the significance of the Resurrection is as 'evidence for the type of person God is willing to eternalize'. Jesus' life being so holy, God shows us that his is the kind of life he is prepared to resurrect. He sees this idea as present 'in embryo' in Peter's Acts 10 speech connecting Jesus' being one who 'went about doing good and healing all who were oppressed by the devil' (10: 38) with him whom God raised 'on the third day' (10: 40). But I do not think that Peter is telling us that God raised Jesus simply because of his good life. For he tells us, before telling of Jesus' good life, that 'He is Lord of all' (10: 36), and that God anointed him 'with the Holy Spirit and with power' (10: 38). He did good, Peter says explicitly, because 'God was with him' (10: 38); and I think that Peter is saying that God raised him because of who he was, not because of what he did, though what he did followed from who he was.

[42] Athanasius, *De Incarnatione* 50.   [43] Ibid. 31.
[44] Thomas Aquinas, *Summa Theologiae* 3a.56.   [45] Ibid. 3a.53.1.
[46] Ibid. 3a.55.6.   [47] Ibid. 3a.55.6 ad 1.

There is, however, much less in later writers by way of argument that the Resurrection is the vehicle for the forgiveness of our sins. They tend to repeat the New Testament verses on this, but do little more. Aquinas, for example, replying to an objection that 'the passion of Christ was sufficient for our salvation', acknowledged that, 'strictly speaking, the passion of Christ achieved its effect with regard to the removal of evil; his Resurrection, however, was both the first instance and model of the good effects produced'.[48] That does not give the Resurrection quite the significance which it has with regard to atonement that it has for Paul or the writer to the Hebrews. For both of these the Resurrection was the completion of the Act of Atonement (for Paul, the overcoming of death; for the writer to the Hebrews, the completion of the sacrifice).

However, the New Testament writers, and by and large their successors, recognized the Resurrection as having the significance which I have argued that, if it occurred, it would have (if only through their verbatim citations of Scripture rather than through well-worked-out arguments); and so, in virtue of the status, it would constitute the kind of signature which God would need to put on his incarnate life, if he became incarnate. If there is a reason to expect that God will become incarnate and lead the kind of life considered in Part II, there is reason to suppose that that life would be culminated by an event somewhat like the Resurrection.

---

[48] Ibid. 3a.53.1 ad 3.

PART IV

CONCLUSION

13

The Balance of Probability

I BEGAN this book with the claim that generally available public evidence (not directly concerned with the Christian tradition) favours the hypothesis that there is a God of the traditional kind— omnipotent, omniscient, perfectly free, and perfectly good. I have not argued for this claim here, although I have done so elsewhere. I do not wish to exaggerate the strength of the evidence, and so I have claimed merely that the evidence makes it as probable as not that there is a God. I then went on to claim that a perfectly good God who saw the sin and the suffering of the human race would want to do something about it. He would want to help us to know which actions are good and which are bad (and especially which actions are obligatory and which are wrong), so that we might do good actions and by living good lives could begin to form characters suited to enjoy him for ever. He would want to help us to make atonement for our past sins in a serious way. And above all, if he has subjected us to suffering (quite a lot of it in no way the result of human sin) for the sake of good purposes, he would nevertheless want to identify with our suffering by sharing it. While the first two of these reasons are reasons why it would be good for God to become incarnate (to take a human nature and live a human life on Earth), the third plausibly makes it obligatory for him to do so. Any serious reflection on how a good creator God would react to a race of suffering and sinful creatures whom he has created must give considerable force to the claim that he must become incarnate. Again, I do not wish to exaggerate the strength of this plausibility and I suggested that it is as probable as not that God will be come incarnate.

I have suggested three reasons (or groups of reasons) why God might choose to become incarnate. If he became incarnate for all three reasons, he would need to live a perfect human life (including life under some of the worst human circumstances), provide true moral teaching, encouragement, and healing, show that he believed himself to be God Incarnate, teach that his life was a means of atonement for us, and found a Church to continue his work. I have argued in Part II that there is evidence which it would not be too improbable to find if Jesus did all of these things, and (given what we know about other prophets, summarized in Chapter 3) it is far more probable that Jesus did most of these things than that any other prophet in human history did. If God became incarnate for only two or one of these reasons—and I have argued that he had an obligation to show solidarity with our suffering—then he might not in his incarnate life do all these things; for example, he might not teach that his life was a means of atonement. However, if he became incarnate for any of these reasons, he would almost inevitably do most of these things. For example, even if he became incarnate merely to show solidarity with us, he would inevitably show us how to live, even if that was not a reason of his for becoming incarnate.

If God became incarnate as a prophet and lived such a life, he would need to put a divine signature on that life, to show his acceptance of any sacrifice, to confirm the prophet's teaching and the teaching of the resulting Church, and thereby to confirm the divinity of the prophet. To raise from the dead the prophet killed for his work would be exactly the kind of super-miracle which would provide such a signature. I have argued in Part III that there is evidence which it would not be too improbable to find if Jesus rose from the dead. But there is no other prophet in human history, apart from Jesus, with whose life there is significant evidence of such a super-miracle being connected. Hence, if God has become incarnate during past human history, it is overwhelmingly probable that it was in Jesus that he became incarnate; and it is very improbable indeed that he would have brought it about that the stated evidence should be associated with Jesus, if Jesus was not God Incarnate (for that would constitute a deception). Yet, the coincidence of there being significant evidence for a super-miracle connected with the life of the only prophet for whom there is significant evidence that he satisfied the prior requirements for being God Incarnate would also have been very improbable unless God brought it about.

It is simply not possible to investigate whether Jesus rose from the dead without taking a view about how probable it is that there is a

God likely to intervene in human history in this kind of way. If the reader thinks that all the evidence suggests there is no God of the traditional kind, or that although perfectly good he would not interfere in human history, then the detailed historical evidence about what happened in Palestine in the first century AD is perhaps not strong enough to make it probable that Jesus rose from the dead. And this despite the very striking coincidence that the one prophet in human history about whom there is the kind of evidence not too unexpected if he led the required kind of life was also the one prophet about whom there is the kind of evidence not too unexpected if his life was culminated by a super-miracle. There is significant relevant historical evidence that Jesus did satisfy the requirements, and the coincidence to which I referred must be taken seriously. If the background evidence leaves it not too improbable that there is a God likely to act in the ways discussed, then the total evidence makes it very probable that Jesus was God Incarnate who rose from the dead.

Appendix: Formalizing the Argument

Logical Probability

Almost all the argument of this book so far has been given in purely qualitative terms. I have assumed that 'natural theology makes it as probable as not that there is a God', and there is evidence which 'it would not be too improbable to find', and that 'it is far more probable' that Jesus did certain things than that any other prophet did, and so on. Let us see if we can give a sharper, more nearly numerical form to the argument. The tool for doing so is the traditional probability calculus, developed since the seventeenth century and given axiomatic form by Kolmogorov in the nineteenth century.[1] The maximum probability for an event is 1, the minimum 0, and if something is as probable as not it has a probability of ½.

There are three kinds of probability. First, there is physical (or natural) probability. The physical probability of some possible future event is a measure of the degree to which it was predetermined to happen by past events. The physical probability of an event is 1 if past events (with laws of nature) made it inevitable that it would happen. The probability is 0 if past events made it inevitable that it would not happen. But if nature is to some extent indeterministic, as quantum theory suggests, then events can have intermediate probabilities. If nature is biased in favour of some event happening (say, some atom decaying within the next forty years), then physical probability is a measure of the extent of the bias. If the physical probability of the event is ⅔, then nature is biased towards it happening twice as much as towards it not happening. Physical probability is relative to time. As time moves on towards the time of the possible occurrence of an event, so the probability of that occurrence may change.

The second kind of probability is statistical probability, which is simply a

---

[1] For full discussion of the probability calculus and its application to measuring how probable some evidence makes some hypothesis, see my *Epistemic Justification* (Clarendon Press, 2001), chs. 3 and 4.

proportion in a class, actual or hypothetical. The probability of a Londoner voting Labour in the 2001 general election just is the proportion of Londoners who voted Labour then, say 0.52. When we are dealing with a hypothetical class of events, e.g. tosses of this coin (not all of which will have been made or even could be made), then probability of an event of some kind is the proportion of events of that kind which would be generated by that process if you went on for ever. That we are talking about a statistical probability is often indicated in English by the indefinite article: the probability of 'a' toss of this coin being heads (that is, any toss chosen at random), which is not necessarily the same as the probability of the next toss being heads.

The final kind of probability which is the kind of probability with which I am concerned in this book is a measure of the extent to which one proposition makes another one likely to be true. (I only describe the other kinds of probability in order to distinguish them from this kind.) It is often called 'inductive' or 'epistemic' probability, but (in conformity with my own usage elsewhere) I shall call it logical probability, to emphasize that whether some proposition makes another one probable and by how much is a necessary truth. Once we have assembled all our evidence, whether that evidence makes it probable that a certain hypothesis is true or false cannot depend on further evidence. Whether it does or does not make it probable depends on the nature of the evidence and of the hypothesis; and we do think, for example, that there is a truth about whether a scientist's evidence (fully stated) makes a particular theory (fully stated) probable or not probable. But since it is not a contingent truth, it must be a necessary truth; and so (in a wide sense of logic) a logical matter.

It is an interesting fact that the same probability axioms can be phrased so as to cover both statistical and logical probability. (It may be that physical probability needs different axioms.) But our concern is with logical probability. Here lower-case letters 'p', 'q', 'r', etc. represent propositions, claims that something is so. '$P(p \mid q)$' means the probability that p, given q (or 'on q'). (If, for example, p is a hypothesis and q is relevant evidence, $P(p \mid q)$ is the probability of hypothesis p on evidence q.) $P(p \mid q) = 1$ then means that, given q, it is certain that p is true. $P(p \mid q) = 0$ means that, given q, it is certain p is false. Intermediate numbers indicate intermediate degrees of evidential support. The axioms of the calculus, phrased as a calculus of logical probability, then have the following form. For all p, q, r,

(1) $P(q \mid r) \geq 0$
(2) If $N(r \to q)$, $P(q \mid r) = 1$
(3) If $N \sim(p \& q \& r)$ and $\sim N(\sim r)$, $P(p \lor q \mid r) = P(p \mid r) + P(q \mid r)$
(4) $P(p \& q \mid r) = P(p \mid q \& r) P(q \mid r)$
(5) If $N(p \leftrightarrow q)$, $P(r \mid p) = P(r \mid q)$.

'$\geq$' means 'is greater than or equal to'. 'N' means 'of logical necessity'. So

'N($r \rightarrow q$)' meaning 'necessarily, if r, then q' is to be read as 'r entails q'. '~' means 'not'. '&' means 'and'. So 'p & q' means 'both p and q are true'. '$\lor$' means 'or' (in an inclusive sense). So '$p \lor q$' means 'either p is true or q is true or both are true'. '$\leftrightarrow$' means 'if and only if'. So 'N($p \leftrightarrow q$)' means 'p and q are logically equivalent'.

It is very easy to see intuitively the correctness of these axioms. Axiom 1 says that the probability of any proposition, given any other proposition, cannot be less than 0. Clearly a proposition cannot have a lower probability than one which is certainly false. Axiom 2 says that if r entails q, then given r, q is certainly true. Axiom 3 says that the probability that p or q (or both) is true, given r is the sum of {the probability that p is true, given r} plus {the probability that q is true, given r}, if r is a logical possibility and if, given r, p and q cannot both be true. Let r be a description of a normal pack from which one card is drawn, and let p be 'the card drawn is a spade', and q be 'the card drawn is a club'. Then the probability that, given that a card is drawn, it is either a spade or a club is equal to the probability that it is a spade plus the probability that it is a club. Axiom 4 is concerned with the probability that two propositions p and q are both true, given r. It says that this equals the probability that one of them (q) is true given r, multiplied by the probability that, given r and also q, the other will be true. If you toss a coin twice, the probability on your evidence (r) that you will get two heads in a row equals the probability that you will get heads first time (given r), multiplied by the probability that if you do (and also given r) you will get heads the second time. Axiom 5 says that if p and q are logically equivalent (that is, if it is logically necessary that when the one holds, the other also holds), the probability of some proposition given the one is the same as the probability of that proposition given the other.

It follows from the axioms that the maximum value of a probability is 1; and that if p is as probable as ~p, given q, P($p \mid q$) = ½. In most cases when the probability is other than 1, 0, or ½, it is not possible to allocate exact numerical values to probabilities; all that can be said is that this probability is fairly high, that one very low, that one less than this one, and so on. But, given the plausible principles which I shall describe below for attributing rough values to some probabilities, interesting conclusions will follow about the rough values of other probabilities.

Among the theorems which follow from the axioms is a crucial theorem known as Bayes's Theorem. I express it using letters 'e', 'h', and 'k' which can represent any propositions at all; but we shall be concerned with it for the case where e represents observed evidence (data), k represents 'background evidence', and h is a hypothesis under investigation.

$$P(h \mid e \& k) = \frac{P(e \mid h \& k) \, P(h \mid k)}{P(e \mid k)}$$

This theorem sets out in a formal way the factors which determine how observational evidence supports a hypothesis (or theory). The relevant points can be made easily enough in words, but less rigorously and with their implications less clear. $P(h \mid e \& k)$ may be called the posterior probability of h, that is its probability on e as well as k. The theorem brings out that a hypothesis h is rendered probable by observational evidence e and background evidence k, in so far as (1) $P(e \mid h \& k)$ (the posterior probability of e) is high; (2) $P(h|k)$ (the prior probability of h) is high; and (3) $P(e \mid k)$ (the prior probability of e) is low. Background evidence typically includes evidence about how things behave in neighbouring fields of inquiry (e.g. if you are investigating the behaviour of the inert gas argon at low temperatures, there may be background evidence about how neon, another inert gas, behaves at low temperatures). But when we are dealing with big theories of physics, and above all theories of metaphysics, there are no neighbouring fields of inquiry (since these theories purport to explain so much that there are no 'neighbouring fields' outside their scope), and so we can ignore k (in technical terms, by putting it as a mere tautology). $P(h \mid k)$ and $P(e \mid k)$ will then have values determinable a priori, dependent solely on what h and e are. We may then call $P(h \mid k)$ and $P(e \mid k)$ the intrinsic probabilities of h and e.

The first condition above ($P(e \mid h \& k)$ high) is satisfied to the extent to which you would expect to find e if h is true. Obviously a scientific or historical theory is rendered probable, in so far as the evidence is such as you would expect to find if the theory is true. However, for any e you can devise an infinite number of different incompatible theories h_n which are such that for each of them $P(e \mid h_n \& k)$ is high, but which make totally different predictions from each other for the future (i.e. predictions additional to e). Let e be all the observations made so far relevant to some theory of mechanics, let's say general relativity (GTR). Then you can complicate GTR in innumerable ways such that the resulting new theories all predict e but make wildly different predictions about what will happen tomorrow. The grounds for believing that GTR is the true theory rather than these alternative new theories will be that GTR is the simplest theory. When k is a mere tautology and so $P(h \mid k)$ is the intrinsic probability that h is true, that is, the measure of the strength of the a priori factors relevant to the probability of h, these factors are, I suggest, its scope and its simplicity. A hypothesis has large scope in so far as it makes many precise claims; and the larger the scope (that is, the more it tells us about the universe), other things being equal, the lower its intrinsic probability. But we can ignore this factor if we are comparing theories of similar scope (as I was supposing, in the GTR example), and, even when we are considering theories of differing scope, scientific examples show that simplicity is more important than scope for determining prior probability, for theories (which satisfy the other criteria well) of large scope are regarded as probable, so long as they are simple. The simplicity of a theory, like its scope, is something internal to that theory, not a matter of the relation of the theory to external evidence.

Let me illustrate the importance of the criterion of simplicity by using again the example of personal explanation (that is, a purported explanation of data in terms of the action of persons) used in Chapter 1. A detective investigating a burglary finds various clues: Jones's fingerprints on a burgled safe, much of the stolen money found in a garage of which Jones possessed the key, witnesses reporting seeing Jones in the neighbourhood of the burglary at the time when it was committed, etc. (which we summarize by e). The detective then puts forward a hypothesis (h) that Jones robbed the safe, which is such that it leads us to expect the clues that were found: (P$e \mid h$ & k) is quite high. But there are an infinite number of other hypotheses which have this property. We could suggest that the fingerprints were planted by Smith; the money stolen by Robinson, who dropped it; Brown picked it up and hid it in the garage, of which, coincidentally, Jones had the key; etc. This new hypothesis would lead us to expect the phenomena which were found just as well as does the hypothesis that Jones robbed the safe. But the latter hypothesis is rendered probable by the evidence, whereas the former is not. And this is because the hypothesis that Jones robbed the safe postulates *one* subject, Jones, doing *one* deed, robbing the safe, which leads us to expect the several phenomena which we find. The simplicity of a theory is a matter of its postulating few entities, few kinds of entity, few properties, few kinds of property, and ways of behaving which are unchanging in simple respects. The latter, if we are postulating persons as our entities, involves attributing to them purposes, beliefs, and powers which are constant over time, or only change in regular ways. If we are postulating natural laws, it involves using few mathematical terms and mathematically simple operations. Of course, many accepted scientific theories these days seem to some of us quite complicated, but they are accepted because they are simpler than any other theory which satisfies the other criteria equally well. We may have contingent background evidence k, e.g. about whether Jones has committed other crimes, which will determine the value of P($h \mid k$), the prior probability of h. But in the absence of such evidence, the prior probability of h will be its intrinsic probability and this will be largely dependent on how simple is h. (It will also depend on the scope of h in that if you were to add to the original hypothesis that Jones robbed the safe a further hypothesis—for example, that he robbed all other robbed safes in the neighbourhood—then the prior probability of the conjunction would be lower than the prior probability of the original hypothesis.)

P($e \mid k$), the prior probability of e (which for tautological k is an intrinsic probability) is a measure of how likely e is to occur if we do not assume any particular theory to be true. By Bayes's Theorem the lower is $P(e \mid k)$, the higher is the posterior probability of h $(P(h \mid e \& k))$, the probability of h on all the evidence. The normal effect of $P(e \mid k)$ in assessing the probability of any particular theory h is that e does not render h very probable if you would expect to find e anyway (e.g. if it was also predicted by the main rivals to h which had significant prior probability). It follows from the calculus that

$$P(e \mid k) = P(e \mid h \& k) \, P(h \mid k) + P(e \mid {\sim}h \& k) \, P({\sim}h \mid k).$$

The first combined term on the right-hand side $(P(e \mid h \& k) \, P(h \mid k))$ simply repeats the top line of Bayes's Theorem. So if the second combined term $(P(e \mid {\sim}h \& k) \, P({\sim}h \mid k))$ is low relative to the first term, the posterior probability of h will be high; and if the second term is high relative to the first term, the posterior probability of h will be low. Put another way,

$$P(e \mid k) = P(e \mid h \& k) \, P(h \mid k) + P(e \mid h_1 \& k) \, P(h_1 \mid k)$$
$$+ P(e \mid h_2 \& k) \, P(h_2 \mid k) \ldots$$

and so on for all the h_n rival to h (where all these together with h are such that at least and at most one of them must be the true theory in the field). This value will clearly be determined largely by the terms $(P(e \mid h_n \& k) \, P(h_n \mid k))$ for which h_n has a relatively high prior probability, and which give to e a relatively high posterior probability. To the extent to which rivals to h which give e a relatively high posterior probability themselves have a low prior probability (in comparison with the prior probability of h), the posterior probability of h will be high.

The Logical Probability of Theism

I have argued elsewhere[2] that where h is the hypothesis that there is a God, and k is tautological evidence (that is, no evidence at all), and so $P(h \mid k)$ is the intrinsic probability of theism, $P(h \mid k)$ is higher than is $P(h_n \mid k)$ for any other hypothesis h_n purporting to explain why there is a universe. This is because h is a very simple hypothesis, postulating one personal being who has infinite degrees of power, knowledge, and freedom of choice (from which there follows his perfect goodness), three qualities some degree of which all persons have to have. To postulate a being with infinite power, knowledge, and freedom is simpler than postulating a being or several beings with certain very precise finite degrees of power, knowledge, and freedom. I have argued that, if there is such a being, we would expect to find (that is, it is quite probable that we would find) the various data of natural theology: the existence of a complex physical universe, the (almost

[2] Primarily in *The Existence of God*, 2nd edn. (Clarendon Press, 1991).

invariable) conformity of material bodies to natural laws, those laws together with the initial state of the universe being such as to lead to the evolution of human organisms; these humans having a mental life (and so souls), and having great opportunities for helping or hurting each other and having experiences in which it seems to them that they are aware of the presence of God. (It would also not be improbable that we would find the kind and quantity of evil that there is in the world.) So when *e* reports these data (including the existence of evil and the sinning and suffering of humans), I have argued, P($e \mid h$ & k) is as probable as not. Yet, unless there is a God, there is little reason to expect such data, that is, it is most improbable that we would find them. Hence P($e \mid k$) is comparatively low.

Such have been my arguments elsewhere. Whether or not I have correctly assessed the values of the terms considered above, there will be a value of the probability of the existence of God (defined as above) on the generally accessible data of natural theology which I have set out; and what that value is is crucially relevant to whether the historical evidence considered in this book shows that Jesus was God Incarnate or rose from the dead.

The Formal Structure of the Argument of this Book

In order to articulate the structure of the argument of the present book, it will now be necessary to give different meanings to the above letters. Let *k* now be not a mere tautology, but the evidence of natural theology (including the sinning and suffering of humans). Let *e* be the detailed historical evidence, consisting of a conjunction of three pieces of evidence (e_1 & e_2 & e_3). e_1 is the evidence of the life of Jesus set out in Part II. e_2 is the detailed historical evidence relating to the Resurrection set out in Part III. e_3 is the evidence (summarized in Chapter 3) that neither the prior nor the posterior requirements for being God Incarnate were satisfied in any prophet in human history in any way comparably with the way in which they were satisfied in Jesus. The historical evidence may be described in broad general terms or fairly precise terms. By phrases such as 'the kind and quantity of evidence' and 'the degree and way' in which requirements are satisfied, I had in mind a very broad-brush description of the evidence, e.g. 'Jesus said some words on crucial occasions to the effect that his life and death constituted an atonement and let his followers believe this', rather than that he said and they said exactly the words they did. Clearly, on any hypothesis, the former is going to be a lot more probable than the latter. Indeed, it is a theorem of the probability calculus that if one proposition (a precise one) entails another proposition (an imprecise one), the latter is always more probable than is the former (or, in odd extreme cases, equally probable with the former), on the same evidence. But it does not matter just how precisely we construe the evidence. For while the probability of just that evidence given the hypothesis that Jesus was God who rose from the dead will be lower the more precisely the evidence is construed, it will be also lower in the same proportion given the negation of that hypothesis, or given any rival hypothesis. The two diminutions of probability will thus cancel each other out.

Let h_1 be the hypothesis that God became incarnate in Jesus, and h_2 the hypothesis that Jesus rose from the dead. h is the conjunction $(h_1 \& h_2)$. Now at the end of the day this book is interested in $P(h \mid e \& k)$—the probability that Jesus was God Incarnate who rose from the dead (h), on the evidence both of natural theology (k) and of the detailed history of Jesus and of other human prophets (e).

Bayes's Theorem tells us that it is a function of the three elements. But these in turn, according to the calculus, are functions of other probabilities; and to articulate the structure of the argument of this book, we must approach our result gradually. As we go along, I shall suggest numerical values for various probabilities, to be understood as very rough values, middle values out of a considerable range of possible values, based on the arguments of the rest of the book that certain probabilities are high, or low. I shall then point out that these values make h very probable on $(e \& k)$, and that we would have to give some very different values to some of the probabilities to avoid that conclusion.

Let us represent by t theism, the claim that there is a God of the traditional kind. $P(t \mid k)$ is the probability that there is such a God on the evidence of natural theology. I suggested in Chapter 1 that we give this the modest value of ½. Then let us represent by c the claim that God became incarnate among humans at some time with a divided incarnation, a more precise form of the way described by the Council of Chalcedon ('c' for a Chalcedonian incarnation) and set out in Chapter 2. I suggested there that if there is a God (and there are humans who sin and suffer), it is quite probable that he would become incarnate (at some time or other). I suggested that it was 'as probable as not' that he would do this and so in numerical terms the probability of his doing it is ½. The probability of ½ is clearly unaffected if we add to c all the data of natural theology, and so $P(c \mid t \& k)$ = ½. $P(c \mid k)$ is the probability on the evidence of natural theology that there is a God who becomes incarnate. $P(c \mid k) = P(c \mid t \& k) \, P(t \mid k)$. Given my suggested values, that is ½ × ½, $P(c \mid k) = $ ¼.

Now, initially, instead of e_1, e_2 and e_3, let us take the slightly different f_1, f_2, and f_3. f_1 is the claim that there is evidence of the strength that, I claimed in Part II, there is with respect to Jesus, that the prior requirements for being God Incarnate are satisfied in one unnamed prophet. (f_1 is compatible with even more evidence than there is with respect to Jesus that one of the requirements is satisfied, and less evidence that some other requirement is satisfied.) f_2 is the claim that there is evidence of the strength that, I

claimed in Part III, there is with respect to Jesus, that the posterior requirements are satisfied with respect to the same prophet (that is, that his life was
culminated by a super-miracle). f_3 is the claim that there is evidence (of the
strength of e_3) that neither set of requirements is satisfied with respect to
any other prophet in human history in any way comparable to the way they
are in the unnamed prophet. Now if c is true, if there occurs an incarnation,
how probable is it that there will be evidence f, the conjunction (f_1 & f_2 &
f_3)? I argued in Chapter 3 that if God becomes incarnate (given the state of
humanity), his reasons for doing so are such that one would expect there to
be a holy prophet who lives a perfect human life, gives good moral teaching, heals, shows that he believes himself to be God Incarnate, claims that
that life provides a means of atonement, and founds a Church (with the
Church continuing the prophet's teaching including the teaching that the
prophet was God Incarnate and provided atonement for human sins); or at
any rate one would expect there to be a prophet who does almost all of
these things. I claimed in Part II that the evidence we have about the life of
Jesus is largely the sort of evidence we would expect to have about a
prophet if that prophet was God Incarnate. But I also suggested that
perhaps that was not true of some of the evidence—that maybe if God
became incarnate in a prophet, we would expect that prophet to make it
more evident that he believed himself to be God than did Jesus. I also
argued in Chapter 3 that if God becomes incarnate, we would expect that
life to be culminated by a super-miracle; and I claimed in Part III that the
sort of detailed historical evidence we have about the Resurrection of Jesus
is the sort of evidence (not too much of it, but of the right kind) we would
expect to have if there was such a super-miracle. I suggested in Chapter 3
that if God becomes incarnate, there is no obvious reason to suppose that
he would become incarnate more than once. So f_3 is also to be expected.
How probable, then, is it that if God does become incarnate (into a human
race sinning and suffering), we would have evidence of the strength
described, connected with one and only one prophet? Let me not exaggerate my case and suggest (despite my strong feeling that this value should be
higher) that we give it a fairly low value and put it provisionally at $1/10$: P(f |
c & k) = $1/10$. (That part of k which includes the sinning and suffering of
humans is important for the kind of evidence of incarnation we would
expect to find, e.g. that the prophet claimed to be making an atonement).
So:

$$P(f \ \& \ c \mid k) = P(f \mid c \ \& \ k) \ P(c \mid k) = 1/10 \times 1/4 = 1/40.$$

Now let us turn to P($f \mid k$). This equals {the probability, given k, that
there is a God who becomes incarnate and leaves evidence of kind f} plus
{the probability, given k, that either there is no God or he does not become
incarnate and you still have f}:

$$P(f \mid k) = P(f \,\&\, c \mid k) + P(f \,\&\, {\sim}c \mid k)$$
$$P(f \mid k) = P(f \mid c \,\&\, k)\, P(c \mid k) + P(f \mid {\sim}c \,\&\, k)\, P({\sim}c \mid k).$$

The first combined term on the right-hand side of the latter equation is the one I have just calculated and to which I have given the provisional value of $\frac{1}{40}$. What of the second term? $P({\sim}c \mid k) = \frac{3}{4}$, given that (as I have provisionally assumed) $P(c \mid k) = \frac{1}{4}$—since by axiom 3 of the calculus $P(c \mid k) + P({\sim}c \mid k) = 1$. What next of $P(f \mid {\sim}c \,\&\, k)$? That is the probability that if there is no incarnation (either because there is no God or he does not become incarnate) and yet there is the evidence of natural theology, f still occurs. The argument of Chapter 3 is that it is not improbable that there might be evidence (of the strength there is in connection with Jesus) that there has been a prophet for whom the prior requirements are satisfied, even if God did not plan it. It is also not totally improbable that there might be evidence (of the strength there is in connection with Jesus) that there has been a prophet for whom the posterior requirements were satisfied, if there is no God. (In that case the evidence that a super-miracle had occurred would be deceptive because no God has violated nature.) But it would be immensely unlikely that there would be evidence of these degrees connected with the same prophet unless God so planned it.[3] It would have been deceptive of God to bring about this combination of evidence (or permit some other agent to do so), unless he had become incarnate in this prophet; and so God would not have brought this about.

So let's say that

$$P(f \mid {\sim}c \,\&\, k) = \frac{1}{1000}$$

$$\text{So } P(f \mid k) = \frac{1}{40} + \left(\frac{3}{4} \times \frac{1}{1000} = \frac{103}{4000} \right).$$

Hence,

$$P(c \mid f \,\&\, k) = \frac{P(f \mid c \,\&\, k)\, P(c \mid k)}{P(f \mid k)} = \frac{100}{4000} \times \frac{4000}{103} = \frac{100}{103},$$

a number very close to 1. This represents the probability on the strength of

---

[3] Or, if there is no God in the traditional sense, unless some supernatural being planned it. But I ignore this possibility as far less probable, because it is a far less simple supposition than the existence of God. I have argued in various places that an omnipotent, omniscient, and perfectly free (and so perfectly good) being is by far the simplest kind of personal being there could be; see e.g. *The Existence of God*, ch. 5. Hence, it is far more probable that there is such a being—that is, God in the traditional sense—than that there is no God, but instead lesser gods or evil gods.

evidence about some prophet that we have about Jesus, that God has or will become incarnate. But, now our evidence is somewhat greater than *f*. It is the evidence *e* that the prophet whom *f* concerns is Jesus, and that the detailed evidence (of the given strength) relevant to the satisfaction of the prior and posterior requirements is as it is. It cannot make any difference to the probability that *f* (with *k*) gives to *c*, if we add to *f* who the prophet is, and the details of the evidence, since we have already taken account in *f* its strength in supporting *c*. So,

$$P(c \mid e \ \& \ k) = P(c \mid f \ \& \ k) = \frac{100}{103}.$$

But given (*e* & *k*) and *c* (that God did or will become incarnate in the sort of way specified which makes probable the occurrence of a super-miracle culminating his life), it would be immensely improbable that the Incarnation took place or will take place in any prophet except Jesus, or that it was culminated in any other way than by the Resurrection. We cannot seriously suppose that although God plans to become incarnate in order to live the sort of life which, as far as our evidence shows, Jesus did, and which would be culminated by the sort of super-miracle which, as far as our evidence shows, was the life of Jesus, yet it was not in Jesus but in some other prophet that God will become incarnate. That indeed would be a grand deception by God. So, $P(h \mid e \ \& \ k)$ will not be very different from $P(c \mid e \ \& \ k)$. So let's say $P(h \mid e \ \& \ k)$ equals something like 0.97. In other words our total evidence (*e* & *k*) makes it very probable indeed that God became incarnate in Jesus Christ who rose from the dead.

To avoid this conclusion, an objector will have to give very different values to some of the probabilities by means of which we have reached this result. He may claim that the evidence of natural theology (for example, because of the phenomenon of natural evil—pain caused by natural processes) makes it very unlikely that there is a God; and/or that if there is a God, he is (despite my arguments) very unlikely to become incarnate. So he will assert a value of $P(c \mid k)$ well below the value of ¼ which I give to it. But if he leaves intact all the other values I have suggested, except in so far as they are functions of $P(c \mid k)$, he would have to ascribe a value of slightly less than $1/100$ to $P(c \mid k)$, to get the probability of h on (*e* & *k*) below ½. If, for example, he thinks that natural theology only gives a probability of $1/51$ rather than ½ to the existence of God, or that there is only a probability of $1/51$ that if there is a God, he will become incarnate, it becomes marginally less probable than ½ that God became incarnate in Christ.

Alternatively, the objector may claim that if God became incarnate in Christ, Christ would leave a lot more evidence of this than he did: he would have said often and openly during his life, 'I am God'; he would have made his disciples learn the Nicene Creed by heart, and so on. So the objector would judge $P(f \mid c \And k)$ to be much less than $1/10$. If he reduces it to $3/1000$, again the posterior probability of h on ($e \And k$) falls below $1/2$. Or the objector may claim that it is not at all unlikely that we would get as much detailed historical Resurrection evidence as we do in connection with a prophet who has satisfied the prior requirements even if that prophet was not God Incarnate. But he would need to increase the value of $P(f \mid \sim c \And k)$ from $1/1000$ to above $1/30$ to get the posterior probability of h falling below $1/2$.

Now I stress again that we cannot really give exact values to these probabilities, nor to analogous probabilities in science or history. You cannot give an exact value to the probability that quantum theory is true or to the probability that King Arthur lived at Glastonbury. But we can conclude that these things are probable, or not very probable on the basis of other things being very probable, or not very probable or most unlikely; and that is all I am doing here. But I am giving artificial numbers to capture the 'not very probable' etc. characters of these other things to bring out what is at stake. I have ascribed values of $1/10$ to $P(f \mid c \And k)$ and $1/1000$ to $P(f \mid \sim c \And k)$ on the basis of the arguments of this book that although it is somewhat unlikely that if Christ was God Incarnate we would have the kind and amount of prior and posterior detailed historical evidence we do, it is not very unlikely; and that it is very unlikely indeed that we would find this evidence if Christ was not God Incarnate. Someone who disagrees with these values will have to find fault with the arguments of Parts II and III and of Chapter 3. $P(c \mid k) = P(c \mid t \And k) P(t \mid k)$. I argued in Chapter 2 that, to put it very loosely, if there is a God and humans sin and suffer, there is a good chance that he might choose to become incarnate, and I have captured that here by $P(c \mid t \And k) = 1/2$. Someone who disagrees with this will have to find fault with the argument of Chapter 2. But I have not argued in this book for it being as probable as not that there is a God, given the evidence of natural theology. I have given my arguments for this elsewhere, and others have argued against these arguments. I believe that in this appendix I have ascribed numerical values to the probabilities involved, which, in my view, do not exaggerate the force of the arguments by which they are supported. If this is right, it is indeed very probable that Jesus was God Incarnate who rose from the dead.[4]

---

[4] In his *Warranted Christian Belief* (Oxford University Press, 2000), Alvin Plantinga drew attention to what he called the 'principle of dwindling probabilities' (p. 280), and he suggested that this principle had the consequence that any probabilistic argument for a Christian creed from such historical evidence (in addition to the evidence of natural theology supporting bare theism) would be very weak. This is the principle that if one argues 'p therefore very probably q, q therefore probably r, r therefore probably s' until we get to 'therefore probably x', the conclusion may be very improbable given the starting point, because at each step of the argument there is a diminution of probability. That is certainly so, though the crucial word is 'may' because it might be that even if (improba-

bly) not-*q*, that still made some other proposition probable which gave some small degree of probability to *x*. To get the total probability of *x* on evidence *p*, you need to *add* together the probabilities of different routes from *p* to *x*, and that may mean the diminution of probability in going from *p* to *x* may not be nearly as great as it would be, if you consider only the main route. (There will never be an increase of probability when you take into account the different routes, but the diminution may not be very great.) Plantinga made this point in criticism of a previous book of mine, where he in effect implied that I supposed that it was enough to establish a certain creed by giving an argument which purported to do so by one long chain of probabilistic inference. Whether or not that was a fair criticism of that book, I hope that I have phrased the argument in this book so as to be immune to any such criticism. I allowed that while $P(t \mid k) = \frac{1}{2}$, going from t to c meant that $P(c \mid k) = \frac{1}{4}$; and going from c to f meant that $P(f \& c \mid k) = \frac{1}{40}$, and so on. But while taking steps typically diminishes probability, adding evidence may increase it enormously. When we find by observation that f is true and that it is most improbable that it would have come to pass unless c, the probability of c increases dramatically.

Index of Biblical References

Index of Names and Subjects